ECONOMETRICS

By

DR. J. TINBERGEN
Professor at the Netherlands School of Economics,
Rotterdam

Translated from the Dutch by

DR. H. RIJKEN VAN OLST
Lecturer at the State University,
Groningen

LONDON
GEORGE ALLEN & UNWIN LTD.
1951

Copyright, 1951, *by* The Blakiston Company

This book is fully protected by copyright, and no part of it, with the exception of short quotations for review, may be reproduced without the written consent of the publisher

PRINTED IN THE UNITED STATES OF AMERICA

PREFACE

This book is intended as a travelling guide for those who want to go sightseeing in the domain of econometrics: a guide through the literature, trying to depict the character of the territory and indicating its highest peaks on the map.

It has been assumed that those interested are not mathematically trained economists. Economic knowledge, therefore, has been presupposed, but no more mathematics than some elementary secondary-school algebra and some knowledge of graphic presentation. An attempt has been made particularly to lay bare the logical foundations; and, in addition, to describe somewhat more systematically the results achieved thus far. As a young branch of science, econometrics can only be learned from periodical articles; as yet it has no textbooks.

May this guide stimulate the desire for travelling!

We acknowledge our thanks to Mrs. J. W. Rijken van Olst, who has rendered valuable assistance in the translation and in the preparation of the English manuscript, and to Professor Harold M. Somers of the University of Buffalo, who revised the English manuscript for publication.

J. T.

H. R. v. O.

FOREWORD

Teachers of economics and statistics have felt acutely the need for a textbook which would give students an adequate introduction to the large and growing number of econometric studies which have appeared in recent years. The present book is designed to fill precisely this need.

The field of Econometrics covers both the mathematical formulation of economic hypotheses with a view toward their statistical testing and the actual process of subjecting these hypotheses to a statistical test. The econometrician must be competent in three directions: he must be an economic theorist, he must be a mathematician, and he must be a statistician. This being the case, it is not at all surprising that econometric studies have been criticized from one or more of these three points of view by specialists in these fields. Econometrics is an interdisciplinary science; and one must be patient with all interdisciplinary sciences. It is easy to throw stones from the unbreakable glass house of our own field of specialization.

Econometrics has much to commend itself as a technique of analysis. The powerful tools of mathematics make possible first of all the formulation of economic hypotheses without the confining boundaries of rigid ceteris paribus assumptions; and the equally powerful tools of statistics enable us then to confront these hypotheses meaningfully with the facts. Thus the use of mathematical symbols in economic analysis does not mean that the analysis becomes "more abstract," "more theoretical," or "more useless." Precisely the opposite is true.

Mistakes have been made and will be made by econometricians. The use of mathematical symbols does not—as is sometimes believed—guarantee against hidden or contradictory assumptions. Least of all does it guarantee against poor judgment or downright stupidity. Econometrics is no better than the econometrician! This does not impugn the technique of analysis itself.

Professor Tinbergen is well known to English-speaking readers as the author of numerous articles in the technical journals, director of the League of Nations study on *Statistical Testing of Business-Cycle Theories,* and co-author of a recent book on *Dynamics of Business Cycles.*

The present volume is a translation of a widely used Dutch book and has been revised and enlarged for the English edition. Up-to-date references have been included throughout, and Part IV and the Appendix have been added. The book explains the relationship of Econometrics to Economics and Statistics and outlines the process of formulating economic hypotheses mathematically and of subjecting them to a statistical test. It explains the methods of obtaining the various component equations of the system—psychic, technical, and business; and it describes the process of setting up an economic model of the system as a whole. Finally, it illustrates the use of econometric methods for policy purposes.

The beginning student requires very little knowledge of mathematics and statistics. With careful study he will find himself carried into some of the most interesting and important aspects of economic theory and policy.

HAROLD M. SOMERS.

Buffalo, New York
December, 1950

CONTENTS

PART III. RESULTS OF ECONOMETRIC RESEARCH

PART IV. ECONOMIC POLICY

APPENDIX

Part I
INTRODUCTION

1
The Relationship of Econometrics to Economics and Statistics

§ 1. Economics

Econometrics is the name for a field of science in which mathematical-economic and mathematical-statistical research are applied in combination. Econometrics, therefore, forms a borderland between two branches of science, with the advantages and disadvantages thereof; advantages, because new combinations are introduced which often open up new perspectives; disadvantages, because the work in this field requires skill in two domains, which either takes up too much time or leads to insufficient training of its students in one of the two respects. As a boundary science, econometrics is younger than the adjacent regions, which fact likewise has advantages and disadvantages. As a disadvantage, the lack of an established doctrine, and also the lack of established textbooks, can be felt; as an advantage, is the fresh enthusiasm, with which its students work. The purpose of this book is to provide an orientation. For this purpose, the most important results of econometric research will be discussed. If one reviews these results, which for the greater part have come into being during the last two decades, a considerable vitality becomes evident.

To understand the position of econometrics, it is necessary to pay some attention to its older neighbors, economics and statistics.

Economics, the science of the satisfaction of human wants, is itself not yet very old, dating from the end of the eighteenth century. It has taught us to distinguish the various functions which can be exercised in the satisfaction of wants, such as that of the entrepreneur, the workman, the landowner, and the moneylender. It has taught us to distinguish different sorts of goods and services, such as consumption goods, production goods, labor, capital services, and so on. It deals with the production process, and exchange and distribution; with prices of goods and services and income formation; with forms of wealth and money; and with international relations in all these fields. It has set up a number of laws in a very general form, which —under certain circumstances—govern the satisfaction of wants, such as the laws of price formation, and it has been able to explain a number of very important facts and tendencies. Economic thinking in business and government circles has developed strongly during the past decades, and it has benefited the technique of economic policy in many respects, despite many failures.

The insight which economics has brought, however, has been mainly qualitative. Even with simple quantitative problems, it has to indicate several possibilities without being able to say which of these possibilities will be realized. For instance, the answer to the question, whether a lowering of railroad rates will bring about an increase or a decrease of the proceeds, cannot be given. It depends, of course, on the elasticity of demand for railroad transportation. If the elasticity is greater than unity, the proceeds are increased by a lowering of rates; if it is smaller than unity, the proceeds will diminish. The elasticity, however, is not known.

With problems containing a greater number of causal links, as do most problems which affect the economy as a whole, this difficulty is even greater. If one combines the various effects which a given change in phenomenon A has on phenomenon B—i.e., the effects along various paths—one has to know the relative importance of these effects. To this end, measuring is indispensable.

Our inability to reach definite answers using qualitative methods only, led to attempts to find such answers on the basis of very general principles, for instance, of the principle that a free society would always lead to the most desirable situation. This method, however, soon degenerated into a dogmatic and sterile conflict of one slogan against another. The state of affairs in economics was comparable to that of the natural sciences in the middle ages; texts of old writers were sworn by and no new investigations were made. Even in 1926, a well-known author referred to various concepts in economics as "empty boxes," without definite content.

These objections applied in nearly the same degree to mathematical economics, because the latter was also confined to very general and abstract formulations, especially of a statistical character. When, after 1900, the problem of the explanation of and the influences working on economic fluctuations came more and more to the fore, it became clear that statics could not render sufficient help. Again, what could be said about the deviations existing between statics and reality was not concrete enough.

So the pressure for concrete formulations and for measurement grew increasingly. Various schools of thought in economic science had already realized this and had begun the collection and adaptation of factual data; insofar as measurement was concerned, increasing use was made of the services of statistics.

§ 2. Statistics

Statistics has made available very comprehensive collections of concrete data. It has determined the relations between the magnitudes in economic life; for instance, the relative importance of the various branches of industry, the incomes of various population groups, the national income of countries, together with an enormous quantity of detailed data. Statistics has likewise brought quantitative knowledge concerning the development of production, prices, and incomes, and concerning the undulating motions of divergent sorts, which are shown by these phenomena. It has also been able to register the development of the phenomena after certain decisions of economic policy have been made; for instance, whether, in certain cases, after the levying of an import duty, trade increased or decreased, and how much.

However, statistics remained relatively superficial, even when refined computing procedures were employed. It could ascertain that the development of a certain type of production moved around a "trend"—i.e., a line indicating the general tendency—which rises in geometrical progression. But an explanation could not be given. It could also determine that the undulating movements in economic life show certain regularities which can be depicted by the so-called "Harvard-barometer." But it could not explain why the line of the stock market leads, compared to that of the commodity markets, and the latter compared to that of the money market, and why these three lines go up and down approximately together. Neither was it clear whether this barometer had some deeper significance or whether it indicated a more or less accidental or self-evident coincidence. Nor could it be stated that the changes which occurred *after* the levying of an import duty, were actually the consequence of that levying.

So statistics undoubtedly made matters more concrete; but rather the problem than the solution. When the economist tried to reach the solution by reasoning—which, in principle, was the only way—he needed various concepts, like supply and demand curves, which the statistician could not procure for him in a statistically measured form. These could not immediately be derived from superficial observation of the facts: a profounder type of analysis was necessary.

In fact, that profounder type of analysis has gradually come. In certain very simple cases—to be judged by the economist—it is possible to derive a supply or demand curve from the facts. A few theories of the business cycle could be rejected, even on the basis of relatively simple statistical observations; for instance, the more primitive overproduction theories. According to these theories, the fall in prices in the depression is a consequence of a rise in production, and the rise in prices in a boom period is a consequence of increasing scarcity of goods. Such a theory would require an opposite course of prices and quantities sold. Economic observation, however, shows that prices and quantities sold increase and decrease simultaneously. Equally, the theory that during the boom period the production of production goods increases at the cost of that of consumption goods, can, if confronted with the statistical data, be shown to be purely fanciful.

With the help of certain statistical inquiries, which provide cross-sections of economic life, the structure and the functioning of the latter can be approximated; for instance, by means of household budget statistics or cost curves. A further extension of the more profound type of analysis, however, was urgently needed; viz., the statistical measurement of the concepts of theoretical economics, especially of demand and supply curves. In particular, not only the measurement of the size and the course of certain phenomena was important, but also the connection between phenomena causally related to each other.

The technique of this measurement was developed by mathematical statistics as early as the nineteenth century, and was for the time being applied mainly to problems of the natural sciences, especially biology. This measurement technique was the so-called "correlation analysis" and "curve-fitting." In the case of those sciences in which one can conduct experiments, one can see to it that only those two phenomena whose interrelationship is under research are varied while the others remain constant.

In economics, experiment is seldom possible. Nature experiments with the economy by the alternation of day and night, winter and summer, and bad and good harvest years. Further, the authorities of a number of countries sometimes experiment in the field of business-cycle control. But the majority of the relations which exist between economic phenomena cannot be discovered through an experiment. This means, that in reality, not only phenomena A and B, the correlation between which we try to determine, change, but simultaneously other phenomena, say C and D, change as well. The alterations in A which appear now, are not only a consequence of those in B, but also of those in C and D. The economist, however, wishes to know how B influences A, all other phenomena remaining equal ("ceteris paribus"). If the statistician wants to be useful to economics, he must be able to eliminate the influence of C and D, or he must confine himself to the relatively rare cases in which the influence of these factors is slight.

Statistics has taught us—often with the economist's help—to eliminate these disturbances in an increasing number of cases. Instances thereof will further be discussed in Chapter II. The most refined method is that of the so-called "multiple correlation analysis," which makes it possible, in certain cases, to determine not only B's influence on A, but also that of the other factors, C and D, on A. In this way, an instrument is provided which fits exactly into the economist's concepts, since these concepts, likewise, always deal with functions of several variables. The typical example is the demand curve, which, under the influence of other phenomena than the price—income, for instance—shows a "shift." It can be said that once the formal analogy between the "regression equation" (see § 21) in multiple correlation analysis and the shifting demand curves of theoretical economics is realized, the gap between economic theory and statistical analysis has been bridged. Part of the next chapter will deal further with these concepts.

Mathematical statistics, however, has still another task. Statistical observations often contain errors. And relations in economics are, in fact, more intricate than even the economist generally assumes in order to keep his reasoning within bounds. For both these reasons there are deviations and errors in the figures and these lead to errors in the results. How great is their influence? What, in other words, is the accuracy of the results? What is the margin of error? Mathematical statistics can inform us of this in many cases. Its task for the future lies in this direction.

§ 3. Econometrics

As we have seen, there is a need for concrete formulations and measurement in economics and for more intensive statistical research; for a mutual influence, therefore, of these two branches of science on each other. Econometrics tries to realize this. If a person wants to coöperate with another he has to be willing to meet the other halfway. This should be done in economics by formulating its theories so as to permit measurement, and in statistics by developing a desire to measure relevant things. We have already mentioned the example of the demand curve. The economist should not, for instance, maintain the point of view that, except for income, the prices of *all* goods influence the demand for butter, because this makes it impossible for the statistician to measure. He must make a choice and say that as a first approximation, the price of butter and that of margarine will determine the demand for butter. The statistician, on the other hand, should not content himself by measuring the quantity of butter consumed each year and the prices of butter and of margarine separately, but he should try to find the relation between these magnitudes and to answer the question, for instance, how much the demand for butter will decline if the butter price rises by 1 per cent and the margarine price by 3 per cent.

Of course, econometrics had its precursors even before it was christened. Econometricians like to think of Cournot the same way as economists think of Adam Smith, whereas the great modern precursor or, rather, pioneer, has been Moore. In 1931, the realization of the necessity of econometric work had become so vivid that the "Econometric Society" was founded. This international association includes practically all workers in this field and counts its members in all civilized countries.* Its periodical, *Econometrica,* disseminates the results of econometric research work and at the same time forms a tie between the members in expounding their scientific ideas. Articles on econometric work, however, can be found nowadays in nearly every scientific periodical on economics or statistics, while in some countries, special periodicals exist dedicated to econometric or similar researches.

It is difficult to draw sharp boundaries between econometrics

---

* According to the latest statistics (*Econometrica,* **17**:292, 1949), the number of members is 866; 477 of whom are in the United States, 56 in France, 43 in England, 35 in the Netherlands, 28 in Norway, 17 in Italy and in Canada, 16 in Sweden and Argentina, 12 in Spain and in Brazil, 11 in India, Czechoslovakia, Switzerland, Denmark and Japan, 10 in Germany, and so on.

and statistical analysis or between econometrics and mathematical economics. Econometrics could be defined as "statistical observation of theoretically founded concepts," or, alternatively, "mathematical economics working with measured data."

It should not be inferred from the preceding that econometric research is only concerned with the use of correlation calculations. Any other method which promises results can be made use of as well.

It is hoped that by a closer coöperation between theory and observation we shall be able to reap the profits of the mutual impregnation of these two parts. The natural sciences have shown an exceptionally rapid progress of scientific research as a consequence of this. Examples of the stimulating influence exerted by statistical research on economic theory will be dealt with in the next chapter.

Part II

THE WORKING METHODS OF ECONOMETRICS

2
Mathematical Formulation

§ 4. The Function of Mathematical Economics

We have already seen that in econometric research, mathematical economics and statistics go hand in hand. For a good understanding of the working methods of econometrics, it is, nevertheless, necessary to distinguish clearly between the functions exercised by each of them. The order of succession in which they are applied is not always the same. "Living" research work constantly adapts itself to the circumstances. The investigation sometimes is like a game of tennis between the economist and the statistician—even if they are one and the same person—or a discussion in which each makes a contribution in turn. In general, the investigation will begin with an economic analysis of the problem. After that, in many cases, a statistical testing of the theory set up concerning the phenomenon under consideration will follow. After the testing, there is often occasion to draw further conclusions with the help of the theory. But it is also possible that the theory has to be revised as a consequence of the testing. The revised theory, then, has to be tested again, before further conclusions can be drawn; the tennis ball goes back and forth twice.

We shall begin with what happens in the first stage and what eventually may repeat itself in the later intermediary stages.

The role of mathematical economics also is a many-sided one in the first stage, and does not easily take on a definite form. We shall only try to give a more or less systematic anthology from the experience acquired in this work.

Speaking very generally, it is the task of mathematical economics to derive a relationship from the premises by which it is determined and to specify that relationship in greater detail.

The problem usually is to explain the changes in the magnitude of a phenomenon, X, from the changes in the size of other phenomena, Y, Z, and so on, which we may call the causes of X. We often speak in this connection of the *phenomenon to be explained* as X and the *explaining phenomena* as Y, Z, and so on. In case X relates to a great complex of homogeneous phenomena—for instance the total demand for consumption goods exerted by all laborers—we may speak of a *macroeconomic* problem as opposed to a *microeconomic* one as in the case where we are concerned with the demand of one laborer for bread. This boundary, again, cannot be drawn sharply; in every case we can distinguish various degrees of macroeconomic research, depending on whether we are investigating more or less comprehensive totals of elementary phenomena.

A distinction of more importance, about which much discussion has been going on, is the one between a *static* and a *dynamic* method of treatment. We may not use these words in an economic argument without first defining them; they have already been used in too many different meanings. In our analysis, we shall follow Frisch's definition and speak of dynamic research only when a relation is sought between economic phenomena referring to various moments of time. So, if today's price determines the quantity to be supplied a month or a year later, we speak of a dynamic relation; if we make use of that relation in our investigation, the investigation is dynamic.

The usual method of analysis of equilibrium economics is, therefore, nondynamic. It is assumed that price and quantity supplied are stationary and the relation between them which will keep them stationary is determined. To that end, the price must be equal to the marginal cost pertaining to that quantity supplied under competitive conditions. With stationary magnitudes, it is not necessary to take a possible time difference into account, as it makes no difference whether we consider the quantity supplied now or next year.

According to our definition, however, the relation between two nonstationary magnitudes is also nondynamic if the movements of the one immediately adapt themselves to those of the other; if, therefore, the quantity supplied depends on the price at the same moment. In that case, both magnitudes may very well change in time. Many writers call this a case of "dynamics." With our definition, however, this case, like the previous one, has a static character, because the situation is not at any moment determined by what has happened before. Should we assume that the quantity supplied also depends on the size of the production plant, which itself is a cumulation of investments in earlier periods, then we have a dynamic relation. Finally, we speak of a dynamic relation when a phenomenon, X, depends on the speed with which a phenomenon, Y, changes, because we can only ascertain a speed by comparing two figures at different moments.

For a long time it has been held that statics is simpler than dynamics and therefore economics has been built up in a static form, from which attempts were made later to derive dynamics by reducing the degree of abstraction. In many respects, this can be done. In other respects, however, statics is less simple, less lucid, than dynamics, because the direction of the causal relation is hidden.

Applying a dynamic method of treatment, we can distinguish between the following two cases, which are intended here as examples only:

1. With a given price, y, the supplier determines the quantity he supplies, x, in such a way, that the marginal cost is equal to the price.

2. With a given amount of orders determining the supply, x, the supplier fixes his price, y, in such a way that his marginal cost is covered.

In static terms, there will be no difference between the cases 1 and 2: in both cases, the price is equal to the marginal cost. In dynamic terms, in case 1, y is the cause and x, the consequence, in case 2, x is the cause and y, the consequence. As every reaction, in principle, requires a certain amount of time —even though it may be very small—in case 1, x will lag behind y, whereas in case 2, y will lag behind x.

In both cases, the application of statics is correct by way of an approximation; the picture of reality, however, is somewhat poorer. It does not matter when the stationary situation has actually been reached: cases 1 and 2, then, cannot be distinguished any more. But under changing circumstances, there is a difference between the two cases and the market mechanism is different. By considering the problem dynamically, it is set out more clearly, which becomes evident particularly if one has to go back to the premises in order to take account of a factor neglected thus far.

This will become more obvious after our discussion of complete economic systems or models.

The kind of relationships which can be brought into discussion in an economic investigation can be of widely different types. They can be of a relatively trivial nature if they only reflect the *definition* of the magnitude considered or if the relations are of a *natural, technical,* or *institutional* nature. An example of a definition is: Value of turnover is equal to price multiplied by quantity, or profits are equal to the proceeds minus costs. An example of a natural, or technical, relation is the connection between the quantity produced and the quantities of productive services used. An institutional relation is the one between income and taxes to be paid. Although the production relation in particular can be very important and though even a definition can sometimes be tested (we remind the reader of the various methods of determining profits), these relations, nevertheless, are less important to the economist than the second sort of relations which we want to distinguish: the *reaction relations.* These relations depict the reaction of a person, a business enterprise, or another economic subject or group of subjects to the given circumstances. They reflect the psychological or institutional efforts of those subjects; i.e., the attempt to reach a maximum satisfaction or a maximum profit, for instance, depending on the organization of the economy. In ordinary economic language, these reaction relations are the *demand* or *supply* relations; however, they can also assume different forms. They usually constitute the core of the economic model. The majority of our examples, in fact, will be concerned with ordinary demand and supply equations.*

§ 5. Which Variables Should Be Included in the Relation?

The size of the phenomena X, Y, Z, etc., which we shall denote by x, y, z, etc., are called the *magnitudes*, or—as in mathematics—the *variables* in the relation considered. The first question to be answered in setting up the relation required is: Which variables appear in it? Or, expressing the question more simply: Which phenomena influence the phenomenon to be explained? As will be discussed later in another connection, we have in mind here the direct influences; we therefore ask for the proximate causes of changes in x.

Generalizations cannot easily be made; moreover, they have little value. Concrete examples are necessary to clarify the analysis.

A very important question is whether one wants to determine a *demand* or a *supply relation;* i.e., whether one wants to consider the quantities sold from the viewpoint of the buyers or from that of the sellers. In the first case, one is only allowed to include variables which are relevant for the buyers; in the second case, only variables which have importance to the sellers may be taken into account. The quantity bought, x, for instance, may be explained from the demand side by the price, y, the incomes, z, and the price of a competing article, u. There is no sense, however, in also including the prices of the raw materials, v. Those are of interest to the sellers, not to the buyers. Insofar as they affect the buyers, they find expression in the price, y, of the product itself.

In considering the additional variables which might play a role in the *demand relation,* one will have to take into account the characteristics of the commodity dealt with, the motives of the buyers, and the organization of the market.

The characteristics of certain commodities are subject to

---

* In compliance with mathematical practice, the word "equation" here is synonymous with "relation," or "connection"; one could also speak of a "law," according to economic practice.

changes. For instance, those of the commodity called "share of stock." To the buyer, one of the most important characteristics is the yield of the share and, in many cases, also the price rise which can be expected. The buyer's appraisal and, as a consequence, also the price, will, among other things, depend on the yield and on the expected price movement.

It may happen quite frequently that the characteristics of the good sought by the buyer are also present in other goods. In that case, therefore, there are *substitute* goods, and it will depend on the price of these goods in relation to that of the goods concerned how high the demand will be. The same is true when the commodity is *complementary* to another one; this means that it is used in combination with that other commodity. In the first case, the two prices will exert a contrary influence, whereas in the second case, their influences will work into the same direction.

Finally, a demand relation may be influenced by quite a number of factors which are associated with special peculiarities of the good or the market concerned. In every case to be analyzed, the particulars of the market should be studied thoroughly before a general theory can be developed. As an example, see § 29.

In case we are concerned with a *supply equation,* the variables which play a role in the first place will be—except the price of the product supplied—the *production costs,* which may be split up into wage and raw material costs, depending on the prices of those factors and on the quantities. These quantities will be proportional to the productivity of the enterprises concerned, while, on the other hand, the marginal productivities determine *marginal costs,* with which we are concerned in a supply function. In general, the marginal productivities are lower as production is higher, and as a rule they depend on the latter.

In certain circumstances—at full employment for instance—the factor determining supply will be the *productive capacity.* This magnitude itself can practically be taken as a datum; however, if one wants to make sharper distinctions, it can in its turn be considered dependent on other factors.

Another factor of importance, both to the demand and the supply equation, is the *organization of the market.* Up to this point, the assumption of free competition has been made, where demanding and supplying economic subjects consider the price as a datum which they cannot influence and there is only one price. When competition is limited, the situation may be different. In some cases, there are more prices than one; the buyer then has to choose between various prices of different suppliers. The situation in this case is similar to the one of competing goods; the demand for the goods of each of the sellers depends both on his own and on his competitor's price. A monopolist's supply curve, moreover, will depend on the price in a different way from the supply curve of a seller competing with others (see § 9).

§ 6. The Mathematical Form of the Relation

A question deserving separate consideration is, what should be the mathematical form of the relation? In the case of the demand function, should the quantity demanded be determined by the first power of the price or by its second power, or by some other function of the price? Of course, this is of some importance for the process of calculation, sometimes even of great importance. Economic theory tells us very little about this; it usually does not know the answer itself. In a few special cases, it is possible by reasoning to deduce something more definite about the form of the function. For instance, if the demand for a certain good is connected with the quantity of another good, by a purely technical relation, and is, say, proportional to that quantity, then at least the mathematical relation with respect to the quantity is determined. When it is certain that somebody will spend a certain amount for a certain commodity, then the quantity he will buy is inversely proportional to the price. These cases, however, are rare. Usually, this sort of information is lacking, and precisely in such cases theoretical economics will only be able to make headway through econometric research. Sometimes it is possible on the basis of further reasoning to detect certain characteristics of the mathematical relation sought after. The way in which demand for a certain good depends on income is a good instance of this. We can let income vary from zero to infinity and ascertain that with zero income, nothing can be spent on the article in question. Further, we can never spend more than the amount of the whole income. In the case of an article which is one of the necessaries of life and has no substitution possibilities of any importance, it can be assumed that there is a certain saturation quantity, above which demand does not rise.

Another consideration which can sometimes be applied is the following: For the real satisfaction of a buyer, it makes no difference if all prices and his income are twice or n times as high as they actually are. Therefore, in such a situation, his reaction will not differ from the one actually in existence. This means, among other things, that also the quantity demanded of each good remains the same, if all prices and money amounts with which the subject is concerned, increase in the same proportion. When this is the case, we say that the quantity demanded is a *homogeneous function* (of zero degree) of the variables mentioned. It should be kept in mind that this homogeneity is subject to the conditions that the changes referred to really take place in all prices and money amounts and that the buyer is not subject to the so-called "money illusion," through which the absolute value of the prices have an independent significance for him. This condition means that the money amounts not mentioned explicitly and which are of some importance for the buyer must also be taken into account.

From such considerations, some general characteristics of the function sought after can be deduced. This limits the choice of functions to some extent (see § 26).

A very general mathematical theorem is of advantage in all these cases; namely, that within a small range of variation, nearly every function can be approximated by a *linear one.*

For that range, the curve representing the relation is replaced by part of the tangent. If the changes in the variables concerned are small, a linear function of those variables will always suffice; in other words, an attempt can be made to approximate x by an expression $x' = a + by + cz + du \ldots$, where a, b, c, etc., are constants. This does not mean, by the way, as is sometimes thought, that a proportionality between x' and y is assumed. The only proportionality assumed is between a small increment of y, for instance, and a corresponding increment of x', z, u, etc., remaining constant. If we represent these increments, as is usual in mathematics, by Δy and $\Delta x'$ respectively, then by virtue of our assumption, the equation

$$\Delta x' = b\Delta y \tag{6.1}$$

holds good. This assumption, however, does not go as far as one of proportionality between x' and y itself.

There are still other aspects of the mathematical relation which, even with small changes in the variables, cannot be determined in advance and which, therefore, deserve attention. Economic theory does not always make it clear whether a magnitude x depends on y, or on a *cumulation* of y (in mathematical language: on the "integral over time" of y). What is meant by the cumulation of y will be explained briefly with the help of a numerical example. If a series, y, is given in the course of time, for instance:

$$y = 5, 3, 6, 8, 4 \ldots.$$

then by the cumulation of y is meant the series, the first term of which is 5, the second, $5 + 3 = 8$, the third, $5 + 3 + 6 = 14$, the fourth, $5 + 3 + 6 + 8 = 22$, etc. As an economic example of the uncertainty referred to above, the question may be asked, How does the rate of interest influence the stocks of certain commodities? Two solutions are conceivable; either the rate of interest determines the stock or it determines the positive or negative additions to the stock. Economic literature, in this respect, is far from clear, and often one hesitates between two contrary opinions. If the first one is true, the stock, x, is determined by the rate of interest, y. In case the second one is true, however, the stock, x, being itself a cumulation of additions to the stock in previous periods, is determined by a cumulation of the values of the rate of interest, y.

It makes a very considerable difference whether the one or the other assumption is made. Before testing a theory of this type, therefore, one has to decide which assumption to make.

§ 7. The Way in Which the Time Factor Appears in the Relation

We have now come to a further problem; namely, the question in what way the time factor plays its role in the relation concerned. The appearance of a cumulated variable already means a form of influence of the time factor; in that case, as we have seen, we have a dynamic relation. The latter can also make its appearance in a simpler way, if a variable, z, influences x, not at the same moment, but with a certain *time-lag,* T. We can say, then, that

$$x_t = a + cz_{t-T}$$

where the subscripts of the magnitudes x and z indicate the period of time for which those variables should be taken. T is sometimes called the "lag" which x shows with respect to z, or the "lead" which z shows with respect to x. This is perhaps the simplest form of dynamic relation conceivable. Another question is whether economic theory can also give a decisive answer about the way the time factor should appear in the relations when the exact correlation of interrelated phenomena is considered. Such a simple time-lag undoubtedly may present itself, namely, in case there is a causal factor of a technical nature which requires a constant lapse of time for a certain decision to have its effect. The length of a production process can give rise to such a lag.

It may also happen, however, that dynamic relations possess quite different forms if they have a psychological origin. Let us suppose that according to the circumstances prevailing at the moment, t, the demand for a certain good must be equal to x_1 in order to give maximum satisfaction to the buyer. If, now, the circumstances suddenly change, the most desirable demand will perhaps be x_2. But some time passes before the buyer is able to realize this. With a small change in circumstances, he will probably not notice that changing x_1 will be advantageous to him. When the change is greater, this will gradually become clear to him. He will now aim at proceeding from x_1 to x_2. Various obstacles, however, may counteract this and therefore the adjustment does not take place immediately. A process of adjustment will, however, develop. This may happen in such a way that the speed with which he moves from x_1 to x_2 is proportionate to the distance from x_2—the "power of attraction," one could say—and, therefore, decreases slowly. At first it may also increase, and so on. Practically no investigations have yet been made in this field.

In the course of that process of adjustment, the circumstances again change, the process is broken off and replaced by a new one. The result of such a series of adjustment processes is a curve quite different from that of one single adjustment process; as an approximation, however, it may very well result in a line showing a lagged relationship.

It can also happen that the magnitude, z, influences the magnitude, x, in different ways and that each of these has a different lag. If we assume that these lags are 1, 2, 3, etc., time units respectively then

$$x_t = a + c_1z_{t-1} + c_2z_{t-2} + c_3z_{t-3} + \dots$$

If, now, z undergoes a change, Δz, which is maintained for some time, the change Δx in x which appears consequently, can be calculated as follows

$$\Delta x = (c_1 + c_2 + c_3 + \dots)\Delta z$$

It can be said now that $c_1 + c_2 + c_3 + \ldots$ represents the *long-term influence of z on x*. The change in x which has taken place after one time unit, however, is

$$\Delta_1 x = c_1 \Delta z$$

In certain cases it is useful to name the coefficient c_1 the *short-term influence of z on x;* in particular, for instance, when c_2, c_3, etc., are each small but when their sum total is important compared to c_1. Of course, we can also put the boundary between short and long term at some other point; and as a matter of fact, the exact description of z's influence on x can only be given by enumerating all the coefficients c_1, c_2, c_3, etc.

There is still quite a different way in which the time factor plays a role. When striving after maximum satisfaction, which underlies all economic action, it makes a difference over how long an interval of time one looks ahead. Expressed in everyday language, the immediate interests sometimes do not coincide with the interests of a later period, and often it is unwise to be shortsighted. In discussions of a more scientific character, use has sometimes been made of the concept of *horizon;* i.e., the period over which somebody looks ahead. The length of the horizon sometimes influences supply curves and demand curves considerably. The simplest example is the case of an excessively large crop. If the farmer or the merchant would not look further ahead than one year, he would take the whole crop to the market and satisfy himself with an extremely low price. If, however, he looks two years ahead, he will take account of the probability that there will be an average crop in the second year; and if, now, he distributes the total crop of those two years equally over the two years, he will have a greater total yield. He will do well, therefore, not to take the whole surplus crop of the current year to the market, but to keep half the surplus back. The length of the horizon here has a clear and, for simple cases, a calculable influence on the amount supplied.

The same occurs in the valuation of shares. If a company does not pay out dividends in a certain year, a shareholder who does not look further ahead than that year would argue that the share was worth nothing to him; it does not give him any revenue. Usually, however, his calculations will cover a longer period of time in the future and in his valuation he will take account of the possibility that after some time, dividends will be paid again. On the other hand, if, in one year, the dividend is three times the normal amount, the price of that share will not necessarily be tripled. Fig. 4B (p. 70) shows this very clearly. There the dividend percentage is measured along the horizontal axis, whereas the "valuation" is measured vertically. The latter concept is defined as "share price divided by nominal value of the share and multiplied by the long-term interest rate" (the yield of government bonds). This magnitude indicates, as it were, interest-bearing bond which is considered to be equivalent to the share. If the share price is twice the nominal amount and the yield of government bonds is 4 per cent, then apparently the share is considered to be equivalent in value to an imaginary bond yielding 8 per cent. If one were to be governed entirely by the momentary dividend percentage, a dividend of 8 per cent would also entail a valuation of 8 per cent. In reality, we do not assume this relation, but rather a relation which depends much less strongly on the momentary dividend percentage. We can say roughly that a rise of 1 per cent in the dividend rate causes an increase in valuation of only ½ per cent, so that with a dividend of 4 per cent a valuation based on 4 per cent is made, whereas with a dividend of 8 per cent the valuation is based on 6 per cent. Again, this is an example of the influence of the horizon on the behavior of economic subjects.

Finally, there is a way in which "the time factor" makes itself felt, if the relation sought after (demand or supply relation, etc.) gradually changes in the course of time. Strictly speaking, this is not an influence of the time factor, because the direct influence originates from other phenomena. Examples of these are a gradual increase of technical knowledge, a gradual change of tastes, and many other phenomena. But if it is difficult to find other criteria to measure these phenomena—often there are many present at the same time—and if we are primarily interested in the short-term fluctuations, we often include time as a variable in the relation investigated. This can also be expressed by saying that we add a trend component to represent the influence of the gradually changing factors mentioned above. Of course, this is only correct as long as these factors actually grow gradually and not jerkily. Examples are the influence of the temperance movement—in its divergent direct and indirect forms—on the consumption of alcoholic beverages, and the influence of increasing highway traffic on the demand for railway transport.

§ 8. Connection with Other Relations

The mathematical formulation of economic relations is of particular importance if one wants to illustrate the connection with other, more or less allied relations. It is useful to consider several examples. Let us choose, as a first example, the various relations which are usually distinguished in the description of a single "Walrasian" market, or rather, which are sometimes not distinguished sharply, to the detriment of the analysis! We have already mentioned the demand and the supply relation. If p represents the price and u the quantity sold, both these relations are equations in which u is, among other things, explained by p. But the supply relation explains u from the point of view of the sellers and therefore, beside p, there appear magnitudes in it which we could call *supply factors* and which we shall indicate by $s_1, s_2. \ldots$ Similarly, in the demand equation, the demand factors $d_1, d_2 \ldots$ appear.

Written in full, they are as follows:

$$\text{Supply equation: } u = f\,(p, s_1, s_2 \ldots) \qquad (8.1)$$
$$\text{Demand equation: } u = g\,(p, d_1, d_2 \ldots) \qquad (8.2)$$

By equating demand and supply we obtain a new equation

$$f\,(p, s_1, s_2 \ldots) = g\,(p, d_1, d_2 \ldots)$$

in which u does not appear any more. From this equation, we can solve p in the majority of cases important to us:

$$p = h\,(s_1, s_2, \ldots d_1, d_2 \ldots) \tag{8.3}$$

We shall call this the *price equation.* It expresses the price in terms of the supply and demand factors without the help of the quantity sold. However, we can also solve p both from (8.1) and (8.2) and equate the two expressions obtained in this way; in other words we can eliminate p from (8.1) and (8.2); we then get an expression in u, s_1, s_2, d_1, d_2 . . . from which we can solve u:

$$u = k\,(s_1, s_2 \ldots d_1, d_2 \ldots) \tag{8.4}$$

We can speak here of a *turnover equation.* The equations (8.3) and (8.4) together are equivalent to (8.1) and (8.2); they express the market quantities—p and u—in this simple problem, the "unknowns"—in terms of the market data s_1, s_2, . . . d_1, d_2 . . . For that matter, we can take any pair to describe the market. But it is incorrect, for instance, to try to explain p by *all* the factors u, s_1, s_2, . . . d_1, d_2 . . . . Such a relation has no sense, because u alone can be derived from s_1, s_2, d_1 d_2 . . . as is shown in (8.4) and therefore it would be duplication to include u in an equation for p in addition to s_1, s_2, d_1, d_2 . . .

As (8.3) and (8.4) can take the place of (8.1) and (8.2), there must also be a relation between the coefficients of those equations. This can be seen most easily, if one makes use of a linear approximation or of an exponential form of the equations. Let, for instance,

$$u = v_{11}p + v_{12}s \text{ be the supply relation and} \tag{8.1'}$$
$$u = v_{21}p + v_{22}d \text{ the demand relation,} \tag{8.2'}$$

where, for the sake of simplicity, we have assumed only one demand factor and one supply factor. Introducing more would not be difficult.

The price equation then becomes

$$(v_{11} - v_{21})p = v_{22}d - v_{12}s$$

or

$$p = \frac{v_{22}d - v_{12}s}{v_{11} - v_{21}} \tag{8.3'}$$

and the turnover equation

$$(v_{21} - v_{11})u = v_{21}v_{12}s - v_{11}v_{22}d$$

or

$$u = \frac{v_{21}v_{12}s - v_{11}v_{22}d}{v_{21} - v_{11}} = \frac{v_{11}v_{22}d - v_{21}v_{12}s}{v_{11} - v_{21}} \tag{8.4'}$$

from which it becomes very clear how the coefficients of the last two equations are connected with those of the first two. If it is better for some reason to test statistically the equations (8.3′) and (8.4′) rather than (8.1′) and (8.2′) then with the help of the expressions given above, it is possible to determine the coefficients of the demand and supply relation from the former two equations.

We remind the reader that the coefficients v_{11} and v_{21} are closely connected with the elasticity coefficients of demand and supply, respectively. By elasticity is meant the ratio of a change in demand or supply, expressed as a percentage, to a given price change, also expressed as a percentage, from which the change in demand or supply results; strictly speaking, the changes should be infinitely small, but such small changes are difficult to deal with in practice. If we designate a small price change by Δp, and the resulting change in quantity sold by Δu, the elasticity is:

$$\epsilon = \frac{\Delta u}{u} : \frac{\Delta p}{p} = \frac{\Delta u}{\Delta p}\frac{p}{u}$$

In order to find the supply elasticity, Δu must be derived from the supply equation; we then have:

$$\Delta u = v_{11}\Delta p \text{ or } \frac{\Delta u}{\Delta p} = v_{11} \text{ and } \epsilon_s = v_{11}\frac{p}{u}$$

To determine the demand elasticity, one has to derive Δu from the demand equation, after which one finds:

$$\epsilon_d = v_{21}\frac{p}{u}$$

In this formula, p and u must have values belonging together; i.e., u must follow from p according to the demand or supply equation.

If the *exponential* approximation is used, the supply equation is represented by

$$u = p^{v11}s^{v12} \text{ or } \log u = v_{11} \log p + v_{12} \log s \qquad (8.1'')$$

and the demand equation by

$$u = p^{v21}d^{v22} \text{ or } \log u = v_{21} \log p + v_{22} \log d \qquad (8.2'')$$

The price and turnover equation, now, can be obtained by reading in (8.3′) and (8.4′) log p, log s, log d, and log u instead of p, s, d, and u.

The elasticity in this case is simpler; it is equal to v_{11} for supply and v_{21} for demand and therefore is independent of the values of u and p; i.e., of the appropriate place on the curve. This is the reason why demand and supply curves of the exponential type are usually assumed if no more details are known about their shape. For other purposes, namely for the use of such relations in so-called "complete systems," the application of linear equations, again, is simpler and therefore those are also often used. As has been pointed out, both types are intended as approximations over small intervals and as a rule they are definitely wrong if one moves too far from the starting point.

§ 9. Supply Equation and Price-Fixation Equation

A second example of connections with other relations and of the use of a mathematical method of treatment in investigating them is obtained when it is thought necessary to dig deeper and to investigate the origin of the supply and demand curves themselves.* According to Walras, both are derived from aiming at maximum satisfaction, and therefore the coefficients of the functions (8.1) and (8.2) must be connected with the coefficients of the ophelimity function or of the profit function. An example of the first one will be discussed later (§ 26), whereas a very simple example of the second will be dealt with now, at the same time illustrating another point, namely, how the market organization can influence the coefficients of the supply function. Let us imagine a branch of industry producing a commodity in quantity u, and the demand function of which is as follows:

$$u = V_0 - V_1 p \tag{9.1}$$

Let production costs exist only as a constant part k_0 and a proportional part $k_1 u$, where k_0 represents total fixed costs for the whole production and k_1 the variable costs per unit of the product.

We first assume that the whole production is in the hands of a *monopolist*. Then the profit, Z, of this monopolist at a price, p, will amount to:

$$\begin{aligned} Z &= pu - k_0 - k_1 u \\ &= (p - k_1)\, u - k_0 \\ &= (p - k_1)\,(V_0 - V_1 p) - k_0 \end{aligned}$$

The profit will be a maximum if the price is fixed at the amount p_M, satisfying the requirement that Z be as great as possible. It can be ascertained, as can easily be seen, that:

$$p_M = \frac{V_0 + V_1 k_1}{2V_1} = \frac{V_0}{2V_1} + \frac{k_1}{2} \tag{9.2}$$

If, now, in the course of time, the demand curve shows parallel shifts, i.e., if V_0 is changeable, while V_1 remains unchanged,

* This is generally not necessary; the econometricians here actually follow Cassel, who wishes to consider the demand and supply curves as the basic data.

the course of the price is indicated by (9.2). This equation, however, is not a supply equation, because it is not exclusively in terms of p plus supply factors. The magnitude k_1 is a supply factor, and V_1 is a constant; but V_0 is a demand factor. On the other hand, u does not appear in equation (9.2), which would be the case in a supply equation. In order to find the supply function in this case, we must replace V_0 by u, if possible. This is indeed feasible, with the help of the demand equation. We then obtain:

$$p_M = \frac{u + V_1 p_M}{2V_1} + \frac{k_1}{2}$$

which can be written as follows:

$$u = V_1 \, (p_M - k) \qquad (9.3)$$

This supply equation must not be understood in the strict Walrasian sense of an equation, which determines the behavior of the suppliers independently of the demand side. But judging by its form, it is such an equation. The remarkable thing is that it contains a constant from the demand side, namely V_1. It shows that a monopolist's supply elasticity depends on V_1 and is equal to $V_1 \frac{p}{u}$. This makes it possible to test statistically whether the supply on a given market is controlled monopolistically.

If free competition prevails, the supply function would look quite different, namely

$$p = k_1 \qquad (9.4)$$

If, finally, some form of limited monopolistic competition prevails, still different supply functions would be valid. At this moment, however, we shall not go further into these details.

This simple example forms a good starting-point for a further consideration of the supply function and its significance. If one looks into what exactly is going on in a market, and in particular, if one looks at the sequence in time of the separate "economic actions"—i.e., if one proceeds dynamically—it will happen in many cases that the supplier does not consider the price as a datum and that he does not use it as a basis for his decisions on how much to produce. If he produces to satisfy market needs through the depletion of inventories, this can approximately be the case. If, however, he produces to order, it is certainly not so. In that case, his production is based rather on the amount ordered; i.e., on the quantity demanded, whereas he fixes the price more or less independently. Of course, he is forced in the long run to follow his competitors when fixing his price; too great a deviation would make his customers disappear after some time. But for a short period he is autonomous in his price fixing, at which time he will take his costs into account. These depend on the supply factors mentioned earlier; namely, the wage rate, the price of raw materials, and the labor productivity in his enterprise, and in addition, on the level of his production. The latter determines which marginal machines and laborers are just needed and what organization of labor can be used. Should we wish to reproduce the reaction relations describing this situation, we could write:

$$u = v_{21}p + v_{22}d$$

being the demand equation described earlier, representing the buyer's reaction on a given price p, and

$$p = g\,(s, u) \tag{9.5}$$

which represents the seller's reaction, namely the *fixing of the price,* which takes place on the basis of the supply factors mentioned, and on the level of production. The only factor still neglected in these equations is the possible difference in time between the variables. This does not concern us at the moment; we only want to demonstrate now that equation (9.5) is a supply equation according to the variables included; it is a relation between the magnitudes u, p, and s. If we neglect time differences, therefore, there is no distinction, and a supply equation can also be interpreted as a *price-fixation equation.* In many cases, this will lead to a more realistic method of treatment.

§ 10. Macroeconomic Investigations

As we have already mentioned, these refer to *groups* of persons or markets, for instance, to the total demand for a certain article exerted by all consumers, or to the total demand for all consumption goods exerted by all consumers. If we start by confining ourselves to the first case, and assume that free competition exists in the market, with an equal price to each of the buyers, it is not difficult to determine the dependence of the total demand for the good considered on the price. If the individual demand functions are

$$u_1 = f_1(p),\ u_2 = f_2(p) \ldots \qquad (10.1)$$

where the subscript refers to a certain person, the total demand is $u = u_1 + u_2 + \ldots = f_1(p) + f_2(p) + \ldots = f(p)$, i.e., again a function of the price.

The situation is different if we want to determine the total demand for consumption goods as a whole. In that case, there are various prices; namely, one for each of the goods, say p^1, p^2, $p^3 \ldots$ etc., where the superscripts refer to the various goods. The demand for each separate good depends on each of these prices, or perhaps, as a first approximation, only on the price of the good itself. In both cases, the total demand for all goods depends on all the prices mentioned. In macroeconomic investigations, however, we usually do not consider all the prices separately, but only one average price of consumption goods, since the very idea of macroeconomic investigations is to simplify the picture. It is by no means certain beforehand, however, that a function of the prices p^1, p^2, $p^3 \ldots$ may also be taken as a function of some average of those prices:

$$p = \frac{a^1p^1 + a^2p^2 + \ldots}{a^1 + a^2 + \ldots} \qquad (10.2)$$

Of course, there are functions for which this is the case. For instance, the function $F(p^1, p^2 \ldots)$, which is defined as follows:

$$F(p^1, p^2 \ldots) = A\,(a^1p^1 + a^2p^2 + \ldots) \qquad (10.3)$$

is equal to A $(a^1 + a^2 + \ldots)p$. But another arbitrarily chosen function as a rule cannot be written as a function of p alone. Does this prove that such macroeconomic methods are inadmissible? It does not; a few conditions can be enumerated, under which macroeconomic procedures are very useful as approximations.

The situation is simplest when a single relation is involved. When the changes in the variables are small, it is always permissible to use linear functions. The total demand for all goods, therefore, may also be written as follows:

$$u = b^1p^1 + b^2p^2 + \ldots + c \qquad (10.4)$$

It is not certain, however, that now the coefficients b^1, b^2, etc., of the terms p^1, p^2 . . . are related in the same way as the coefficients a^1, a^2 . . . in the definition of p in (10.2). Otherwise there would be no objection against defining p differently, namely with the coefficients b^1, b^2 . . . instead of a^1, a^2. . . . On the contrary, this is an example of the fact that index numbers should always be constructed in such a way that they are suitable to the problem we want to solve with their help.

We shall illustrate this with a concrete example. We assume that the demand for every separate good depends only on its own price and also that these relations have a linear form; for instance,

$$u^1 = b^1p^1 + c^1,\ u^2 = b^2p^2 + c^2,\ u^3 = b^3p^3 + c^3 \qquad (10.5)$$

The magnitudes b^1, b^2 . . . depend on two circumstances. A certain b^1 is greater as the quantity consumed of that good is greater, and it is also greater as the demand for that good is more elastic. If the elasticity is indicated by ϵ^1, then, as we have seen before (§ 8),

$$\epsilon^1 = b^1\frac{\overline{p}^1}{\overline{u}^1} \qquad (10.9)$$

where $\bar{p}^1$ and $\bar{u}^1$ are the values of p^1 and u^1 at some reference point. It follows that

$$b^1 = \frac{\epsilon^1\bar{u}^1}{\bar{p}^1} \tag{10.7}$$

Instead of (10.5), therefore, we can write

$$u^1 = \frac{\epsilon^1\bar{u}^1}{\bar{p}^1}p^1 + c^1,\ u^2 = \frac{\epsilon^2\bar{u}^2}{\bar{p}^2}p^2 + c^2 \ldots$$

From this it can be seen that the total demand

$$u = \frac{\epsilon^1\bar{u}^1}{\bar{p}^1}p^1 + \frac{\epsilon^2\bar{u}^2}{\bar{p}^2}p^2 + \ldots + c^1 + c^2 + \ldots \tag{10.8}$$

and also that the definition of the general price level in this problem must be such that the weights used are equal to

$$\frac{\epsilon^1\bar{u}^1}{\bar{p}^1}, \frac{\epsilon^2\bar{u}^2}{\bar{p}^2},$$

etc. These weights are different from the ones which are generally used in a price index number. There we usually take $\bar{u}^1$, $\bar{u}^2$, etc., as weights. In our case, goods with a strongly elastic demand are weighted extra heavily.*

As we have said, there is no objection against this procedure, as long as we are dealing with only one relation. If, however, in another relation, the price level p also has to play a role, it can happen that the weighting system which would be most suitable does not coincide with the weighting system required for the first relation. Strictly speaking, another index number p′ would in such case be necessary for the second relation. This index number will possibly not coincide with p, and then the intended

* For a practical application, the reader is referred to my "Business Cycles in the United States of America, 1919-1932" (League of Nations edition), § 3.4, which has been worked out by Dr. J. J. Polak.

simplification is partly illusory. If, however, the movements of the separate prices do not diverge strongly, the difference between p and p′ will remain within very narrow limits, so that as an approximation we may put $p = p'$. In many cases, this parallelism of the separate prices is actually present. This is particularly the case if the systematic factors which are the cause of the price movement are present in all prices, for instance, wages as an element of costs or general overproduction as a cause of declining prices. The component parts of price indices have, for the most part, moved parallel to one another. This does not alter the fact that, in principle, it is always desirable to investigate whether the conditions are satisfied.

A good example of the complications which a macroeconomic concept may entail can be given if we investigate in greater detail the dependence of demand on *income.**

Let income for an individual family be i and the demand for consumption goods, c; further, let the total income of all families be I and the total demand for consumption goods, C. If c is a linear function of i, C will depend on I in a simple way; if, namely,

$$c = a + bi \text{ (a and b constant)}$$

and if these relations are added for all families,

$$C = aN + bI$$

where N is the number of families. But as soon as c depends on i in a more complicated way, the sum total of all c's is no longer dependent on I only. This makes the question, how an increase of the income I influences the demand for consumption goods, a difficult one to solve. An increase of I can take place in so many ways that it is no longer a matter of indif-

* The following is quoted from an article by P. de Wolff: Income elasticity of demand, a micro-economic and a macro-economic interpretation, *The Economic Journal,* 1940.

ference how it actually happens. Further computations in the article cited above indicate that an unambiguous relation between I and C exists only in those cases where the income distribution contains only two "parameters," and secondly that even then there is no sense in supposing that C depends also on the distribution of incomes. By "parameters" we mean those magnitudes which "describe" a frequency distribution; a well-known example is the one of Pareto's law of income distribution, which contains as one of the parameters the magnitude α. Although the details of the argument cannot readily be clarified without higher mathematics, we call the reader's attention to it as a good example of what mathematical analysis can achieve here.

Also in the case mentioned before of linear dependence of c on i, we have an example of an unambiguous dependence between I and C and of the absence of any influence of income distribution on the total demand. It is a happy circumstance for macroeconomic research that actually within wide limits c depends linearly on i (see § 26).

§ 11. The Description of Complete Systems

We shall now go somewhat deeper into the contribution of mathematical economics to what we have called the last stage of the investigation; i.e., after the testing of the relations discussed in the previous section has taken place. In order to see the sense of the following, we have to recall what is the ultimate purpose of all economic analysis. We formulate this purpose twofold: (1) to explain the historical course of economic phenomena from their noneconomic causes, or "data," and (2) to ascertain how a change of these data—for instance, a certain form of economic policy—will have its effect on that course. So far, we have only been occupied with one single relation between economic phenomena. Changes in one phenomenon have been reduced to changes in other economic phenomena and to certain data of a natural, a technical, or an institutional character. If, however, we want to explain the whole of economic activity, we have to consider not one relation but a number of these together, enough, in fact, so that the number of phenomena to be explained is equal to the number of relations. Only in this case can we hope really to explain the course of economic phenomena from noneconomic phenomena. Expressed more concretely: it is not sufficient to derive the demand for consumption goods from incomes and prices; the latter, in their turn, must also be explained.

In order to do this, the network of causal relations which together form the economic structure of a certain area should be investigated systematically. Some preliminary defining of the concepts used cannot be avoided here. We think this can best be carried out by using a "system of arrows" (see Fig. 1).

In this figure, every dot represents a certain economic phenomenon during a certain time-unit, say during a certain quarter. Horizontally, the same phenomenon has been symbolized in subsequent quarters. Vertically we find the various phe-

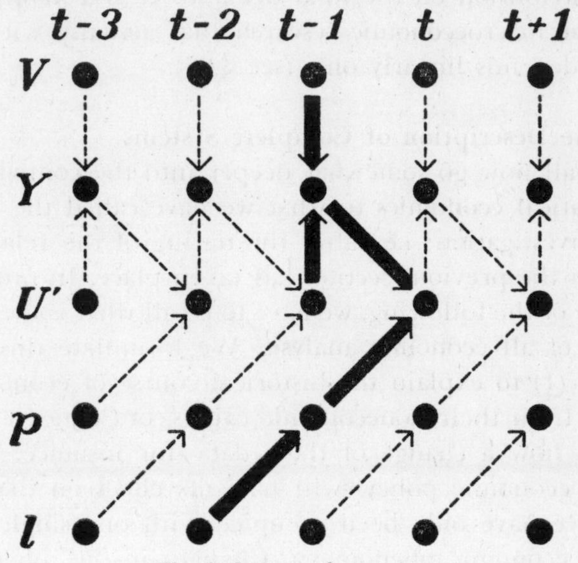

Fig. 1. System of arrows.

nomena taken into consideration for the same quarter. Now the value of a certain phenomenon in a certain quarter, say of the demand for consumption goods U'_t during the quarter t, will be determined by the values of some other phenomena during the same or another quarter. To clarify this, let us assume that it is determined by the level of income in the previous quarter, Y_{t-1}' and by the prices in that same quarter, p_{t-1}. We indicate this by the arrows running from Y_{t-1} and p_{t-1} to U'_t. These arrows indicate a direct causal relation. They repeat themselves quarterly, if the structure of the economy is assumed constant. The values of U′, Y, and p do not necessarily repeat themselves—that would only be the case in a stationary situation—but the causal relation does repeat itself.

In their turn, the incomes Y again depend on other magnitudes, say on the value of consumption U′ and on the value of investments V during the same quarter. That will be indicated by arrows from U′ and V to Y, without lags. The prices p and the investments V′ will also have their determining factors. In this way we obtain a whole scheme of arrows which repeat themselves. By inquiring again and again after the direct causes of phenomena which have not yet been explained, a growing number of relations is obtained. In the beginning we shall also have to consider a growing number of phenomena. But at some point this becomes unnecessary: now, phenomena which have already been considered, again act as causes; at that point the phenomena not yet explained have all been reduced to explained ones. If the number of phenomena then is equal to the number of relations, we have a complete system, or *model,* which word stresses the fact that such a system is always more or less *simplified* in comparison to reality. In such a model, unexplained noneconomic phenomena can still appear as data, but it is not the task of economics to explain these.

The entire set of arrows now forms the *logical structure* of our system. These arrows can be arranged in two ways. We can consider all arrows ending in one point; we then see at a glance the various *causes* of one phenomenon, characterized by that point. We can also take together all arrows which start from one point; we then consider the *influence* of one phenomenon on the others. This last arrangement is, so to speak, directed forward; it is used in most verbal arguments. The first arrangement is the one which corresponds with our equations: the various terms of the latter indicate the various arrows which end in the variable to be explained. With both methods of arrangement, of course, in each column every point should be considered successively, i.e., all phenomena should be taken into consideration. Moreover, as we have already pointed out, the whole picture obtained in this way repeats itself in time.

In both arrangements mentioned, we work exclusively with direct causal relations. This is sufficient because each arrow may be considered in turn. It must not be inferred, however, that the *indirect*—i.e., the "deeper"—causes are neglected. But every direct cause at the same time is an indirect cause. If p has a direct influence on U′ and if the wage-level l has a direct influence on p, then l has an indirect influence on U′. Going backward along the arrow ending in U′ and coming from p, we first arrive at p, and subsequently we can go further back to l, etc. Thus we can detect the secondary and tertiary causes, etc. The system, therefore, is completely defined by the equations which we have introduced indicating the "elementary laws" which connect the variables. We shall speak, consequently, of the *elementary equations* or of the *structural equations.*

We have to go a little further into the form of these equations: What kinds of variables appear in them? As an example, we again take the demand equation for consumption goods:

$$U'_t = v_1 Y_{t-1} + v_2 p_{t-1} + v_3(t) + v_4 + R_t^{U'}$$

We have added a few terms, which will be discussed presently. The following variables appear now:

1. the *variable to be explained,* U′ (demand for consumption goods);

2. the *explanatory variables* Y′ and p (income and the price level);

3. a number of *constant magnitudes:* coefficients v_1, v_2, v_4 and lags (of one time-unit in this case), which together determine the *structure* of the system (we shall discuss this term later);

4. a term $v_3(t)$ depending on time, which reflects the changes

of *systematically* changing *data* or of explanatory phenomena which have not been included separately, such as changes in technique, seasonal influences, influences coming from foreign countries or from the rate of interest;

5. a term $R_t^{U'}$ which has not been discussed earlier, representing the *nonsystematic* changes of *data* or explanatory variables which might occur and which are not included elsewhere. Here we have to think first of a number of influences, each of which is small in itself, and which has been omitted in the simplification process; and second, of the influence of less important data which are usually considered as having a random character. The demand for consumption goods may be lower because more people happen to be ill or because more rain has fallen than usual, etc. Such magnitudes have an irregular influence, but also a small one, and as a rule they do not interest us. By way of exception, influences of some more importance may be included, such as, for instance, crop yields and possible technical improvements of great importance, or the influence of a strike, a political event of major importance, and so on.

We have used the word *structure* in particular when referring to statement 3 preceding. As a matter of fact, by the structure of an economy we mean in particular the permanent characteristics of it. Much may be said, however, in favor of including also the systematically changing variables mentioned under statement 4, particularly the natural, technical, and institutional factors which are included in that group. With an "open" economy, however, we also have under statement 4 those variables which may perhaps not be considered as data and consequently not as structural magnitudes in economic science taken as a whole.*

In our example, v_1 and v_2 have been considered as structural constants, i.e., the coefficients by which income and price level influence consumption. As we have remarked earlier, we can also dig deeper here and consider those magnitudes which lie behind the first ones as structural, as for instance the coefficients

* For instance, the world price level.

in the ophelimity functions and the technical coefficients. It is only for purposes of exposition that the coefficients of the demand curve themselves have been considered as data; a device to be compared to Cassel's working method.

As we have seen above, in the system of structural equations describing a certain economic model, the following kinds of magnitudes appear:

1. variables at the moment t
2. variables at earlier moments
3. data

The equations for the period t may be, for instance:

$$u_t = \upsilon_1 Y_{t-1} + \upsilon_2 p_{t-1} + \upsilon_3 T_{t-1} + R_t^u$$
$$Y_t = \eta_1 u_t + \eta_2 p_t + R_t^Y$$
$$p_t = \pi_1 Y_{t-1} + \pi_2 q_{t-1} + R_t^p$$

where:

u_t = the quantity demanded of all goods and services
p_t = the average price of these
Y_t = national income
T_t = the temperature and
q_t = the crop.

The first equation is the demand equation for all goods and services taken together; the second is the definition equation of national income put into a linear form, and the third is the price-fixation equation. It has been assumed that the total demand has also been influenced by the temperature, and the price by the crop size.

The categories under (2) and (3) together are sometimes called the *predetermined variables.* They form the whole of those magnitudes which are known at the beginning of the period t and which determine the magnitudes with t-subscripts except the R's. The three equations actually enable us to determine these magnitudes because there are precisely three such magnitudes. It may be noticed that each of these appears in several of the equations. If the system of structural equations is *solved* for the variables of period t, they assume the so-called *reduced form.*

In order to clarify the importance of the reduced form of the equations, we consider another example of a very simple system of equations, namely the demand and supply equations which together describe a certain market. The variables in such a system are the price p and the sales u; all the other magnitudes may be considered as data. The reduced form now is obtained by solving the demand and supply equations for p and u; as we have seen in § 8, we then have the so-called price equation and the turnover equation. These together form the reduced form of the structural equations of one market.

§ 12. The Movements of Complete Systems

The elementary equations taken together, now, enable us to learn the movements of all economic phenomena, if we only know:

1. the structure of the system, embodied in the given coefficients, lags, and trend terms;
2. the values of the other systematically changing data for each period of time;
3. the values of the nonsystematically changing data, R, and
4. certain initial values of the economic variables. What these values are can only be determined in a concrete case.

If we possess these data, we can determine the course of the final figures by a process of computation. We shall demonstrate this with the help of a very simple example referring to a single market which is in isolation and forms a system of its own. Let the demand u_t be dependent only on the price p_t, and without lag:

$$u_t = -p_t + 200 + t \qquad (12.1)$$

Let, further, the supply likewise be dependent on the price only, but with a lag of three time-units:

$$u_t = p_{t-3} \qquad (12.2)$$

In the demand equation we have also included a gradually increasing term, brought about, say, by population growth. The positive constant, here taken equal to 200, is necessary, because otherwise for every positive value of the price p at the moment O, a negative demand would appear, which is unacceptable.

As has been said, we also have to know a few initial values of one of the magnitudes in order to be able to compute the further course of the figures. In this case it can easily be seen that we must know the course of one of the magnitudes during the first three periods, say for $t = 1$, 2, and 3. We therefore assume that we know u_1, u_2, and u_3, which respectively amount to:

$$u_1 = 100; u_2 = 120; u_3 = 130$$

In fact, with the help of (12.1), we can now calculate p for $t = 1$, 2, and 3 and with the help of these, we can determine the values of u for $t = 4$, 5, and 6; from (12.2); then again, with (12.1) we can find p for $t = 4$, 5, and 6, etc. The result of this *numerical extrapolation* is as follows:

$t =$	1	2	3	4	5	6	7	8	9	10	11	12
$u_t =$	100	120	130	101	82	73	103	123	133	104	85	76
$p_t =$	101	82	73	103	123	133	104	85	76	106	126	136

The peculiarities of this movement will be dealt with presently. The calculations do not offer particular difficulties, but the method, in general, has two disadvantages. First, in order to become acquainted with the movement of one of the magnitudes, we always have to compute those of the other one as well. With systems containing a great number of variables, this involves a considerable amount of work. Second, in the method used above we can only learn something about the type of movement, and its dependence on the assumptions made, after much laborious work. The results are obtained only after a large amount of experimentation. Mathematics, however, offers us the means to overcome both objections.

In order to be able to leave undesired variables out of consideration, we must and can *eliminate* them, an operation well-known in elementary algebra. In the simple case of our example, we only have to substitute (12.2) into (12.1):

$$p_{t-3} = - p_t + 200 + t \tag{12.3}$$

This means that from a consideration of "first causes" we change over to the study of "second causes"; in other words, that we change over from elementary economic laws to *"derived economic laws."* There is quite a hierarchy of such derived laws, namely, derived laws obtained by combining 2, 3, etc. elementary equations. It is not easy to speak about these laws in words instead of in formulas, because most of them have not been given separate names. For this reason the method has sometimes been rejected as "streamlined analysis." The only thing to do about this is to choose the system as simple as possible, but of course, its closeness to reality will suffer by this procedure.

The end of this elimination process is reached when we are left with one equation with only one variable. It is not always possible to get as far as this; but it can be done with linear equations and similarly with a number of other types. In this *final equation* the remaining variable in general appears with values pertaining to various periods; the equation is, therefore, *dynamic.* Its coefficients are combinations of the coefficients appearing in the elementary equations. Moreover, in this final equation, various random disturbances from the elementary equations will be included. We have neglected these in our example, but they can easily be included in the model.

Both for the final equation and for the system as a whole, we can compute the further course by numerical extrapolation, if we know a few initial values of the variable. We shall now consider more systematically which results we can expect when doing so. To this purpose we first write equation (12.3) somewhat differently:

$$p_t = - p_{t-3} + 200 + t \tag{12.4}$$

Disregarding the random disturbance terms, which are neglected here, we now have three kinds of terms in the right-hand side of the equation.

The first kind of term for which we ask attention is the constant; in our example, the term 200. If this were the only term, the value of the variable p_t would also be constant, i.e., a stationary situation would exist and we would be dealing with *statics* in the narrower sense. This constant value of p would depend on the constant additive terms in the elementary equations and on the constant coefficients (for instance, elasticity coefficients and so on). It would be what we usually call the *equilibrium value* of p. If in the final equation (12.4) also random deviations R appear, p will show random deviations, which, however, group themselves around this equilibrium value.

The second kind of term is that *in which time appears explicitly* and which is a consequence of systematically changing data, such as increasing population and technical knowledge, or seasonal fluctuations or, also, changes originating abroad. If these appear—whether accompanied by those of the first kind, or not—the variable p cannot be constant any longer—i.e., a static equilibrium is impossible—but p will change in the course of time and, consequently, show systematic movements. These movements take place *simultaneously with the movements in the data* which give rise to them. On account of the absence of lag terms like p_{t-3}, the system immediately adapts itself to changes in data. If these changes of data were not present, no movement would be possible, i.e., *endogenous movements could not exist.* This system is not static in the narrower sense; it is static, however, according to our definition, and the corresponding theory is sometimes called *comparative statics.* The same formulas can be used for mutual comparison of two stationary situations, in which the data possess different values.

Finally, let us consider the influence of the third kind of term, namely, the term in which the variable appears for other moments of time. Let us first imagine that these terms—p_{t-3} in our example—are the only ones, with or without the constants. We can now conclude that in this case movements are possible without changes of data, i.e., *endogenous movements may occur.* We can only speak of this sort of movement, however, if this third kind of term is present; in other words, the system must be dynamic.

It can be shown mathematically that the movements which follow from the presence of terms with variables at various moments of time form a special type. They consist of one or more of the following movements, which may manifest themselves with various degrees of relative intensity:*

1. damped, nondamped, or antidamped periodic movements,
2. one-sided movements, gradually approaching a certain limit (convergent one-sided movements),
3. one-sided movements leading further and further away from the initial situation.

These one-sided movements are of certain mathematical types, but we shall not go into this further. The periodic movements may have various *periods.* These periods, however, are determined by the structural constants; they show some analogy to the so-called self-vibrations of various mechanical systems, the periods of which are also determined by their mass, their dimensions, elasticities, deflection resistances, etc.

In our example it can easily be seen that the movement is a purely periodic one (i.e., nondamped) with a period of six time-units. Omitting the last two terms, the equation becomes:

$$p_t = -p_{t-3}$$

From this it follows that

$$p_{t+3} = -p_t = p_{t-3}$$

which means that the value of p_{t-3} is equal to that of p_{t+3}. This is true for every arbitrary t, and therefore p is equal for any two periods of time with a mutual distance of six units. If, instead of $p_t = -p_{t-3}$ we have

---

* For exact proofs we refer to "Einige Grundfragen der mathematischen Konjunkturtheorie," Archiv für mathematische Wirtschafts- und Sozialforschung III (1937), pp. 1, 83.

$$p_t = -a\,p_{t-3}$$

and therefore

$$p_{t+3} = a^2 p_{t-3}$$

a damped movement would originate with $a < 1$ and an anti-damped movement with $a > 1$, as can easily be shown. In this simple case the period only depends on one of the structural data, namely the "lag" of three time-units, which, for instance, could represent the duration of a production process. In most cases the period will depend on other structural data as well, which will make the relation less simple.

The *amplitude* of the fluctuations, however—i.e., the size of the maximum deviations which appear—depends on the deviation from equilibrium existing in the beginning; this could be called an inheritance of history, although it need not always be old history. In general, influence will be exerted by the intensities with which the random deviations—for instance, the consequences of crop changes, possible wars, etc.—make themselves felt.

What happens if all terms are present at the same time? In case we are dealing with a linear equation, which, as a first approximation, can often be assumed, it can be shown that the movement is the *sum total* of:

1. an equilibrium level,
2. an endogenous movement as described above and
3. "exogenous" movements brought about by the change of data, with the same period as the movements of the data, insofar as these are periodic, and which show a linear growth in time if the data show a linear growth.

To these, we have to add the possible random deviations which are cumulated in a certain way. We shall explain this in more detail. For the sake of simplicity, let us assume that only the first term of the right side of (12.4) and a random deviation are present; we then have:

$$p_t = -p_{t-3} + R_t^p$$

If p_{t-3} is given, p follows from this equation. For p_{t+3} we have:

$$p_{t+3} = -p_t + R^p_{t+3} = p_{t-3} - R^p_t + R^p_{t+3}$$

Here the combined influence of two random deviations can be seen. For p_{t+6} we would have:

$$p_{t+6} = -p_{t-3} + R^p_t - R^p_{t+3} + R^p_{t+6}$$

and so on.

If we survey the result, it becomes clear that the movements shown by economic phenomena, under the influence of changes in data and of the dynamic character of the relations, show the following components:

1. one-sided movements brought about by one-sided changes of the data, for instance, growth of the population;
2. one-sided movements brought about by internal dynamics, for instance, capital formation;
3. periodic movements brought about by periodic movements of the data, for instance, foreign business-cycle influences and seasonal fluctuations;
4. periodic movements brought about by internal dynamics, for instance, the movement of the business-cycle;
5. random movements brought about by random (irregular) changes of the data, for instance, crop changes and many small structural changes.

§ 13. Stable and Unstable Equilibria. The Purpose of Economic Policy

We have already seen that the economic systems with which we have occupied ourselves thus far possess no static equilibrium. Nevertheless, the purpose of economic policy, especially of business-cycle policy, is often formulated as a more balanced development of economic life. In the light of the preceding we have to understand by this, a development where the movements under 3, 4, and 5 are restricted as far as possible. The aim of econometric research in this field, therefore, is to determine whether such an aim can be attained by the measures which are being proposed from various sides. The investigations in this respect are only in their first stage; a few preliminary results will be given in § 41. In this methodologic chapter it is appropriate to indicate briefly the concepts of *equilibrium* and of *stability* and *instability* of equilibria. Whereas by equilibrium in the limited static sense, a situation is meant which can be maintained, such a definition has only little value for our systems as it requires a situation which cannot exist. There is more sense in the definition of an *equilibrium development,* indicating a movement as gradual as possible, or, more precisely: that movement of all possible movements of the system which conforms itself most closely to a straight line. From the preceding it can be inferred that, for a given system, these movements are certain well-defined ones, namely the components 1 and 2 of the series mentioned at the end of § 12. The movements taking place in reality and containing also the components 3, 4, and 5, are fluctuations around the former ones.

If these fluctuations are damped, we can call the equilibrium development *stable.* In case they are nondamped or antidamped, we call the equilibrium development *unstable.* It is the task of business-cycle policy to change the structure of the national economy—or the world economy—in such a way that its stability becomes as great as possible; in other words, that the *degree of damping becomes as great as possible.* Expressing this in everyday language, but perhaps easier to understand: we must learn to nip the fluctuations in the bud and, if possible, not incidentally but systematically, i.e., by changing the structure. Such a structural change will perhaps have to be found in the financial or monetary government policy, but possibly also elsewhere. Here the econometrician has no vote: he only has to investigate the problems put before him.

This problem, however, cannot be separated from the other aims of general economic policy, namely the requirement to reach the highest possible average level of prosperity. If it would turn out that a greater stability could only be reached at the cost of a lower average level of prosperity, a choice would have to be made on welfare grounds.

3
Statistical Testing

§ 14. Statistical Testing; Measuring Phenomena

We have already stated that econometric investigations should be started by setting up one or more relations between the magnitudes to be studied, with the help of mathematical-economic methods. When this has been done—we have called it the first stage of the investigation—the statistician has the floor. He will try to ascertain whether the supposed relations agree with the facts and if so, whether the measuring of certain magnitudes will make it possible to obtain more concrete information concerning those relations.

The first question the statistician has to answer is whether all phenomena the economist deals with are *measurable*. It is often stated that so many imponderables play a role in economic life that it is fundamentally incorrect to expect that reality can be laid bare by measurement.

This question is not new. It was asked in connection with the natural sciences before it was asked for economics. Physicists have been reproached because they considered heat as something measurable. Practically everyone is now convinced the day has been won by the "measurers," who by their delight in measuring have contributed to enormous progress in the theory of heat. Nor do the contemporary psychologists shrink from measuring many imponderables. However, we shall not reason by analogy, but prefer to go into the question directly. The main problems of economics are concerned with measurable phenomena. We speak of production, of unemployment, of real wages, etc. As far as the influence of imponderables on these measurable phenomena is concerned, we must distinguish between these imponderables themselves and their influence on the measurable phenomena. Even if expectations themselves are perhaps not measurable, their influence on investments can only be in the form of a certain increase or decrease of the investments, a measurable phenomenon therefore. This latter fact alone interests us. It must moreover be remarked that the expectations themselves are usually based on very concrete and measurable phenomena. It is obvious, therefore, that we may try to investigate the influence of these phenomena on investments, disregarding the fact that expectations themselves might not be measurable.

Another example refers to the "degree of satisfaction." This magnitude is generally considered nonmeasurable. But after examination of the problem it becomes clear that it is not necessary to know the degree of satisfaction if we want to explain the behavior of economic subjects. We only need know the combinations of goods which bring about the same degree of satisfaction—all lying on "indifference-surfaces"—and these are measurable in principle.

We therefore believe that it is not necessary to worry unduly about this matter.

A similar question is: Do psychological relations take place *according to certain laws* in such a way that they can be expressed in mathematical equations? Often doubts are expressed on this question; it is pointed out that free will can, under the same circumstances, lead at one time to a certain reaction and at another time to a different one. The answer to this objection is that if another reaction follows the second time, there must have been a reason for it. Therefore we should speak of different situations when completely describing the circumstances. Moreover—and this is of particular importance to macroeconomic investigations—there is a great likelihood that the joint behavior of large groups of persons shows a more regular pattern than the behavior of separate persons, because individual deviations greatly compensate each other. This is confirmed in many cases by observation; as will become clear from a few of our examples, there is often a surprisingly great regularity in mass reactions.

The simplest form of measurement with which we are concerned in statistics is the measurement of a separate phenomenon: the determining of a price, of the quantity consumed, of national income, or of the part of the latter accruing to the working class. From the point of view of econometrics, little can be added to the achievements which were made in this field by government statistics, by statistical evaluation methods, and by theoretical statistics long ago. It is of primary importance that we obtain an impression of the margin of uncertainty in the statistical results. This can often be attained by comparing various alternative observations or calculations; if an average price is concerned, we have to study the variance of the component price data and to apply the formula for the standard deviation of an average. Similar but rougher methods can be applied in other cases where fewer observations are available.

The *standard deviation* σ of a set of figures is computed by ascertaining for each of them the deviation from the average, by squaring these deviations, adding the squares, dividing this total by the number, and finally by taking the square root from the average of the squares of the deviations which has thus been obtained. Expressing this in a formula:

$$\sigma = \sqrt{\frac{1}{n}\left(x_1^2 + x_2^2 + \dots + x_n^2\right)}$$

where $x_1 \dots x_n$ are the deviations from the average.

The real econometric problems begin when we study whole series of observations, in particular series indicating the course of a certain magnitude in time, the so-called *time series.*

§ 15. Determining the Components of Time Series

Only rarely are all aspects of the behavior of a time series made the subject of econometric study at the same time. Usually various components in this behavior are distinguished; the traditional classification made by business-cycle research workers is in four categories, namely:

1. the trend or general direction of the series, or better, of the curve representing the latter;
2. cyclical fluctuations;

3. seasonal fluctuations, i.e., the fluctuations with a period of usually one year, which are the consequence of the natural change of seasons or of conventions with respect to the calendar and
4. random and incidental changes.

The underlying principle of classification here is the length of the waves. It could be stated that waves of 15 years and more and the one-sided movements (to be considered as waves with an infinite period) belong to group 1, those of from three to 15 years to group 2, those of one year to group 3, and the still shorter ones to group 4. Something, however, will be said about this presently.

As a consequence of the irregular form of most waves, their length often cannot be stated with certainty, or at any rate it is liable to changes. Some waves are not genuine waves, at least according to some writers. The so-called "long business-cycle waves" (Kondratiefs), which have a period of about 40 years, are, according to some authors, only more or less accidental alternations of rising and falling movements. Group 4 also shows rising and falling movements, but we certainly cannot speak here of a real periodicity, or a tendency to it. Changes which occur *only once (structural breaks,* as they are sometimes called) are difficult to classify. Finally, waves of different lengths do not always have different causes, which would make it illogical to separate them.

A few things can be said against the classification itself, i.e., against the choice of the boundaries. There are fluctuations which in origin are perfectly analogous to seasonal fluctuations, but which have a much shorter period, namely, a month, a week, or a day. Examples are the fluctuations in retail sales, in production of electric power, or in traffic. They therefore belong to group 3. On the other hand, there are random fluctuations with a much longer period than one year. The variations in crop yields are a very important example of a random influence. Should we want to ascribe a period to these, a time interval of three years could best be used. Nevertheless, they must be considered as belonging to category 4. Wagemann only partly meets these objections by his distinction between "free" and "tied" fluctuations.

Much confusion has arisen in the use of the words *long and short* waves in economic life. By "long business-cycle waves," sometimes the waves of 40-years length which have just been mentioned, are meant, sometimes also the waves of approximately nine years; by "short waves," the latter are sometimes meant and in other instances the reference is to the waves of approximately three years which appear in the United States. Schumpeter has proposed to prevent this difficulty by calling the three sorts of waves after the authors who have discovered them, and consequently to identify them as *Kondratiefs, Juglars,* and *Kitchins.* As regards business-cycle fluctuations, there is the additional difficulty that the various writers do not yet quite agree on the causes and therefore a causally founded definition cannot be given easily. Here we usually think of movements generated by endogenous causes. For certain special markets we can also distinguish cycles differing in length from the other ones, for instance, a cycle in house-building activity in the United States (15 years), a coffee-market cycle (also about 15 years), a hog-market cycle (three years), etc.

As regards *seasonal fluctuations,* we can distinguish between the normal or *average* seasonal movement, which is considered to be determined by strict laws—purely periodic, for instance—and the fluctuations which can be ascribed to the seasonal changes actually taking place in a certain year. During a very cold winter, for instance, water traffic will show a deeper trough than it does normally. This trough belongs to the individual seasonal influence of the year concerned, but not to the normal seasonal movement.

These remarks reflect a number of facts which can be useful to the econometrician. At the same time, they can protect him against mechanical application of some of the calculation schemes which have been set up in order to determine the components. Every case should be considered separately. Taking all these reservations into account, we think that our classification of components is fundamentally sound; in particular the isolation of seasonal fluctuations, of the short random fluctuations, and of a theoretically justified trend, because separate complexes of causes can be made responsible for their presence. We also think that we have given a foundation—albeit conditional—of the method in § 12, because we have shown there that the total movement of an economic variable can—under certain conditions—be split up into a number of additive components.

In the following we shall go a little further into the computation of the separate components; we do not intend, however, to discuss the actual calculation rules in detail, nor to illustrate them by examples. For this, we refer to the literature on the subject.

So far as the distinction based on the length of the periods makes sense—which is often the case—a general method can be given to determine all the components, namely that of *moving averages.* The seasonal fluctuations and all shorter fluctuations can be eliminated, for instance, by taking, instead of a series of monthly figures, the series of the averages of the terms Nos. 1 to 12, Nos. 2 to 13, etc. This series is called a 12-months moving average. Each of its terms has been built up from figures of all seasons, and therefore no seasonal changes are present in this series: the seasonal fluctuations have been eliminated. At the same timc, all shorter fluctuations have practically been eliminated. It is true, complete elimination can only be spoken of if the period of the fluctuations goes a certain number of times into 12 months. But all other fluctuations appearing in reality can be assumed to be approximately eliminated. If we want to become acquainted with the shortest of the fluctuations eliminated—let it be assumed that these have a period of three months—we have to determine the three-months moving averages and to subtract these from the original series: we then are left with the shortest fluctuations. If the next period is a 12-months one, we can find the corresponding component by subtracting from the original series both the shortest fluctuations which have just been determined and the 12-months moving average. In similar ways each of the components can be computed. This method, by the way, is rather rough. Moreover, for seasonal fluctuations it does not show the average or normal seasonal movement. To this end, we can take the averages of all January figures, of all February figures, etc., of the seasonal component determined in the way described previously. More refined methods, however, exist. With these we shall now deal in some more detail.

§ 16. More Refined Methods; the Trend

We shall first consider the determination of the *trend* more closely.

If the wavelength of the longest fluctuations which we do not want to consider as part of the trend amounts to nine years, these fluctuations and the shorter ones will be eliminated if the nine-years moving averages are determined; we then are left with the trend series. By doing this, we make use of the property of shorter fluctuations; that the sum total of their deviations is equal to zero, if taken for one or more periods. This property, strictly speaking, is only valid for nondisturbed, purely periodic movements. It does not exactly apply to damped or antidamped movements or to disturbed movements. In order to avoid this inaccuracy, we can also try to base the computations on a property of the trend itself. In that case we speak of a *mathematical trend* in contradistinction to the method just described.

When calculating a *mathematical trend* we assume *a priori* that the trend is a mathematical graph, a curve of a certain form. The simplest form is the *straight line;* also simple is the *exponential line,* the ordinates of which form a geometric series at mutually equal distances. If we change from the given series to the series of the logarithms of the figures, the trend, if originally an exponential line, will become a straight line. This property is often made use of to reproduce the original series on a logarithmic scale: the exponential trend then is a straight line. Whereas the straight line is characterized by a constant absolute increase per year, the exponential line shows a constant percentage increase. More intricate lines have been used as trends, namely, so-called *parabolas* (of arbitrary order) and also the *logistic curve*. The latter deserves more explanation, on account of its fundamental and practical importance. The simplest numerical example is obtained if the trend x_t for each moment t is calculated according to the formula:*

$$x_t = \frac{120}{1+2^{-t}} \tag{16.1}$$

where t goes from $-\infty$ to $+\infty$. The following values are obtained:

$$\begin{array}{cccccccccc} t = -\infty \ldots & -3 & -2 & -1 & 0 & +1 & +2 & +3 & \ldots +\infty \\ 0 & 13\frac{1}{3} & 24 & 40 & 60 & 80 & 96 & 106\frac{2}{3} & 120 \end{array}$$

Representing this graphically (see Fig. 2, curve B), we obtain a curve rising slowly at first, then quicker, and finally approaching a certain saturation value, 120 in this case. In the beginning, the increase is slow if measured in absolute figures, but quickest proportionately.

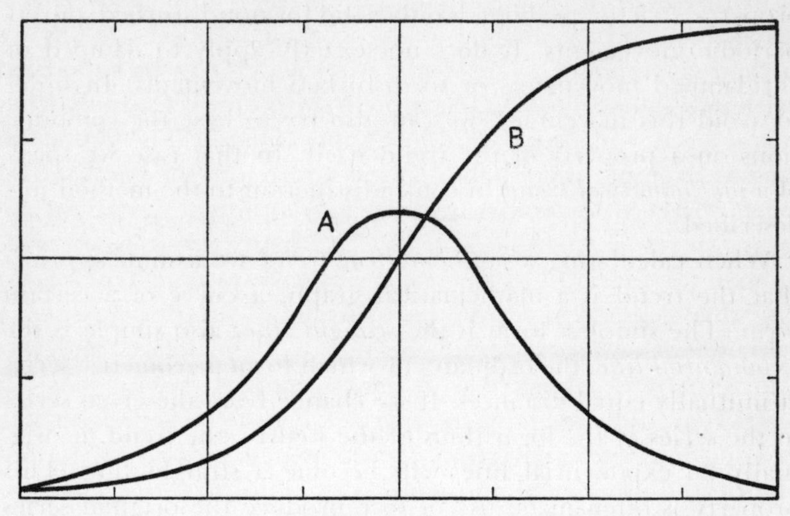

Fig. 2. Course of the Gauss curve (A) and of the logistic curve (B).

* The figures 120 and 2 are only examples; other figures could be used.

Which of these various lines should be used in a concrete case—what is the criterion? In principle, this should be decided by the law determining the generation of the trend. This means that we must have an explanation, a theory, about that movement. In certain simple cases this is actually so. In the case of population growth, for instance, under certain simplifying circumstances, both mortality and birth will be proportional to the size of the population and so will, therefore, the yearly increase of the latter. If this is true, the population line will be exponential. A similar case will be found if the growth of the stock of capital goods under simplified circumstances is studied: the increase of that stock is determined by the savings and these are determined mainly by nonlabor income, which in its turn is often proportionate to the existing stock of capital goods. Also in this case we obtain an exponential growth.

The logistic curve originates if a somewhat more complicated process of growth takes place; namely, if the increase of a population of size x is proportionate both to x itself and to the distance of x to a higher constant figure, a. This law of growth has been found in colonies of lower animals having a fixed stock of food or food source at their disposal. The figure a then corresponds to the population which can be supported with that source of food. The growth slows down if x approaches a and a is not surpassed, but only approximated. The figure 120 in our example corresponds to the figure a. This law has also been observed for human populations, although deviations appear. Moreover, the source of food is usually not constant with human populations. In general a growth approximately following this logistic curve can be expected if after some time a certain slackening, a certain saturation, takes place, and this can actually be observed with many economic phenomena. In particular, the development of the quantity of a new article coming into use often shows approximately this curve, for instance, the number of automobiles or radio sets, the length of the network of railways or of the telephone network, and the size of the production of artificial silk. This development can also be considered somewhat differently. Some people immediately want to have a commodity that is new on the market. Others prefer first to see which way the cat jumps; others, again, have to overcome a great inertia before deciding to buy. The speed of reaction, therefore, is widely divergent for various people and it can be assumed that like other human qualities, it is approximately distributed according to the "normal law" or Gauss-Laplace law (see also § 17). By accumulating the values of the new purchases, which are distributed in time according to the Gaussian law, we obtain the total number of objects in use, and the course of the cumulated Gaussian curve is very much like that of the logistic curve.

The exponential curve can be considered as an approximation of part of the first stage of the logistic curve; namely, where the saturation tendency practically cannot be noticed yet, because x is so small in comparison to a that from a to x may be considered constant. The increase in this case is only proportionate to x. Besides, the straight line can be considered as an approximation over still smaller intervals of each of these lines, also of the higher parts of the logistic curve; every curve can be approximated by a straight line. Parabolas usually cannot be founded theoretically, and therefore are not recommended strongly; they are usually chosen on the basis of a more external resemblance with the general course of the series to be dealt with.

The presence of an exponential trend in a series x has as a consequence that in the series x′ of percentage increases of x, no trend is present; the figures x′ are all grouped around a figure not equal to zero. Instead of eliminating the trend and working with deviations from trend we sometimes use percentage increases, known in American literature as "link relatives."

§ 17. Determining and Eliminating the Random Component

By a "random component" we mean in the broad sense a variable which can assume more values than one, and where it is not certain beforehand which of these values will be assumed in certain circumstances—for instance, at a certain moment of time. A clear example which tells us more than abstract definitions is the number of times we can throw heads with one or more coins. If we throw with one coin, that number can be 0 or 1 on each throw; if we throw with three coins, it can be 0, 1, 2, or 3. The number of times each of these values appears is its frequency; the table of these frequencies is the frequency distribution. If the latter is expressed relatively, i.e., in figures the sum total of which is 1 and which are proportionate to the frequencies, we speak of a *probability distribution.* The probability or relative frequency of the appearance of one certain result indicates which part of the observations leads to that outcome.

The probability distribution of the outcomes of a head or tail game with one coin, repeated a great number of times, can be given by the following table:

Number of "heads"	Probability
0	½
1	½

Quite a number of other probability distributions of random variables is possible. One very well-known one is the Gaussian distribution. It refers to a continuous random variable, i.e., a random variable which can assume all values in a certain interval and not only integers. The *Gauss law* can be represented graphically by the well-known bell-shaped curve (Fig. 2, curve A); the probability that the observation lies in a very small unit-interval near the value x is

$$y = \frac{1}{\sigma\sqrt{2\pi}}\epsilon^{-\frac{\alpha^2}{2\sigma^2}}$$

If a random variable shows this distribution law, it is called "random" in the narrower sense. Such a distribution can originate from various sorts of mechanisms. It is found approximately, for instance, if the value of the variable at each moment is the result of a very great number of mutually independent forces, each causing a small deviation which itself is random in the wider sense.

A series of figures satisfying some frequency distribution, for instance, the Gauss law, may show various properties as regards the *sequence* of the figures. It is conceivable that the figures are arranged according to size. It is also conceivable that no regularity can be detected in the sequence. In particular, it can be investigated whether any dependence exists between two successive terms. This can be done by considering the frequency distribution of the second item of a number of arbitrary pairs, if the first items of these pairs are all equal to a fixed number a, and checking whether this distribution would be different from the one which is found if the first items are equal to another fixed figure, b. If the frequency distribution of the second items is always the same, no matter which value the first figure has, the subsequent terms are said to be *independent* of each other. If the series of figures we are dealing with has originated in the way described previously, namely, as the result of a very great number of independently working forces, each in itself causing a small deviation which is random in the wider sense, the subsequent terms will also show this independence. In general, the subsequent terms of a series of figures will be mutually independent, if the laws governing the origin of each figure do not depend on the preceding figure.

The determination of the random component in a series of observed figures usually takes place as follows. First, a hypothesis is drawn up concerning the behavior of all other components. On this basis the random component is ascertained and it is subsequently checked whether the latter satisfies the requirements which can be put to a random series. The hypothesis made regarding the sum total of the other components usually is that these have a "smooth course." This can be specified mathematically by assuming that the curve representing this sum total is of the first degree (straight line), or of the second, third, fourth degree, etc. These curves are "smooth" to a decreasing extent; they become more and more complicated and are liable to more and greater oscillations. We can distinguish here between an integral and a differential method. With the former, it is assumed that the sum total of the other components, taken over the whole period under consideration, is a straight line or one of the higher-degree curves. Actually this total then is equated to a trend, namely, to a mathematical trend. With the differential method it is only assumed that these requirements are satisfied for small parts of the period, in other words, that in the vicinity of each point the systematic components together form a straight line or one of the higher-degree curves. Calculation shows that this is equivalent to the assumption that the sum total of these components can be approximated by a moving average. If a straight line is taken as an approximation, it is an ordinary moving average; if, however, higher-degree curves are assumed, it turns out to be a weighted moving average, where higher weights are given to the middle terms than to the extreme terms. The number of terms of these moving averages—nonweighted or weighted—again depends on the length of the shorter periods for which the assumption is made. If it is assumed, for instance, that for every five points the total of the systematic components forms a second-degree curve (an ordinary parabola), we obtain a weighted moving average of the following shape:

$$\frac{1}{35}(-3x_{-2} + 12x_{-1} + 17x_0 + 12x_{+1} - 3x_{+2})$$

The total of the other components is determined, therefore, either as a mathematical or as a nonmathematical trend. The remaining part which pretends to be the random component is found by subtraction of these trend figures from the given series. Finally, we check whether this remaining part satisfies the requirements.

These can be twofold, namely, independence of the subsequent terms and a Gaussian frequency distribution. The independence is checked by determining the *autocorrelation,* i.e., the correlation (see § 19) existing between the subsequent terms of the series. The checking of the frequency distribution can take place, either rather roughly by drawing up a graph of the distribution and comparing graphically, or more accurately, by making use of the mathematical-statistical methods devised for this purpose (the chisquare test).

§ 18. Determining the Seasonal Fluctuations and the Business-Cycle Component

As seasonal fluctuations as a rule have a fixed period, more refined computational procedures are sometimes possible than with the other components. In accordance with the aim of this book we shall only clarify the fundamental significance of some of the most important methods of calculation.

We shall first confine ourselves to determining the normal seasonal movement (see § 15). The first question which is often asked is whether the seasonal influence is *additive* or *multiplicative*. By this, the following is meant: If the general level at which a variable is situated changes, will the addition in the top season remain the same or will it be proportionate to the height of that general level? Further investigation shows that it depends on the mechanism of the seasonal influences whether the first or the second possibility is realized. Moreover, there are many other possibilities. Mostly, however, the statistical material does not allow us to make an exact decision in this case. The ideal scientific research would require an accurate investigation; this however, in general, is still in the realm of unfulfilled wishes.

Further, we can imagine a *fixed* and a *systematically changing* seasonal pattern. With a fixed pattern the seasonal influence is assumed equal every year—be it additive or multiplicative. It is conceivable, however, that the peaks become gradually less high and the troughs less deep. An example is egg prices: it has been possible to stimulate winter laying by night illumination in the henhouses, which has led to a decrease in seasonal differences. This lowering of the peaks can be considered to be regular in various ways: usually it will be assumed that they diminish by an equal amount every year and it can be determined statistically what the size of that amount must be in order to obtain the best possible adaptation to the statistical material.

The systematic change can be conceived to be even more intricate; with Wald's method, for instance, the height of the peaks and the depth of the troughs are considered to be proportionate to the standard deviation of the seasonal fluctuations, the latter being determined from the deviations of 12-months moving averages.

Shifting seasons offer a particular difficulty. If the shifts take place systematically, they can sometimes be regarded as a special case of the example of changing the seasonal pattern mentioned first: offset against a decline in one of the months there can be a rise in another month. If, however, the shift does not continue in the same direction, this method cannot be applied. One example is the shifting of seasons as a consequence of the change of

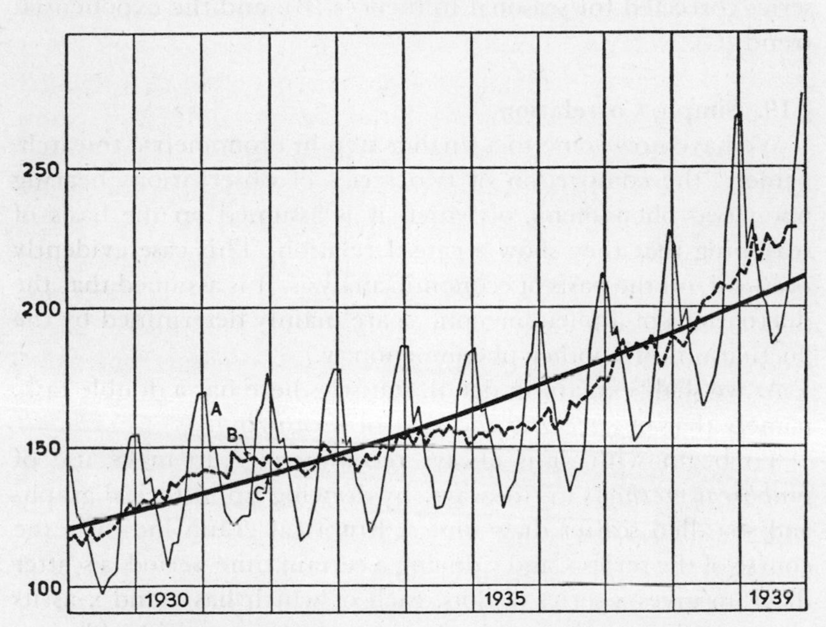

Fig. 3. Example of the computation of the components of a series (A) (electricity consumption in the Netherlands in millions of kwh, thin line). The heavy drawn line (C) indicates the trend, computed according to the exponential method. The dotted line (B) is the series after elimination of the seasonal fluctuations according to the multiplicative method, which is the method to use here because the seasonal fluctuations are proportionate to the yearly averages. The dotted line therefore gives the total of trend, business-cycle component and random component.

the dates of Easter and Whitsunday. Of course, we can try to make the necessary corrections as we go along. Another instance is a changing season brought about by weather conditions. This gradually brings us to the subject of the individual seasonal movement, i.e., the seasonal movement which differs from year to year as a result of a known cause.

The ideal of scientific treatment here is the causal explanation, for instance, the explanation of seasonal movements based on the temperature, the rainfall, etc. They then become correlation problems, to which we shall now turn.

In Figure 3, finally, we give an example of a series (A), a series corrected for seasonal influences (B), and the exponential trend (C).

§ 19. Simple Correlation

We have now come to a further step in econometric research, namely, the comparison of two series of observations bearing upon two phenomena, of which it is assumed on the basis of reasoning that they show a causal relation. This case evidently occurs if, on the basis of economic analysis, it is assumed that the fluctuations of a phenomenon, x, are mainly determined by the fluctuations of another phenomenon, y.

As we shall explain in detail, statistics here has a double task, namely that of *checking* and that of *measuring*.

To begin with, it is always recommended to make use of *graphical methods* in two ways: by drawing up historical graphs and so-called scatter diagrams. A historical graph indicates the course of the series x and y during a certain time period, a scatter diagram gives a series of dots, each of which has y and x as its two coordinates. As a rule the independent variable (the explanatory series, in this case y) will be measured along the horizontal axis and the dependent variable (the series to be explained, in our case x) along the vertical axis. If there is a distinct relation between the two series, the scatter diagram is a finer tool than the historical graph. But the latter shows more clearly whether there is a difference in *trend,* or a *lag.* In those cases scatter diagrams are sometimes so poor that it cannot be seen what the relation really is. This last remark, by the way, refers to attempts to give suggestions to the econometrician to change the economic hypothesis to be tested, in case the first statistical check has taken place and has given a negative result.

If the two phenomena actually show a close relation, this will manifest itself in the dots obtained, which will lie nearly on one line (see Fig. 4A). If this is the case, the *correlation* is said to be high, possibly complete. If the dots are more scattered, there is incomplete or low correlation. According to the form of the line around which the dots group themselves, we have *linear* or *non-linear* correlation. In the case of linear correlation we also speak

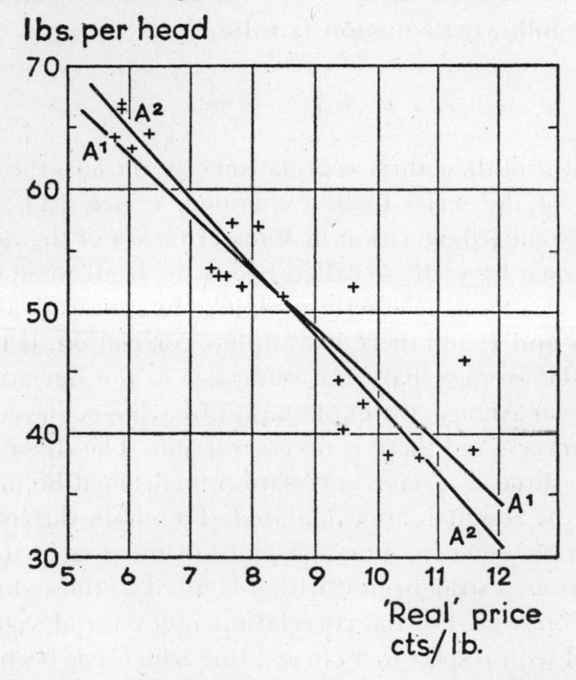

Fig. 4A. Example of simple correlation (the demand line for sugar, taken from Schultz, The Theory and Measurement of Demand). The two straight lines indicate the first (A^1) and second (A^2) regression lines.

of *normal correlation* if for every value of y the deviations of the x values follow the Gaussian frequency distribution with a standard deviation independent of y, and similarly as regards the deviations of y for every value of x.

If the graphical method has shown that there is a certain relation, and therefore, a chance of success, a further refinement of the analysis can take place by algebraic methods.

The *checking* function of statistics must give a reply to the question: Is there any relation between y and x? A reply in the affirmative or in the negative is not adequate here; we need a quantitative reply, because there are various sorts of possible intermediate forms. The relation, therefore, is close to a greater or less extent, and this can be expressed by the *correlation coefficient,* by the *correlation index,* or the *correlation ratio.* For all three, the following equation is valid:

$$r^2 = 1 - \frac{\sigma^2_{x,\,y}}{\sigma^2_x}$$

Here r is one of these three correlation criteria, σ_x is the standard deviation of the series to be explained, x (see § 14), whereas $\sigma_{x,y}$ is the standard deviation of some criterion of the deviations not explained by y, the so-called residuals. If all these residuals are zero, every x can be exactly explained by the assumed relation between y and x; and there is complete correlation. If the residuals, on the average, have the same size as the deviations of x from its own average, the explanation by y has achieved a minimum of success and there is no correlation. The differences between the three criteria of correlation mentioned lie in the way in which the residuals are calculated. To obtain the correlation coefficient, we calculate the deviations of the dots in the scatter diagram from a straight line which is fitted to those dots in the best possible way. For the correlation index the deviations are calculated with respect to a curved line which has been fitted as well as possible. Finally, in the case of the correlation ratio we take the deviations with respect to the averages of all x values belonging to each value of y. The deviations in all these cases are measured vertically, i.e., in x direction. The correlation coefficient is the severest judge; it is 1 only if the dots lie on a straight line. With the correlation index, the statistical material has, so to speak, been given some more chance, as the curve has been drawn according to requirement; the correlation ratio has even more been fitted to the material by taking the line of the averages, which may jump rather arbitrarily. It is even possible—namely, by measuring the y values finely enough—to see to it that every y value only appears once, so that the corresponding average x value is equal to the (only) x value which appears in that group. Then there is complete correlation in every case in which the y values all differ. This, however, is of course unacceptable and in general such a fine subdivision will not be made. Strictly speaking, no use may be made of the correlation ratio, if the relation to be tested has actually been described beforehand by the economist.

Whether a correlation will be considered satisfactory depends on the tolerance (room for free play) which is allowed, and some difference of tastes exists in this respect. With a great number of observations, moreover, we can be satisfied with a lower correlation than with a small number. We must set a standard for ourselves here.

If this standard has been met, we come to the *measuring* function of statistics. It is now important to determine what relation there is between y and x. In the case of a straight line this question can be expressed as follows: By how much will x increase, if y increases by unity? This amount is called the *regression coefficient;* also in case we have to deal with other than straight lines, the curve indicating the relation is called the *regression line* (or regression *curve*); the equation indicating the relation is called the *regression equation.* The regression coefficient and, in general, the constants appearing in the regression equation can of course not be determined exactly, but with a margin of uncertainty; mathematical statistics offer several criteria for this. The higher the correlation and the greater the number of observations, the smaller this uncertainty will be.

In Fig. 4B a second example of simple correlation is given, about the result of which some remarks have already been made in § 7.

The line or curve indicating the relation can be determined unambiguously if there is complete correlation. As soon as the correlation is not complete, several lines are possible, varying according to the principles applied to make the line fit to the scatter diagram in the best possible way. The line is usually determined by minimizing the sum of the squares of the residuals in the x direction, i.e., by applying the principle of least squares to the residuals in the direction of the variable to be explained. The line obtained in this way, particularly if a straight line has been chosen, is called the *first* regression line.

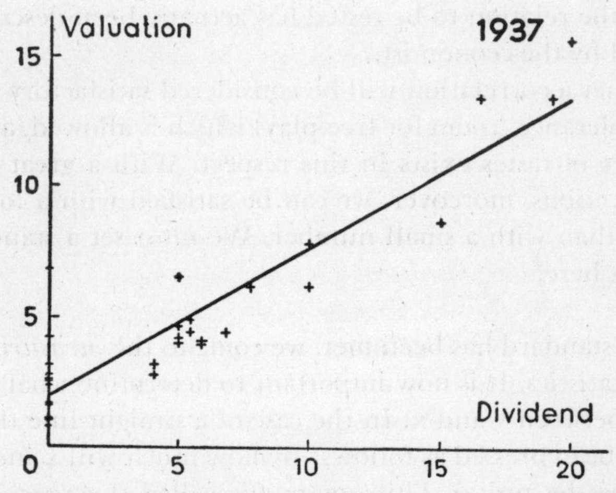

Fig. 4B. Example of simple correlation: the relation between dividends and "valuation" of shares. See § 7.

If the principle is applied in the y direction (that of the explanatory variable), we have the *second* regression line. In case of complete correlation the two lines coincide. If the correlation coefficient is zero, they are perpendicular to each other and coincide with the axes. The deviation between the two lines (the angle, or another criterion) therefore, can also be adopted for measuring the correlation.

If the first regression line is taken, it is assumed that the deviations between the actual and the calculated values are exclusively a consequence of (1) measuring errors in the series to be explained, and (2) incompleteness of the theory. As a rule the greatest importance will have to be attached to (2). If there is reason also to suppose errors of measurement in the explanatory variable, still other regression lines can be used.

§ 20. Possibilities of Application in the Economic Field

As has been mentioned previously, the method of testing by simple correlation can only be used if a magnitude x can be explained by another magnitude, y. We know that this is only rarely the case in economic science. As a rule a variable x is influenced by many other variables. Of old, this has been the difficulty in testing economic laws; the theoretical laws actually do relate two magnitudes at a time, but under the "ceteris paribus" condition: that other factors remain the same, which usually is not the case. Simple correlation, therefore, is important for econometric work only if the theory can show that there are cases in which the ceteris paribus clause is nearly fulfilled. We shall consider to what extent this actually turns out to be the case, in particular as regards demand and supply functions. We therefore interrupt for the moment our consideration of the technical problems of statistical testing. We allow ourselves this encroachment on our systematic treatment of the problem because also when actually carrying out an investigation, the ball has to go to and fro between statistician and economist again and again.

We now come to a classic problem: the statistic determination of demand or supply curves, i.e., the relation between price and quantity sold. This is only possible if the other (demand or supply) factors remain constant; for the demand curve, it is sometimes referred to as the Cournot-case. These other factors are: for the demand function, particularly income and possibly the price of competing articles; and for the supply function, production costs and capacity. Before enumerating a few cases which, in our opinion, satisfy this requirement, we have to correct somewhat the conception which we have just given. It is not necessary, namely, that the other factors remain constant, even approximately; it is sufficient that their influence is small. This happens when they appear in the reaction relation with a small coefficient.

We think that in the following cases there are indeed reasons to expect that the remaining factors will have a small influence.

1. The demand for *primary necessaries of life* will depend little on income; at least as long as they are not highly substitutable or complementary goods their demand will mainly depend on their own price.

2. The demand for goods whose prices *fluctuate very greatly* through circumstances on the supply side will depend relatively little on the other factors. Examples are goods with very strong fluctuations in crop yields, in particular if they are perishable, such as fruits and vegetables; and articles with very strong production fluctuations as a consequence of small adaptation possibilities of supply to demand through the long duration of the production process, such as pork and coffee. An article with very heavy supply fluctuations, moreover, is anchovy, where the catch in one year is sometimes a hundredfold that of another year (see § 40).

3. The demand for goods with very *rapid* supply fluctuations. As changes of income—for the economy as a whole—usually take place relatively gradually, we can reduce the influence of this factor by considering short periods. Examples are various goods with a strong seasonal movement in supply, and which cannot be stored. Fruit and vegetables have already been mentioned in another connection; eggs are another instance, especially in those times when less of them were stored in cold-storage warehouses.

4. The *supply* function of goods with relatively stable costs but great fluctuations in demand, such as mineral raw materials, may also be mentioned.

In a number of other cases the ceteris paribus clause is not satisfied, so that x has to be explained by several variables y, z, etc. Nevertheless, it is often possible to reduce the multiple relation appearing now to a simple one, which subsequently can be tested by a simple correlation calculation. Usually certain *corrections* are carried out beforehand with the material, or other variables are substituted. We shall enumerate a number of the best-known ones.

1. If in a demand function the most important other factor which has changed is the *size of the population,* the quantity demanded *per capita* is considered. The correction here consists in dividing the quantities by the number of the population.

2. If the most important other factor which has changed is the *price level of all other goods*—where all other goods are assumed to be competitive with the good considered—the price of the good under investigation is divided by the general price level; we work with *deflated prices.* It is tacitly assumed here, by the way, that the influence of the general price level is such that in the demand function exactly the quotient of the price and the general price level appears. It is conceivable that this function is different.

3. If, in a *supply function,* the other factors to be considered are the costs of production per unit, these are subtracted from the price, and the *profit margin* is introduced as a new variable. If these costs, in turn, are supposed to be built up from raw material and wage costs, an index of the raw material prices and a wage index should be merged into an average in such a way that their weights correspond to the composition of the production costs.

4. If, likewise in a supply function, changes in production *capacity* should be taken into account, the quantities supplied are expressed as percentages of the capacity.

5. If, in a demand function, account should be taken of the influence of *prices of competing goods,* it may be assumed that the ratio of the price to that of the competing good appears in the demand function. Moreover, the same remark made under statement 2 applies here. We can even go a step further and also replace the quantity by the ratio of the quantities of the two competing goods. If, therefore, a quantity x_1 of the good considered and a quantity x_2 of the competing good are demanded at prices p_1 and p_2, respectively, it is assumed that

$$\frac{x_1}{x_2} = f\left(\frac{p_1}{p_2}\right)$$

A similar line of reasoning underlies a demand function for investment goods, which has been put forward by some authors. This demand is supposed to be dependent on the quotient

$$\frac{z}{mq}$$

where z is the expected profit,

q is the price of the investment good, and

m is the rate of interest. This quotient can be regarded as a ratio of "profit percentages," namely, $\frac{z}{q}$ for the good to be invested, and m for the amount of money sacrificed.

6. If, in a demand function, *income* is a factor which has to be taken into account besides the price, its influence can be estimated *a priori* on the basis of family-budget statistics and the observed quantities can be replaced by "quantities corrected for changes in income." This may not, however, always be correct.

7. If the remaining factors can all be assumed to change only gradually—for instance, size of the population, changes of tastes and habits, possibly also income changes in very quiet times—it can be assumed that these only influence the trend of consumption. By taking deviations from trend, both for the quantities and for the prices, we then obtain two variables the coherence of which is not disturbed. It would be incorrect to eliminate only the trend in consumption and not in the price, because the trend of the price will also exert its influence on the trend of consumption. The fluctuations in consumption, however, can only be explained by the price fluctuations, if by fluctuations we mean deviations from trend.

If one of these *a priori* reductions cannot be changed to a single relation, we have to make use of multiple-correlation calculations.

§ 21. Multiple Correlation

The problem here is to explain the changes in a series x by the changes in a few other series y, z . . . . Also in this case, *graphical reconnaissance* is very desirable. Time graphs can be used without any difficulty for this purpose. The question now is not whether the fluctuations of x and y are the same—possibly after corrections for trend or lags—but whether the fluctuations of x can be built up from a combination of the fluctuations in y, z . . . etc. Although more general methods are possible, we shall confine ourselves mainly to *additive* relations and we shall ask whether a function

$$x' = ay + bz + \ldots + a'y^2 \ldots \qquad (21.1)$$

with constants a, b, a′ . . . can be found, in such a way that the deviations between x and x′ are as small as possible. In the previous formula, higher-degree terms have been included. Usually even these are omitted in the beginning, and we see whether a *linear* function is sufficient:

$$x' = ay + bz + \ldots \qquad (21.2)$$

With the help of the method of time graphs it is possible to determine by observation whether there is any likelihood of such a relation. This means (see Fig. 5) that it should be possible to approximate the series x satisfactorily by a sum total of y, z, etc., where these last variables may first be enlarged or reduced in a certain proportion, which can be determined freely.

The particulars in the course of x should be found, therefore, either in y or in z, or in both. (See Fig. 5.)

The method of the scatter diagram should be used in this case. If there is a close relation between the variables, the dots are situated in a surface, possibly in a plane. Operating with a spatial diagram, which by the way could only be used if there are only two explanatory variables, however, offers some practical difficulties, and therefore we have to manage to get along in some other way, as, for instance, with Ezekiel's method. We therefore refer to Ezekiel's book *(Methods of Correlation Analy-*

sis) and we shall not go into the methods of finding the best relation along these lines, but only into the way of representing this relation, after it has been determined by calculation.

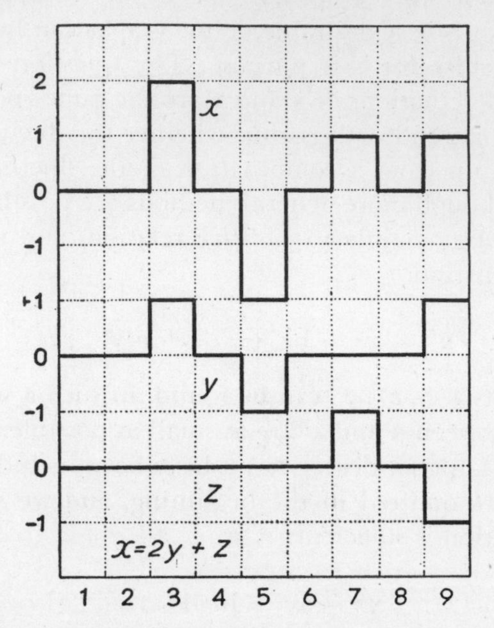

Fig. 5. Theoretical example of multiple correlation. It can be seen that the line x can be built up from the lines y and z, if we take $x = 2y + z$.

The calculation is again carried out by the method of least squares. We determine a, b . . . (and, as the case may be, a′ . . .) in such a way that the sum of the squares of the residuals

$$x - x'$$

is a minimum. We now have obtained the equation of the *first regression line*. Also in this case, other regression lines can be distinguished, namely, the second, third, etc., to the nth, if there are n variables in total and consequently n-1 explanatory variables. The second regression line is obtained by assuming a relation

$$y' = cx + ez + \dots \qquad (21.3)$$

and requiring that the sum of the squares of $y - y'$ is a minimum. (In the mathematical literature about this subject, a systematic method of indicating all the coefficients appearing in these equations is in use. For the sake of simplicity and in accordance with the purpose of this book we shall not go into this here.) If the correlation is complete—i.e., in the case of a linear regression equation, if the dots lie in a plane—the relation between x and the remaining variables found from the second regression equation will be identical with the one derived from the first.

In equation (21.2), which as a rule is used, because it can usually be assumed that the deviations are consequences of incompleteness of the theory, we call the term ay "the influence of y," the term bz, the influence of z, etc. This term is independent of the unit in which y is measured, because if y is indicated by a smaller number (as a consequence of a greater unit), the term a will automatically be enlarged in the same proportion. If we assume, by way of example, that the investigation refers to a demand curve where

x is the quantity demanded and
y is the price; and where also appear
z and u, two demand factors,

then we shall call

$$x - bz - cu \qquad (21.4)$$

"the value of x corrected for the influence of demand factors." This magnitude must show a simple correlation with the price, y. The character of this relation can be represented graphically by drawing a scatter diagram with these two magnitudes as its coördinates; we then speak of a *partial scatter diagram.* Similar scatter diagrams can be made for each of the explanatory variables, for instance, between z and $x - ay - cu$, the values of x corrected for y and u.

The equation

$$x' = ay + bz + cu \qquad (21.5)$$

can also be given an interpretation showing its connection with the theory of demand curves. The term $bz + cu$ can be called the "shift." This name fits in with the usual graphic representation of the demand curve, where constant values are allotted to the "remaining factors," in this case z and u, and where we are left with a relation between x and y which is represented graphically. If, now, z and u assume other values, this means that the demand curve is shifted parallel to itself. This method of representation can also be related to the method of representation in space, which we have discussed earlier. For the sake of simplicity we confine ourselves to one demand factor, z. The relation $x = ay + bz$ is represented by an inclined plane, as we have already seen. If a fixed value is given to z, only the points on the plane lying in one straight line are considered. If another value is taken for z, the points of another straight line in the plane are obtained. The projections of these straight lines on the xy plane, then, are the demand lines for the various values of z, "the shifting demand curves."

The determination of the regression coefficients is impossible in a fundamentally important case, namely, if another linear relation exists between two or more of the explanatory variables. The simplest case occurs when the fluctuations in two of those variables, for instance y and z, are proportionate. In that case y can be substituted a certain number of times for z. If a regression equation is to be found, an arbitrary number of other ones could immediately be derived from it, leading to equally satisfactory results. The result, therefore, is not unambiguous. In other words, the influences of y and z cannot be separated.

More complicated cases are also possible. It may happen that y is not proportionate to z but that

$$y = pz + qu \tag{21.6}$$

where p and q are constants. In this case, y can be substituted wholly or partly by the right-hand side of this expression and so the number of possible results is increased.

It should not be inferred that in such cases where *multicollinearity* is said to exist, nothing can be learned from the calculation. If y and z are proportionate, their influences certainly cannot be separated, but u's influence can be determined. If (21.6) is valid, the influence of none of the three explanatory variables can be ascertained, but certain functions of that influence can. Whether the result can be used or not depends on the ultimate purpose of the calculations.

The appearance of multicollinearity may be the consequence of the presence of other structural relations between the magnitudes included in the equation investigated. As an example, we shall take a demand equation

$$u = v_1 Y - v_2 p \tag{21.7}$$

where u is the quantity demanded,
Y is income, and
p is the price.

If, besides, a price-determination equation

$$p = \pi Y \tag{21.8}$$

is valid, the latter is the cause of collinearity of p and Y. It is also said in this case that equation (21.7) is not *identifiable*. This means in practice that if a number of numerical values of u, Y, and p are given, the coefficients v_1 and v_2 cannot be determined. In order to see this, suppose that certain numerical values v_1' and v_2' would have been found, for which the numerical values of u, Y, and p satisfy (21.7). It would now be possible to increase v_2' by any arbitrary figure α, if only v_1' is increased by $\pi\alpha$. By this procedure we would obtain:

$$u = (v_1' + \pi\alpha)\, Y - (v_2' + \alpha)p$$

This equation, which is of the same type as (21.7), would now also be satisfied, as a consequence of (21.8).

This difficulty would not have appeared if in (21.7) the term with p were missing. It would not have appeared either, if in

(21.8) another variable were included besides p and Y. It depends on how the various variables appear in a number of structural equations, whether a certain equation is identifiable or not.

§ 22. Evaluating the Uncertainty of the Results

There are two main reasons why the results of a multiple-correlation calculation are not completely accurate. In the first place, there are random deviations, manifesting themselves in the spreading of the dots in the scatter diagram and caused either by errors of measurement or by neglecting part of the explanatory factors in the underlying theory. In the second place, there may be multicollinearity or a situation approximating it. The two causes may appear independently of each other, but often both will be present.

The uncertainty in the results, in particular in the regression coefficients and also in the correlation coefficient—a consequence of the presence of random deviations—is usually expressed by the size of the *standard deviation* of these magnitudes. The latter indicates the standard deviation which—calculated according to the ordinary definition of this expression—would be obtained if not one complex of observations would be present, but a great number of similar complexes, in which the random deviations would have been different in every case. These complexes, like the one which has appeared in reality, are considered as representing *samples* from a greater imaginary complex indicating "what could have happened just as well." This greater complex, of course, is of a more or less hypothetical character. Fisher, who has given the theory on the basis of which these standard deviations are usually calculated, has assumed that the explanatory variables are exactly known, but that the variable to be explained possesses a random component, which is distributed according to the Gauss law. The usual formulas have been derived from these premises.

These formulas lead to results which themselves can be uncertain to a high degree, if the complex of observations is approximately multicollinear, as has been pointed out by Frisch. The latter, therefore, has tried to reach an estimation of the uncertainty of the results in another way. In order to understand a few main points of his method, consisting in the determination of so-called *bunch maps,* we start from the theorem that if perfect correlation is present without multicollinearity, all regression equations lead to the same result. This means that the second regression equation (21.3), when solved for x:

$$x = \frac{y}{c} - \frac{e}{c} z \ldots \tag{22.1}$$

leads to coefficients which are the same as in the first regression equation:

$$x = ay + bz + \ldots$$

Therefore: $a = \frac{1}{c},\ b = -\frac{e}{c}$, etc.

If, on the contrary, a situation of multicollinearity is approximated, great deviations will be found between the regression coefficients determined in the two ways indicated. Bunch maps (see Fig. 6) give a survey of the various values which are obtained for the same coefficient.

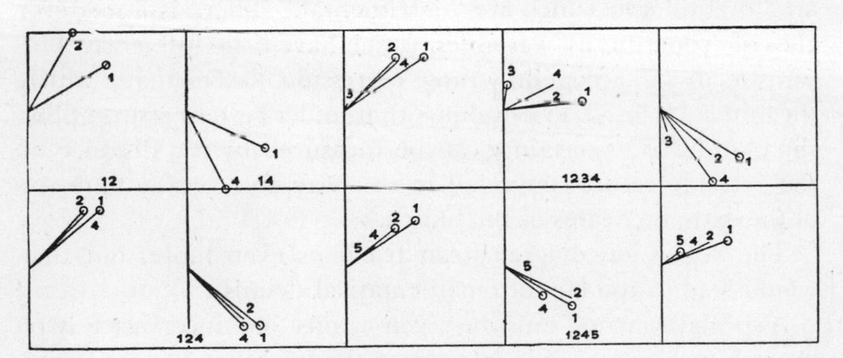

Fig. 6. Example of a bunch map.

These values are indicated by the slope of the lines drawn from the origin, or "beams." These beams carry a number, each indicating a variable. Two of the beams are always indicated in a particular way; they are the main beams. Their numbers indicate the variables between which the regression coefficient has been determined; the undermost number is the one considered as the dependent variable, the uppermost number indicates the variable considered as the independent one. The numbers further indicate the number of the regression equation from which the value of the coefficient belonging to each beam has been computed, or the direction in which the residuals have been minimized. The number of beams is equal to the number of variables included in the investigation.

Frisch's method consists in particular in a gradual extension of the number of variables. If a new variable is added, we can observe in the regression diagrams what influence this fact has on the bunches of beams. If a variable is added which is essential for the explanation from a statistical point of view, i.e., which approximately explains the residuals not explained so far, it will be seen that the bunches of beams close up. If, however, the added variable is nearly a linear combination of variables already present, the bunches will "explode," whether this new variable is essential from an economic point of view, or not. A typical indeterminateness in the regression coefficients appears. It can be observed, therefore, which newly added variables are "useful" and which are "detrimental." There is a medium class of "superfluous" variables, which have little influence. The statistician will accept only those regression coefficients in which the bunch is closed. Frisch shows that under certain assumptions the margin of uncertainty can be measured by the distance of the extreme values computed in this way, i.e., by the tangents of the extreme beams of the bunch.

The regression diagrams can teach us even more, but that would lead us too far into mathematical details.

A special warning must be given against one incorrect way of using bunch maps. It is sometimes thought that the explosion of a bunch of beams after the inclusion of a new variable is an indication that this variable should not be included. This, however, can only be decided by economic theory, not by regression analysis. It may happen that according to economic theory the variable in question is essential. The conclusion then must be that we cannot determine all coefficients because—accidentally or not—a few of the most important variables are mutually correlated. As has been remarked, it depends on the problem under investigation whether useful conclusions still can be drawn in such a case.

T. Koopmans has combined the elements of Fisher's and Frisch's theories into one theory which, however, has a complicated mathematical character and therefore cannot easily be paraphrased. We therefore refer to the literature.

§ 23. Simultaneous Equations

The preceding discussion referred to the testing of only one relationship at a time between the economic magnitudes considered. Strictly speaking, it can only be applied if there is but one relation between the magnitudes considered as variables to be explained. As soon as more than one equation exists at the same time, its validity is limited. This is nearly always the case if more than one variable to be explained appears in the problem. T. Haavelmo* has pointed out that the application of the method of least squares to each of the relations separately would mean that mutually contradictory assumptions were taken as starting points. The logical setup in this case should be to consider together the random deviations appearing in each relation as a sample from a higher-dimension complex of such deviations. If each of the relations is considered separately, it is assumed that each deviation is "drawn" from a one-dimension frequency distribution. If, for instance, the deviations in two simultaneous relations are u and v, their joint frequency distribution could be

$$F(uv) = \frac{1}{2\pi\sigma_u\sigma_v}\epsilon^{-\frac{1}{2}\left(\frac{u^2}{\sigma_u^2}+\frac{v^2}{\sigma_v^2}\right)}$$

---

* T. Haavelmo, The probability approach in econometrics, Econometrica, 12 (1944) Supplement. For a more simplified explanation, see T. Koopmans: Statistical estimation of simultaneous economic relations, Cowles Commission Papers, New Series, No. 11.

If, now, in analogy to § 21, u and v in this equation are replaced by the residuals of the two relations, for instance

$$u = x - x' = x - ay - bz \ldots$$

and an attempt is made to determine the values of a, b, etc., at which a maximum is reached for the probability of the appearance of the observed values of x, y, etc., other values will be found than with the method of least squares (multiple correlation).

The deviations from the regression coefficients found by this last method are only small if high correlations are found for each of the relations. The intricate method can be avoided, however, if the relations are brought into a special shape, namely, the *reduced form* discussed in § 11. The coefficients of the relations in their reduced form may, under certain circumstances, be determined by the method of least squares. We may continue to apply the method of least squares, for instance, if in each equation on the right-hand side only lagged values of the explanatory variables appear.*

§ 24. The Use of Regression Analysis in Econometrics †

The way in which the econometrician makes use of the methods described above has been described systematically by Koopmans along the following lines.‡ The statistician, when testing a relation set up by economic theory, may draw unconditional and conditional conclusions. The *unconditional* conclusions, however, are only *negative*. These conclusions may play a role when the theory is checked. If, namely, the correlation coefficient turns out to be too low (in comparison to the standard set before), the conclusion must be that the relation is incompatible with the facts. In other words, the theory is incorrect, or at least incomplete. The positive conclusions which

* For a simple explanation see Appendix A.

† See Appendix A for a further elucidation.

‡ Koopmans, T.: The logic of econometric business cycle research, Journal of Political Economy, 1940.

can be drawn do not appear when the theoretical relation is checked: it cannot be *proved* statistically that a theory is correct. The correlation may be high: other theories, however, may also lead to a high correlation. Positive conclusions do appear with the measuring function, but then they are *conditional,* for instance; if the assumed relation is correct as regards the choice of the variables and the lags, then the most likely value of the influencing coefficients is such and such.

If we want to draw positive conclusions, additional information is necessary to satisfy the conditions mentioned; this information must be given by economic theory. It is reasonable to submit this additional information to the following principles:

a. the principle of *statistical censorship:* it must not be contradictory to the data;
b. the principle of *scientific efficiency:* it must not be a consequence of theses already assumed, together with the data;
c. the principle of the *solid basis:* it should be as plausible as possible; and
d. the principle of the *sufficient basis:* it should be such that positive conclusions can be drawn. Between these last two principles a certain tension may often exist; we should try to find an optimum.

In most econometric investigations carried out with the help of multiple correlation, the additional information is approximately as follows:

1. The factors not included in the relation only lead to small random deviations or to
2. a trend influence or to
3. deviations in individual years which can be left out of consideration.
4. The factors included in the relation (explanatory variables) are active in a given mathematical way (often linearly, or only additively), whereas
5. the lags are given, or at least should be positive, and
6. certain regression coefficients also have a prescribed sign: sometimes the value of those coefficients is bound within certain limits.

The last three points require further explanation. As we know, the restriction embodied in statement 4 is not serious if the deviations of the variables from their averages are not large. The lags need not be given beforehand; they can be left undecided and be determined by the requirement of the best possible fit between x and x'. This can be done by trial and error, or alternatively, by including in any relation with the explanatory variables y and z, not only these variables for the same moment of time, but also for other moments, for instance

$$x' = ay + a'y_{-1} + bz + b'z_{-1}$$

The relative size of the regression coefficients a and a' shows approximately how large the lag between x and y should be taken. If, for instance, $a = 2$ and $a' = 1$, then, by rough approximation (at least, if the time unit is small with respect to the period of the fluctuations in y):

$$x' = (a + a')y_{-\frac{1}{3}} + \ldots$$

Point 6 is the most important one. Certain regression coefficients must have a certain sign or a certain value, on account of their economic significance. For instance, the coefficient of the price in a demand equation should be negative, and in a supply equation, positive. A regression coefficient representing wage-price ratio, or the marginal propensity to consume will have to be smaller than 1.

Usually such requirements will not be made at the start, but the regression equation will be computed first.

As has been pointed out earlier, the following results are possible: (a) the correlation is lower than the standard established; the theory is rejected; (b) the correlation is good and the regression coefficients have a small margin of uncertainty; measurement is possible with relatively few limiting conditions; or (c) the correlation is good, but the regression coefficients or lags are relatively uncertain. In this case it is often possible to limit the area of uncertainty with the help of further conditions of the kind mentioned under statements 5 and 6. The value of one or more of the lags or regression coefficients can be wholly or partly fixed.

The greatest success, of course, is obtained if such additional information is not necessary. Even then, relatively unexpected conclusions are sometimes reached: the influence of one of the factors may be small. From investigations made by the author, for instance, it has become clear that under certain assumptions to be mentioned later (see § 37), the influence of the rate of interest on investment activity is small; similarly as regards the influence of the so-called acceleration principle.

If we meet with success, we can try to mitigate one of the conditions; for instance, the mathematical form may be generalized or more factors may be included in the relation. We can divide the premises originally taken as a starting point into *acceptable* and *doubtful* premises, and from now on we can include only the acceptable ones in the calculation. As regards the doubtful ones, the following conclusions may be reached:

1. they are wrong;
2. they are correct, starting from the acceptable premises;
3. it cannot be decided whether they are correct or not, but if they are omitted, measurement is impossible, or
4. same as 3, but they are irrelevant for measurement.

Conclusions of the kind mentioned under 2 form a type which was not present in the first framework.

As an example of doubtful premises, we mention the assumption that one of the regression coefficients must lie within a given interval:

1. now occurs, if there is not a good correlation in which the coefficient lies within the interval;
2. occurs if there are only good correlations where this is the case;
3. and 4 occur if good correlations exist with values both within and outside the interval.

Another example is the following: assume that y exerts some influence on x, but that it is doubtful whether z also has any influence:

1. applies if the regression coefficient of z is approximately zero;
2. applies if the correlation is good with z and bad without z;
3. and 4 appear if the margins of uncertainty in z's coefficient are large.

Other situations, more favorable to the attainment of positive conclusions, occur if the economic theory leads to the formulation of hypotheses alternative to the doubtful ones; in other words, if the economist says, it is not certain whether z has any influence, but if it does not, then u has some influence.

Part III

RESULTS OF ECONOMETRIC RESEARCH

4

The Psychic Reactions

§ 25. Contents and Subdivision of This Chapter

In this chapter some of the most important results of econometric research will be surveyed. We have already seen that the boundaries between econometrics and its older neighbors, economics and statistics, cannot be drawn clearly. We therefore start by more or less marking out the field of econometrics beforehand. Also in economics and statistics, important results have been attained during the last 10 or 20 years. We shall, however, only discuss those investigations which at the same time deal with measurement and have a quantitative-theoretical character. Purely mathematical-economic and consequently theoretical results, such as much of the work by Frisch, Hicks and Allen, and Marschak—to mention a few of the most successful workers in this field—will not be considered here. Also Chait's work, although connected with statistical facts, was originally achieved in the theoretical field, and therefore will not be considered.

Nor will many results of statistical investigations be discussed, as, for instance, the important results in the field of the evaluation of national income and wealth, the enormous progress in the computation of production, price and many other indices, or work like that of Leontief who has elaborated a flow network for production in the United States. The important work of pure business-cycle statisticians like Mitchell, Wagemann, Dupriez, and others, is also left out of account. Of course this does not mean that this work is of less importance. It is only as a result of a somewhat arbitrary limitation which is always necessary with a restricted amount of space that these authors will not be discussed.

The breakdown of this chapter, however, will not be according to authors or schools, but according to the material to be investigated. In broad outline, the breakdown consists in first discussing the psychic, technical, and institutional reaction relations themselves, and subsequently the consequences of the combined presence of these elementary relations for the development of separate markets and for whole economies. A few conclusions concerning economic policy for separate markets and for the economy as a whole will follow.

§ 26. Psychic Reaction Relations; Engel Curves

We explained in § 11 that the structure of an economy can be described by a number of elementary relations, of which the reaction relations are the most important ones. As the most important examples of the latter, we mentioned the demand and supply relations. We shall therefore discuss now what results have been achieved in determining these relations. There are reasons for distinguishing between demand and supply relations referring to goods and services valued psychically, and demand and supply relations based on objective valuation of goods and services. As an example of the last category, we mention the demand for raw materials and labor exerted by an entrepreneur when supplying his products. Mainly technical and market data play a role here. The entrepreneur's psyche may exert some influence through his expectations, but as a first approximation it can be said that much more objective decisions are involved than is the case with the demand for consumption goods by the final consumer and the supply of labor and savings to the final producer. This distinction more or less corresponds to the division made by monetary economics in the achievement of economic aims; instead of considering working and consuming in such a way that a maximum total satisfaction is obtained, the procedure is often followed of first aiming at a maximum money income, and then with this given money income, at maximum satisfaction. The division has not been carried through completely, sometimes not even very far; the tendency, however, is present for the most part. The "psychically based" demand and supply functions should be seen as derived from aiming at maximum satisfaction, the "institutionally based" functions—as we shall call them—from striving after a maximum money income, and in particular a maximum profit in the case of a business enterprise. We shall first concern ourselves with the psychically based reactions.

As we have already explained (§ 5 and following), the quantity demanded depends mainly on various factors, including *income*. This dependence on income has first been investigated statistically by the so-called budget studies, or investigations into family expenditures. We have data here concerning families with divergent incomes, and we can therefore investigate how the expenditures for various goods and services and the quantities bought change according to the size of this income. This relation has first been examined by the statistician Engel; its graphic representation is often called the *Engel curve,* both when the amounts spent and when the quantities bought are represented. A very great number of budget studies have been carried out during the last century, which have enormously increased the available statistical material. This has made it possible for econometric investigations into the character of this curve to develop. There are two ways in which we may determine the form of the curves theoretically. The first is to form an idea directly as to how the increase of incomes will influence the amounts spent. We can consequently distinguish (1) on the one hand, between so-called poverty goods or inferior goods (margarine, potatoes, bread) the expenditures for which in the long run decline with increasing incomes, because these goods are replaced by others; and, on the other hand, all other goods; and (2) on the one hand, between necessary goods, which are bought at every level of income and, on the other hand, luxury goods which are only bought if the income exceeds a certain amount. On the basis of the behavior of the curves, certain general types of formulas describing the Engel curves can be set up.

A good recent example of such attempts are the formulas computed by Törnqvist,* a few of which are mentioned below:

* See his book review in Ekonomisk Tidskrift 1941, p. 216, and in particular, p. 223.

Food: $u = \frac{26x}{x + 31}$ Animal food: $u = \frac{16x}{x + 37}$

Clothing: $u = \frac{21 (x-10)}{x + 160}$ Vegetable food: $u = \frac{26x}{x + 31} - \frac{16x}{x + 37}$

Housing: $u = \frac{54 (x-5)}{x + 290}$ Total expenditures: x.

Another method of obtaining a theoretical formula for the Engel curves has been used by Bowley and Allen.* They assume that the indifference function has a certain shape and from this they find the shape of the Engel curves. The simplest hypothesis which can be made about the indifference function is that it is of the second degree because it must be represented by a curved surface. From this, however, it follows that the Engel curves are straight lines. As can be seen from Fig. 7, this in fact is the case over intervals of considerable length. From the constants describing these straight lines, Bowley and Allen derive a criterion for distinguishing between luxury goods and necessary goods. With luxury goods the line cuts off a positive part of the income (the horizontal) axis, with necessary goods it cuts off a positive part of the expenditure (the vertical) axis. The goods can also be listed in order of urgency, by taking into account the point of intersection with the vertical axis (above or below the origin) and by considering those goods as the most urgent whose point of intersection is highest.

Something can be said against this latter distinction: the height of the point of intersection, among other things, depends on the classification. It is possible, by splitting the item Food—which Bowley and Allen find in several cases would satisfy the most urgent need—to obtain two items each of which would be less urgent than the item House Rent, which comes after food. The sequence, therefore, is not unambiguous.

The straight lines, also, can only be approximations because negative expenditures are not possible (except negative savings). Nevertheless, it is important for further research work that

* "Family Expenditure," London, 1935.

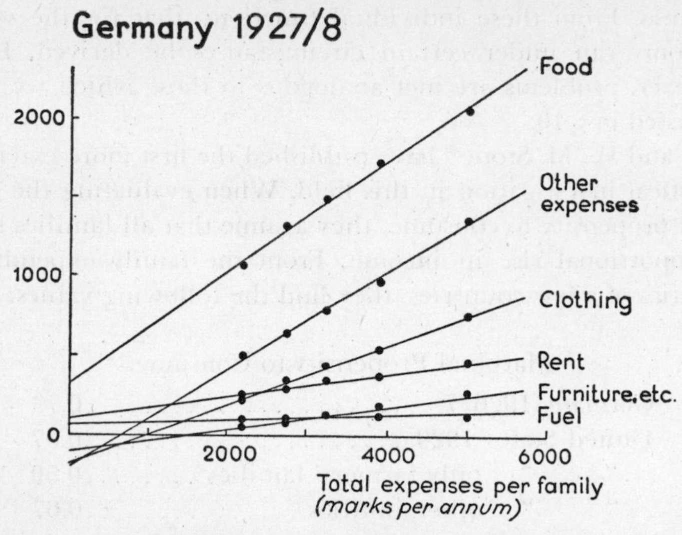

Fig. 7. Example of nearly straight Engel curves, taken from Bowley and Allen, "Family Expenditure."

linear approximation here is possible over long intervals (see § 10 and 12).

§ 27. The "Propensity to Consume" and the "Multiplier"

A special case of Engel curves is the representation of the "propensity to consume," which has been introduced so successfully by Keynes: a general consumption equation indicating how total consumption expenditures depend on the size of the income. This can be expressed in the formula: $C = f(Y)$, where C represents the consumption expenditures and Y is income. If Y undergoes a small increase ΔY, and C a small increase ΔC, then $\Delta C/\Delta Y$ is called the *marginal propensity to consume*. Because of the important influence of this reaction on the degree of activity of the national economy, an exact knowledge of the function is of great importance. Research into this subject is partly possible from family budgets. From these the individual consumption functions are found, if it may be assumed that the reaction of a family on an income change is equal to the difference existing at one moment between families with different incomes. From these individual functions, that for the whole economy can under certain circumstances be derived. Here, however, problems are met analogous to those which we have discussed in § 10.

R. and W. M. Stone* have published the first more extensive statistical investigation in this field. When evaluating the marginal propensity to consume, they assume that all families show a proportional rise in income. From the family expenditure statistics of a few countries, they find the following values:

Marginal Propensity to Consume	
Germany 1926/7	0.73
United States 1929	0.67
" " only farmers' families	0.50
" " other families	0.67

For the Netherlands, A. L. G. M. Rombouts† has computed the following figures:

Netherlands, 1935/6	
Manual workers	0.83
Brain workers	0.82
Agricultural workers	0.79
Farmers	0.44

A second method which has been used is the *historical method.* If the Keynesian assumption is made, that consumption expenditures in fact only depend on the national income—possibly also on a trend—it is not difficult to determine, with the help of the correlation method, the regression coefficient a appearing in the equation

$$C = aY + bt + c \tag{27.1}$$

* The marginal propensity to consume and the multiplier, a statistical investigation, Review of Economic Studies VI (1938/9), p. 1.

† Statistical measurement of Keynes' concepts "propensity to consume," etc. for the Netherlands, Netherlands Business-cycle Studies XI (1940), p. 21. (In Dutch.)

where C is consumption expenditures, Y is national income, t is the time, and a, b, and c are constants. This a, again, represents the marginal propensity to consume. The Stones found:

Marginal Propensity to Consume

Germany	1925–32	0.72
"	1932–36	0.42
Gr. Britain	1929–35	0.52
Netherlands	1923–33	0.47
Poland	1928–36	0.71
Sweden	1896–1916	0.80
"	1923–30	0.60
United States	1920–35	0.75
" "	1919–35	0.70

It may be remarked here that, in general, the correlation coefficients obtained are high, so that Keynes' theory is not contrary to the facts. A few theoretical objections, however, can be raised against equation (27.1), all leading to the wish to include more variables in the equation.

The first variable which is often mentioned in this connection is some criterion for the *income distribution.* This has been stressed in particular by Staehle,* who has shown that in some cases the regression coefficient belonging to Y changes considerably if such a variable is included. The Stones mention that an income distribution criterion which they have used, namely Pareto's α, is highly correlated with Y, and therefore could not be included in the calculation without making the result very uncertain. In their coefficients, therefore, Y's influence is combined with that of α and this remains correct as long as α and Y remain correlated. As the causes of changes in α are not known, we cannot say on what conditions the continuance of the correlation between α and Y depends. From de Wolff's considerations (see § 10) it follows that it is not certain whether in equation (27.1) we can assume a term which includes α.

Another way of taking changes in income distribution into

* Retail sales and labor income, Review of Economic Statistics 20 (1938), p. 128.

account is not to include one series Y for total income as an explanatory variable, but several series, for instance labor income L and nonlabor income E. The difficulty may again be that these series are mutually highly correlated, but in several cases this is not so. In the computations where this procedure has been followed, account has been taken at the same time of the influence of the price level p. We have now arrived at the subject of *demand curves,* which will be discussed in the following sections (§ 28 to § 31).

Before doing this, we shall say a few words about the difference in propensity to consume between farm families and other families. Probably the reaction of business people in general is reflected here, which in family-budget statistics is usually only represented by farmers. Where business firms and households are separated, the household's marginal propensity to consume will be increased greatly; on the other hand, however, the surplus business income in favorable years will not be used for consumption at all. For the economy as a whole, this manifests itself in an important part of the increase in national income assuming the form of retained earnings, through which the propensity to save increases. For the Netherlands in the period from 1923 to 1933, approximately 25 per cent of the increase in national income consisted in profits retained in business. Radice* shows that for Great Britain, in the period from 1922 to 1935, 43 per cent of the increase in profits of limited liability companies assumed the form of retained earnings. The low figures found by the historical method for the marginal propensity to consume must therefore be ascribed for the most part to the phenomenon of retained earnings, and the decline compared with earlier periods must probably be ascribed to an increase in retained earnings.

Evaluations according to the new statistical method of simultaneous equations (see § 23) have been made by T. Haavelmo.† Here the consumption equation and one or two more equations,

* "Savings in Great Britain," 1922-1935, Oxford University Press, 1939.

† Methods of measuring the marginal propensity to consume, Journal of the American Statistical Association 42 (1947) p. 105.

together forming a complete system, are simultaneously tested. In the simplest case, as the best estimate of the marginal propensity to consume for the United States (1922 to 1941), 0.67 is obtained, as against 0.73 obtained by using the old method of least squares (for each equation at a time).

From the values a of the marginal propensity to consume mentioned previously, the "multiplier" M can be computed according to the well-known formula $M = \frac{1}{1-a}$. Of course, it is also possible to measure the latter directly, if we try to explain the fluctuations in national income Y from those in investments I:

$$Y = MI + Y_0$$

where Y_0 is a constant. This formula, however, is only correct for a country without relations with the outside world; if trade with foreign countries takes place, a more detailed formula will have to be chosen, for instance

$$Y = M(I + E) + Y_0$$

where E represents the value of exports. This has been done for Canada by Chang,* where, by the way, the terms with I and E were each taken with their own coefficients; these coefficients, as was to be expected, turned out to be nearly equal, namely 1.4 approximately.

§ 28. Demand Curves; Agricultural Products

In the theoretical analysis of demand, the emphasis has been mostly on the dependence on the price of the commodity, which is not correct in all respects. By the demand curve in the narrower sense, only this dependence on the price is meant. It has been investigated statistically only in fairly recent years, because great difficulties arose, which we partly described in § 20. The great pioneer in this field is Moore; his intellectual heir is Schultz, who in his life's work "The Theory and Measurement

* A note on exports and national income in Canada, Canadian Journal of Economics and Political Science, 13 (1947) p. 276.

of Demand"* has given us the standard work on this subject. In addition to English-speaking countries, much attention has been devoted to the statistical testing and measuring of the demand function in Scandinavia, France, and the Netherlands; and to a lesser degree in a few other countries. The historic method is most generally used; a few attempts to use the geographic method will be mentioned separately.

After the discussion of this subject in § 20 we need not be surprised that of the first attempts, nearly all referred to products of agriculture and horticulture, supplemented later by livestock products, and only in more recent times by services and industrial products. The hypotheses made about the further variables to be included in the demand relation are divergent, but with agricultural products they are in general not so relevant, because the price influence is often dominating. The extensiveness of the literature permits us to give only a rough survey of the results attained; for details we must refer to that literature. It can be said in general, that the correlations which have been attained here, are high, so that the "law of demand" for these products certainly is not contrary to the facts. In most of these demand functions only the price of the article itself plays a role; we shall deal separately with a few cases which show deviations from this rule. Instead of the price we often have to take the price divided by the general price index number. A trend nearly always is necessary, on account of the increase of the population, but an income index only rarely has to be included among the explanatory variables. When using the results it is of course desirable to become acquainted with all these particulars; and especially with the kind of price which has been used. The elasticity with respect to wholesale prices often differs considerably from that with respect to retail prices.

Many figures about *agricultural products* have been given by Schultz, for three periods in each instance; 1875 to 1895, 1895 to 1914, and 1915 to 1929, and with five different formulas.

---

* The University of Chicago Press, Chicago 1938.

The median figures for the elasticity coefficients with respect to wholesale prices follow:

1. Wheat	– 0.15	6. Oats	– 0.58
2. Barley	– 0.24	7. Potatoes	– 0.62
3. Sugar	– 0.29	8. Hay	– 0.67
4. Cotton	– 0.32	9. Maize	– 0.71
5. Rye	– 0.43	10. Buckwheat	– 1.01

Sugar evaluations have also been made for the Netherlands by F. Weinreb.* He found an elasticity with respect to the retail price of – 0.3. For the elasticity with respect to the wholesale price a lower figure would have been found.

We also mention here that Roy† puts the elasticity of the demand for wine in France at – 1.

The demand elasticity for a few *horticultural products* with respect to their wholesale prices is given by G. F. Warren and F. A. Pearson.‡ They give the following figures:

Pears	– 0.2	Apples	– 0.6
Peaches	– 0.3	Cranberries	– 1.6
Bananas	– 0.4	Cabbage	– 1.8

A further investigation into the demand for apples in the United States has been made by W. E. Black.§

The demand for *grapes* and *tomatoes* has been investigated by J. G. W. Ignatius and H. Rijken van Olst.|| The price elasticity with respect to wholesale prices for grapes moved between 1930 and 1939 from – 2 to – 0.4; for tomatoes, elasticities of – 0.8 and – 0.9 were found, varying according to the formulas used.

The demand for *cherries* has been investigated by J. H. van

* "Statistical Determination of the Demand Curve," Haarlem 1936 (in Dutch).

† Etudes Econométriques, Paris 1935.

‡ Interrelationships of supply and price, Cornell University, Agricultural Experiment Station, Ithaca, N. Y., 1928.

§ Consumer demand for apples and oranges, Cornell University, Agric. Exp. Station, No. 800, 1943.

|| The demand for a few horticultural products, Statistical and Econometric Studies, 2 (1947) pp. 27 and 55 (in Dutch).

Stuyvenberg.* He found a price elasticity with respect to auction prices of -2 and an income elasticity of slightly more than 4, making use of time series. From family-budget statistics, however, a "long-term" income elasticity of 0.7 was found. The higher "short-term" income elasticity should probably be ascribed to the luxury character of cherries, which makes it possible to postpone demand.

Much attention has been devoted in various countries to the demand for *livestock products*. Here we have various cases of clearcut substitutability, either mutually or with other products: margarine can be substituted for butter and one sort of meat by another. Consequently, careful distinction should be made between cases where the price of the competing article is supposed to be constant (i.e., where corrections are made for changes in this price or where this price is included as a variable in the multiple-correlation calculation) and cases where it is assumed that this price has moved parallel to that of the article itself.

A first example of the difficulties in this field is the article *butter*. The year-to-year price movement of butter is nearly the same as that of margarine. It is very difficult therefore—in fact, it is only possible in cases of very high correlation between actual and calculated consumption—to separate the influences of these two prices. With Dutch data this turned out to be impossible. The difficulty can be solved, however, by considering the *seasonal fluctuations*. The margarine price does not show such fluctuations, the butter price does. In this way, the elasticity for the Netherlands has been computed at approximately -1 (in summer -0.8, in winter -1.6).† For Sweden, Wold‡ has found an elasticity with constant margarine price

* "Some Economic Aspects of Cherry Growing in the Netherlands," Haarlem 1947 (in Dutch).

† Compare the writer's article "L'élasticité de la demande des industries agricoles," Ve Congrés Intern. technique et chimique des industries agricoles, Scheveningen 1937, Comptes Rendus, p. 475.

‡ Efterfrågan på jordbruksprodukter och dess känslighet för pris-och inkomst förändringar, Statens offentliga utredningar 1940: 16, Jordbruksdepartementet, Stockholm 1940.

of − 1.4 to − 1.5, whereas the retail-price elasticity of the total demand for the two goods taken together amounts to from − 0.4 to − 0.5.

A second example of the influence of prices of other articles on the demand function is formed by the various sorts of *meat*. The evaluation of the elasticities has been solved in greatest detail by Schultz,* who has determined for the United States the influence of the prices of beef, pork, and lamb, each taken separately. The result is as follows:

	Demand Elasticity with Respect to the Price of		
	Beef	Pork	Lamb
Beef	− 0.86	0.10	0.20
Pork	0.19	− 0.70	0.00
Lamb	0.63	0.37	− 1.80

For the Netherlands only the demand for beef and pork have been studied in their mutual dependence. The following results were attained:†

	Elasticity with Respect to the Price of	
	Beef	Pork
Beef	− 1.5	+ 1.0
Pork	0	− 2.1

Wold's investigations for Sweden are somewhat different, as he finds no influence of the pork price on the demand for beef. His results are:

	Elasticity with Respect to the Price of	
	Beef	Pork
Beef and Veal	− 0.5	.
Pork	0.25	− 0.5

Between the demand elasticities of two goods with respect to each other's prices, certain relations must exist, as Hotelling

* Loc. cit., p. 638 and following.

† De Nederlandse Conjunctuur (Dutch Business-cycle Studies) May 1935, p. 15, and November 1935 (in Dutch).

and Slutsky have shown. These are tested by Schultz. The margin of error in the results often turns out to be too great to enable us to draw very exact conclusions. In any case, this problem needs further investigation.

Besides the groups mentioned above, there are a few other stock-breeding products, the results for which follow below:

Article	Country	Author(s)	Elasticity
Milk	Netherlands	Van den Briel[1] .... Smit[2]	− 0.3 to − 0.4
Milk	Norway	Frisch & Haavelmo[3]	− 0.4 to − 1.2
Milk	Sweden	Wold[4]	− 0.2 to − 0.3
Cheese	Netherlands	Van den Briel[1]	− 0.3 to − 0.7
Cheese	England	Ruth Cohen[5]	− 0.3 to − 0.6
Eggs	Netherlands	Central Bureau of Statistics[6]...	− 1.7
Eggs	Sweden	Wold[4]	− 1.0

[1] Ve Congrès int. techn. et chim., Scheveningen 1937, C. R. vol. II p. 477. [2] Ibid. p. 498. [3] Eftersporselen efter melk i Norge, Statsok. Tidsskr. 52 (1938). [4] Loc. cit. [5] The History of Milk Prices. Oxford 1936. [6] De Ned. Conj. (Dutch Business-cycle Studies), March 1931, p. 24.

The demand for *food as a whole* has been investigated in an article referring to the United States, from 1922 to 1941, by M. A. Girshick and T. Haavelmo,* where use has been made of a system of five simultaneous equations. The variables included in this system are the food consumption per head of the population, the retail price of foodstuffs, the disposable income per head of the population (the latter two divided by the cost of living), the agricultural production of foodstuffs (per head of the population), and the prices received by the farmers (divided by the cost of living). This investigation, which is especially important as an example of the method of simultaneous equations (see § 23), results in an elasticity of − 0.25 for the average values of price and quantity demanded.

Finally, the demand for all *durable goods,* all *nondurable consumer's goods,* and all *services* in the United States has been investigated by L. R. Klein for the period from 1919 to 1939.†

* Statistical analysis of the demand for food: examples of simultaneous estimation of structural relations, Econometrica 15 (1947) p. 79.

† A post-mortem on transition predictions of national product, The Journal of Political Economy 54 (1946) p. 289.

The explanatory series used for each of these categories are real national income, the relative price of the category considered with respect to the average price level, and a trend. The correlations for the first two categories were very good; for the services, however, moderate (0.73). The elasticities with respect to the group's own relative price were 2.5, 0.4, and 0.26 respectively; the marginal propensities to consume were 0.12, 0.28, and 0.26 respectively.

§ 29. Demand Curves; Services and Industrial Products

Attempts have also been made in recent years to analyze statistically the demand for other than agricultural products. The difficulties here are greater: the price changes are less frequent and smaller, whereas the goods (and services) do not possess in such a high degree the character of staple products with sharply defined qualities. The success has been greatest for a number of services and goods which are more or less monopolized. Relatively elementary methods can sometimes be made use of here. The prices or tariffs in this category usually remain unchanged for a long time, and then suddenly are brought to another level. At such a moment the other demand-determining factors as a rule do not change much; it is also possible to wait for a moment at which they again reach a level attained earlier. In other instances this is not the case and we have to resort to one of the correction methods described in § 20 or to the multiple-correlation method.

The services investigated all belong to the field of transportation. Roy* mentions that the demand elasticity for passenger transport by local railways in the vicinity of Paris amounts to – 0.25, near smaller places to – 0.50, and for passenger transport by railway for the whole of France to – 0.40. For streetcar transportation in Marseilles, he finds – 0.32.

The Netherlands Central Bureau of Statistics† evaluates the elasticity of streetcar transport with respect to tariff changes at:

* Etudes Econométriques, Paris 1935.

† The demand for transport by tram, Dutch Business-cycle Studies IX (1938) p. 12 (in Dutch).

The Hague . . .	— 0.72	Copenhagen	— 0.73
Amsterdam . . .	— 0.80	Stockholm	— 0.31
Rotterdam	— 0.5 to — 1		

The author remarks that in Dutch towns, as in Copenhagen, the competition of the bicycle is considerable, whereas the latter is much weaker in Stockholm; he thereby explains the higher elasticities in the towns mentioned earlier. Roy, in his study mentioned above, characterizes Marseilles as a town where the streetcar has no competition from a subway. For this town, as low a figure was found as for Stockholm. He could have added that also the bicycle is relatively unimportant there.

In an investigation of passenger transportation by railway* an elasticity of — 0.44 was found for all passenger transportation and an elasticity of — 0.7 for transportation on holiday tickets. It should be kept in mind that all these figures are valid only if all or most categories of passengers are subject to a proportional tariff change. The figure is an average of business transportation and transportation for private purposes. The latter is probably much more elastic (which also follows from the higher figure for holiday tickets) and reacts differently on certain partial tariff changes. The results cannot be applied to such tariff changes.†

Morice‡ found an elasticity of — 0.60 for the demand for mail service around 1870, which gradually decreased to — 0.40 in 1910 and has since remained approximately the same.

As regards the industrial products investigated, Roy§ mentions the demand elasticity for gas in Paris, which he put at — 0.5. Both with gas and with electricity there is a possibility of using the method of "geographical comparison."¶ As the market for these products is usually local or provincial, and as

* J. Tinbergen and P. J. Verdoorn, The demand for passenger transport by railway, Dutch Business-cycle Studies X (1939) p. 79.

† I am indebted to Professor Goudriaan for these critical remarks.

‡ Loi de la demande d'un service monopolisé, Econometrica 6 (1938) p. 291.

§ Loc. cit.

¶ Dutch Business-cycle Studies, May 1935, p. 26; August 1937, p. 83; and November 1937, p. 127 (in Dutch).

there are rather considerable price differences between the municipalities and the country districts, an attempt can be made to determine the demand curve from such local data. This geographic method, of course, is only possible if it can be assumed that the material is homogeneous, i.e., that the other factors influencing demand are the same from place to place. This may be assumed as far as the general economic situation is concerned; it is less certain regarding the general preference and mentality; and it is very questionable whether it is true as regards the "electricity civilization." The latter may easily be developed to a greater degree in places where there have been power stations for some time or in places where intensive propaganda has been made than in places with young or small active enterprises. This lack of homogeneity is not so serious in itself, as long as it is not systematically linked with the explanatory variable, the price. It is not easy to answer this question with certainty. We therefore only mention the difficulty and we remark that it may be neglected only if the elasticity turns out to be very high.*

Of the other, still rather scarce, investigations into the demand for industrial products, we mention in particular that of Roos and Von Szelisky† concerning the demand for automobiles, which is also of importance from a methodologic point of view. The authors start from the assumption that the demand for automobiles is a derived demand, namely, derived from the demand for transportation by car. These services are rendered by all available cars, and the demand for new cars, therefore, depends on the number that the consumers wish to use. It is assumed, further, that for every income level and price level of cars, there is a certain optimal number of automobiles which the public wants to possess. This optimal number, therefore, is variable; moreover, it cannot immediately be realized, but only

* In the article "The Demand for Electricity," Dutch Business-cycle Studies, May 1935, p. 26 (in Dutch), figures are given, from which an elasticity of 1.7 can be computed.

† "The Dynamics of Automobile Demand," edited by the General Motors Corp., with contributions of S. L. Horner and others, New York 1939, pp. 21-99. As another example we mention M. J. Schut, "Tin Restriction and Tin Price," Haarlem 1940 (in Dutch).

be striven after. Here we have a nice example of a dynamic method of treatment.

The hypothetical number can be approximated by making use of a property of the logistic curve.

In this curve there is a linear relation between the percentage increase at each point with respect to the preceding one (during a given small time unit) and the actual level which has already been reached. If, therefore, that percentage increase is measured along the vertical axis (see Fig. 8) and the absolute level along the horizontal axis, we obtain points lying on one line. This is not quite the case in Fig. 8, because besides the normal growth tendency, other influences are active as well, through which the whole growth curve moves, so to speak, up and down. In depression years the points are lower than in years of prosperity. The point of intersection with the horizontal axis indicates the optimal number of automobiles, because for all points

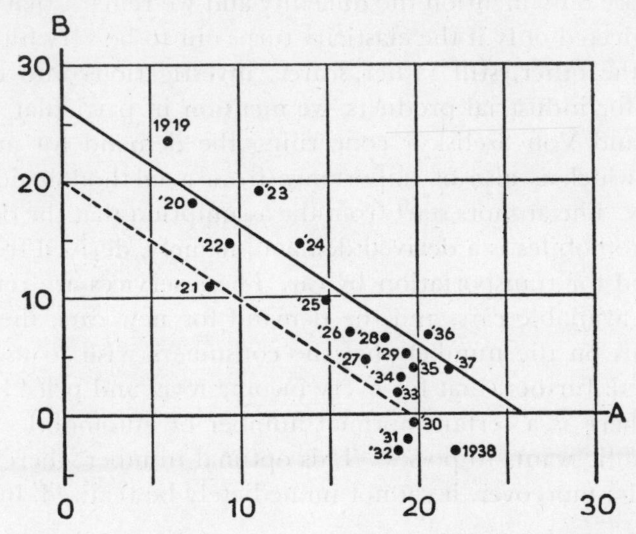

Fig. 8. Determination of the optimal number of automobiles according to Roos and Von Szelisky. Vertically: percentage increase of the number of cars in operation with respect to the preceding year; horizontally: total number of cars in operation. The optimal number can be read off as the abscissa of the point of intersection with the horizontal axis.

on the horizontal axis the vertical coördinate (the percentage rate of increase) is zero.

The authors explain the movements by the price of automobiles and by "free income." This is the part of national income remaining after a certain quantity of goods has been bought by each family for the first necessities of life.

Besides the demand for automobiles for the increase in the total number, of which we have only spoken so far, there is also a demand for the *substitution* of worn-out cars. The latter depends on the age distribution of cars actually in operation and, in a high degree, on the economic situation. Similar results were attained by de Wolff in a study which appeared earlier.*

With this product, as with a number of other industrial products, the demand elasticity cannot be determined so easily, because the price influence, in comparison to that of other factors, is relatively unimportant. Roos and Von Szelisky, therefore, came to the conclusion that it is not possible to determine whether the demand is elastic or inelastic. De Wolff, who used another price series, concluded that the demand is inelastic during a business-cycle boom, and very elastic during a depression.

An example of an industrial product permitting a rather exact determination of the demand elasticity is alcoholic spirits, for which Derksen and Van Lottum found an elasticity of − 1.4† (see Fig. 9).

§ 30. The Demand Function for All Goods Taken Together

For various problems regarding the economy as a whole—especially for problems of general economic policy—it is not so important how the demand for separate goods reacts on price changes of those goods, but how the total demand for all goods as a whole changes. We have tried here to proceed by macroeconomic investigations—in economic theory, by Keynes and

* The demand for passenger cars in the United States, Dutch Business-cycle Studies, Nov. 1936, p. 18 (in Dutch).

† Statistical analysis of the sales of beer and spirits, Dutch Business-cycle Studies 1938, p. 43 (in Dutch).

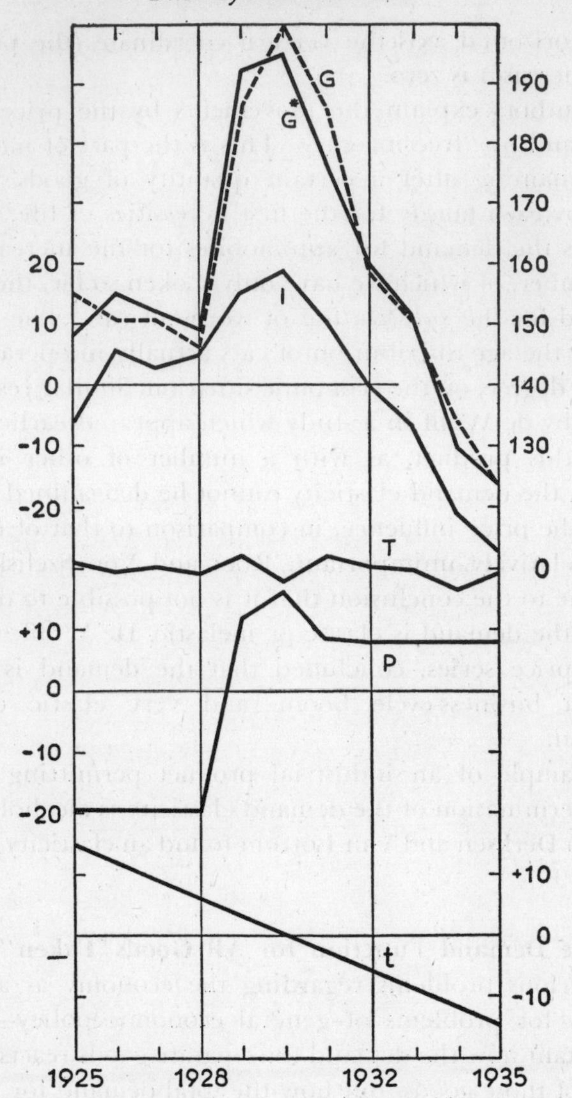

Fig. 9. Determination of the demand function for spirits, according to Derksen and Van Lottum. G: Consumption of spirits, in 10 million liters.

G*: Consumption computed as the sum total of:
I: Influence of incomes
T: Influence of the temperature
P: Influence of the price
t: Influence of gradually changing factors.

his followers; in statistical research, by the econometricians. To begin with, a distinction has been made between consumer goods and investment goods. We shall now only speak of the former; thereby at the same time continuing § 27, which dealt with determining the influence of income changes on total consumption expenditure.

In two investigations* the author has tried to explain total consumption expenditures, C, as far as the fluctuations are concerned, from some income and price series. Use has been made of more than one income series, in order to take the income distribution into account, as has already been indicated in § 27. For the United States, separate series were included in the multiple-correlation calculation for labor income (L), nonlabor income (E), and capital gains, whereas for England only the former two were considered: capital gains there were of much less importance. As a price series, the index number of the cost of living (p) was taken. The possibility of a lagged influence was taken into account only with incomes E and with p.

There were some difficulties through a number of interrelations giving rise to multicollinearity (see § 22). For the United States, L and E are strongly correlated, whereas for England, L and $E_{-\frac{1}{2}}$ show a high correlation. The influences of these variables, therefore, cannot be separated. Use had to be made of one or more of the methods described in § 23. It seemed to be the best solution to allot to series L a regression coefficient chosen beforehand, and to add this condition to the usual assumptions. On the basis of divergent budget inquiries the marginal propensity to consume for laborers' families was put at 80 per cent; the results found for England were such that an alteration of that figure did not seem advisable. For the United States, this figure was finally changed into 95 per cent, on the basis of the requirement that the marginal propensity to consume for laborers' families should be higher than for non-

* For the United States, 1919-1932, together with Dr. J. J. Polak in "Business-Cycles in the United States of America," Geneva 1939; for England 1870-1914 in: "Does consumption lag behind incomes?" Review of Economic Statistics, 1941.

laborers. With a value of 80 per cent this result could not be attained.

A number of further experiments was also undertaken, for which we must refer to the publications themselves. The most satisfactory results finally led to the following figures:

Marginal Propensity to Consume

	Laborers	Nonlaborers	Capital Gains	Demand Elasticity
United States 1919-'32	0.95	0.77 ± 0.32	0.28 ± 0.13	0.95 ± 0.15
England 1870-1914	0.8	0.3 ± 0.1	—	0.2 ± 0.1

The figures behind the ± sign indicate the standard deviation, according to Fisher (§ 22). As would be expected, the marginal propensity to consume for capital gains is lower than for other incomes. The elasticity of total demand for all consumption goods for the United States is nearly equal to 1. For England we find a very low figure both for this elasticity and for the marginal propensity to consume of nonlaborers. Both point to a great stability (or rigidity) in the consumption habits of the English. When we compare the figure mentioned last with the American figure, it should be borne in mind that retained earnings are included in the English E series, as a result of which the figure is somewhat biased downward—although not seriously for the period considered.

Important further studies concerning total demand for consumption goods have been made in the United States since the Second World War. These have partly become possible because more statistical material became available, going back to 1889. It was found that during the whole period since 1889, the average propensity to save has moved about 12 per cent, although the average income has greatly increased. A distinction has been made, now, between short-term influences and long-term influences exerted by income changes; besides, there are gradual and sometimes apparently sudden changes in saving habits. The short-term influence may also be called the cyclical income influence. This very probably is smaller than the long-term influence, i.e., a cyclical rise of incomes leads to a smaller increase in demand than a persistent rise.*

§ 31. Dynamic Demand Functions

The demand functions dealt with in the previous sections, in general, take little account of expectations as to the future or other facts giving rise to dynamic relations. The case of the demand for automobiles was an exception. Most consumer goods do not give rise to that sort of relation. Some of the complications which arise may be demonstrated by the results obtained for the price formation of shares. We have already explained in § 7, that the "valuation" of shares, expressed in their price, does not change proportionately with increases and decreases of the dividend percentage, but "more conservatively," i.e., the share prices are approximately half as much above or below normal as would correspond with the dividend fluctuations. We ascribe this to the expectation that the dividend will in the long run become normal again.

All this is based on the investor's viewpoint, where only the dividend expectation is important. If we consider shares which in a considerable degree serve as objects of speculation, we see in times of extremely active stock-market speculation that their prices also deviate from the level just described. It may be assumed that the expected gains in share prices play a role here. A dynamic relation may be supposed to exist; it may be assumed, namely, that the price rise in a preceding period stimulates the desire for speculation. It could be determined from a number of investigations† that this theory is not contrary to the facts. If we accept the theory, the influence of this speculative demand factor on share-price fluctuations was the greatest

* For a survey of these recent American investigations, the reader is referred to discussions in the Review of Economics and Statistics (1946) pp. 1 and 197, and (1948) p. 45.

† J. Tinbergen, Business Cycles in the United States, 1919-1932, Geneva 1939; J. J. J. Dalmulder, The factors determining share prices, Dutch Business-cycle Studies (1939) p. 111 (in Dutch); J. Tinbergen, The dynamics of share-price formation, The Review of Econ. Stat. (1939) p. 153.

in the United States between 1926 and 1929, weaker in the United States before 1914 and in England during the same period, and practically absent in Germany. The result for the United States is in agreement with the fact that the price for a stock-exchange seat paid about 1929 was several times as high as ever before.

It has also been observed in a few other cases that the demand function is more in harmony with the facts if it is assumed that the rate of increase in prices a little earlier is also an explanatory factor.

§ 32. The Foundations of Demand Curves: Indifference Surfaces

Thus far we have considered the Engel curve and the demand curve as more or less given functions. This is also done by Cassel. It has already been pointed out that most theoretical economists do not consider these functions as the final data, but derive them from *indifference functions* or indifference surfaces. Econometricians have tried to take this step in the reverse direction and to derive the indifference functions from the data concerning the behavior of economic subjects.

A first attempt was made by Frisch.* His purpose was more limited in scope than the determination of all particulars of the indifference lines. He tried to determine the dependence between the size of income and the size of the marginal utility belonging to each income. According to the marginal utility theory, every income is spent on various goods in such a way that the utility of the last cent spent on each good, i.e., the marginal utility of the monetary unit is equal for every cent. This marginal utility is called the *marginal utility of income*. It decreases as income increases, because less urgent needs can be satisfied. The question of to what degree it decreases is of interest to taxation theorists, as it may serve as a basis for the choice of the income-tax progression. Even if marginal utility

* "New Methods of Measuring Marginal Utility," Tübingen 1931 and "Confluence Analysis by Means of Complete Regression Systems," Oslo 1934.

itself is not measurable (which is practically a *communis opinio*), it is conceivable that the relation between the marginal utility of two different incomes is measurable. This is Frisch's opinion. The simplest case he considers is the one where the existence of *independent goods* is supposed. A good is called independent of all other goods, if its marginal utility only depends on the quantity consumed of that particular commodity.

If, now, a certain person in two different situations—for instance, at different moments of time with different prices and different incomes—consumes the same amount of that commodity, the marginal utility per gram is the same. One gram, however, represents a different number of money units; a number proportionate to the price. The marginal utilities of the money unit, then, are inversely proportional to the prices of that independent commodity in the two situations.

In his first investigation, Frisch assumed that sugar is such a good. From the figures of a big Paris coöperative store he selected the months for which the total sugar consumption was equal. The total income of the group of consumers concerned he put proportionate to the total consumption expenditures. (This was an approximation, which of course has nothing to do with the principle.) For these two amounts of income the marginal utilities, therefore, were inversely proportionate to the sugar prices. In this way Frisch determined the flexibility of the marginal utility, i.e., the ratio between a small relative change of marginal utility and the relative income change. He found values of 3.5 for the lowest incomes. An income decrease of 1 per cent, therefore, leads to an increase of the marginal utility by 3.5 per cent. For higher incomes this value rapidly decreases.

Later Frisch made similar evaluations for American families, where he started from demand curves for independent goods. It would lead us too far to discuss the mathematical details; the principle does not differ from the previous one. He also tried to introduce corrections for the case where no independence exists. This was done by assuming that the prices of other goods also exert influence on the marginal utility of the good considered, and by correcting for changes in those prices with the help of multiple-correlation calculations. For the United States he found a flexibility of approximately 1. It is possible in principle to check the results obtained for one commodity with those of another. This check was carried out for one other article; it led to satisfactory results.

Later attempts to determine the indifference functions as a whole have been undertaken by Wald.* Wald assumes that the ophelimity function or utility function in the vicinity of the point for which one wants to determine it is a function of the second degree. Depending on the number of goods considered, there is a certain number of coefficients fixing that function. For instance, if we have three commodities, x, y, and z, the quantities of which are commanded by an economic subject, the utility function is

$$W(x, y, z) = a_{00} + a_{01}x + a_{02}y + a_{03}z + a_{11}x^2 + a_{12}xy + a_{13}xz + a_{22}y^2 + a_{23}yz + a_{33}z^2$$

and this function is known, if a_{00}, a_{01}, a_{02} . . . to a_{33} inclusive are known. Wald shows that if for a number of different price situations the subject's Engel curves are known, i.e., if it is known how much he will buy at various sizes of income, a calculation is possible of the *ratios* of coefficients, except a_{00}. This, however, is sufficient for the solution of all economic problems pertaining to the subject; the absolute height of W is indifferent here, only the course of the surfaces of equal utility is important. Knowledge of the ratios of the other coefficients is sufficient to this end. The number of coefficients increases rapidly if more goods are taken into consideration. It is also necessary that the Engel curves for an increasing number of different price situations are known. The computational work is very intricate for four or more goods, but in principle it is possible.

---

* The approximate determination of indifference surfaces by means of Engel curves, Econometrica 8 (1940) p. 144.

5
The Technical Relations

§ 33. Cost Curves for Separate Industrial Enterprises (Microeconomic Cost Curves)

Concerning cost curves for separate enterprises, of course very much is known inside those enterprises; but these data are usually secret. The research worker outside the business firm, therefore, is handicapped. This handicap is gradually decreasing through the growing number of publications in this field. On the other hand, if the figures are available, they are often not suitable for further research in general economic problems. The structure of most industrial enterprises is intricate and there are many ways in which the available means of production may be used. A textile factory may increase its production in different ways; for instance, the number of looms in a weaving mill operated by one man or woman, may be varied; also the speed of the machines can be varied. The production costs, therefore, do not depend in an immediately discernible way on the rate of production. How costs react on demand fluctuations depends on many individual details. With macroeconomic problems, on the other hand, we are concerned with the total increase of costs of large groups of enterprises or of branches of industry in relation to the rate of production. It can easily happen that in those investigations, tendencies become apparent which, although in principle present in every enterprise separately, are nearly invisible in the latter, through the influence of individual factors outweighing the systematic ones. It is therefore possible that macroeconomic relations which have little use microeconomically are valid, and conversely. This is exactly the same in the psychic sphere.

For the two reasons mentioned, we shall deal very briefly with cost curves for individual enterprises. As regards their role in econometrics, we shall only make a few remarks.

That econometric methods can also be applied within the enterprise for the solution of cost problems becomes clear, for instance, from Dean's work.* With the help of the multiple-correlation method, this author has tried to approximate the variations in real cost by a combination of the following variables: rate of production, average size of orders, number of times the style was changed (furniture), changes of production rate, personnel turnover, and quality of raw materials.

A few very rough tendencies which have become apparent from quantitative investigations and which are of importance for econometrics are the following.

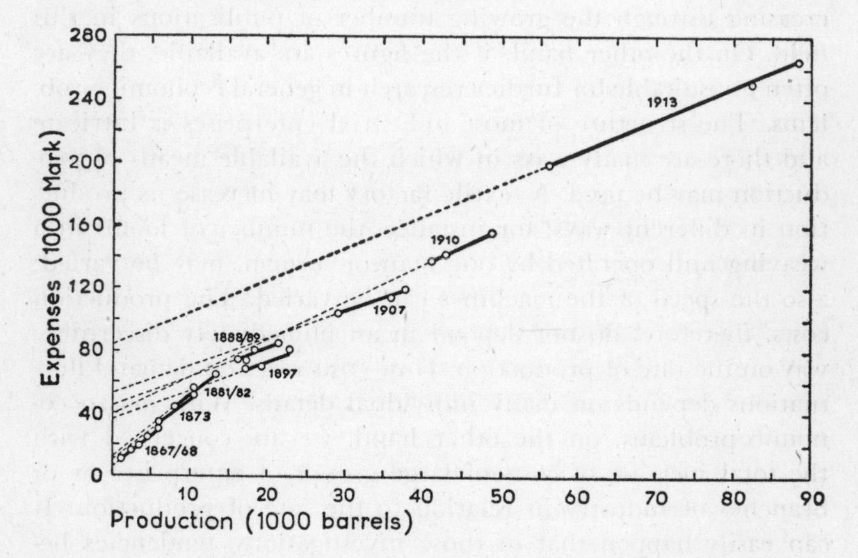

Fig. 10. Example of a number of cost curves in a cement factory, according to Ehrke (Die Überproduktion in der Zementindustrie, 1858-1913, Jena 1933) and Schneider; these curves correspond to the situation in various periods of time. It can be observed that the capacity of the enterprise has increased considerably; the importance of fixed costs (to be read off as the ordinate of the point of intersection with the vertical axis) has increased. The curves are nearly straight.

* Statistical cost curves, Journal of the American Statistical Association 32 (1937) p. 83, and his book: "Statistical Determination of Cost with Special Reference to Marginal Cost," Chicago, 1936.

It has been found in the first place, that in a number of industries the course of total costs in their dependence on the production size can, within rather wide limits, be represented by a straight line. Fig. 10 is an example. At the same time, this graph is an example of the structural changes which have taken place in the course of the last few decades. We see, for instance, an increase of fixed costs, manifesting itself in a rise of the point of intersection of the cost curve with the vertical axis, and a considerable rise in capacity.

A second point of importance is the variance in costs between the separate enterprises in one branch of industry. Very exact material about this variance is not available; but the various more or less serviceable existing data all show that the enterprises (weighted according to their production) are usually distributed over the various cost intervals according to the normal curve. The static supply curve for many branches of industry can consequently be represented by a line with high elasticity in the middle and small elasticities in the vicinity both of very low production and of the capacity limit.

§ 34. The Production Function (Macroeconomic Cost Curves)

We shall now consider what approximate relations can be assumed for great aggregations with respect to the connection between the rate of production and the required quantities of production factors. It is useful to distinguish here between *short-term* and *long-term* changes.

As regards the first, it may usually be assumed that the quantity of fixed factors of production is constant. This hypothesis of economic theory is supported by the gradual trend of such symptomatic factors as the total horse-power and the number of machines of various types and their capacity. The other factors—raw materials, energy, labor, etc.—mostly show a close correlation between the fluctuations of quantities of the factors used with the rate of production. This is in agreement with the simplest theory conceivable, namely, that the variable real costs are proportionate. This does not mean proportionality of, for instance, production and working hours, but proportionality of their fluctuations. For great complexes it is usually found that an increase of production by 10 per cent can be brought about by a 7 or 8 per cent increase in personnel. Of course, there are differences for separate branches of industry; for production of electricity, for instance, the figure is much lower.

If we have more accurate figures at our disposal, the analysis can be refined. For the mining industry* for instance, we find that a tendency existed for an increase of labor productivity shortly after the deepest trough of the depression had passed. This does not mean that at that time the productivity was greatest, but merely that its *increase* was greatest. The phenomenon is more complicated than the automatic influence of a higher and lower level of employment; here probably more purposeful changes in methods, or in the choice of the strata exploited, are involved.

Attempts in another direction to make a further analysis of macroeconomic data can be found in a study by Stone and Tweddle.† They adapt exponential production functions to labor productivity data and in this way set up more complicated (nonlinear) cost functions. They find that marginal labor costs decrease in five cases and increase in three cases; in five or six cases, however, they are practically constant, which would be in accordance with our first approximations.

When studying *long-term* changes, we also have to consider as variable the quantity of fixed means of production. The question now comes to the fore, how great is the quantity of the product which is produced with a given quantity of labor and a given quantity of means of production. By far the most important attempt undertaken in econometrics to set up a general function for this relation (the production function), has been made by Douglas and his co-workers.‡ If the quantity of "capital"—by which Douglas sometimes means only the fixed means of production and in other investigations the whole

* The influence of the business-cycle on labour productivity, Dutch Business-cycle Studies, June 1934, p. 13 (in Dutch).

† A study of costs, Econometrica 4 (1936) p. 226.

‡ See Douglas: "The Theory of Wages," Chicago 1936 and numerous articles in American economic periodicals.

wealth of an enterprise—is denoted by K, the quantity of labor by a and the quantity of product by u, Douglas has tried to find a function

$$u = ca^{\lambda}K^{\mu} \tag{34.1}$$

which finds as close an approximation for u as possible. In this formula, c, λ, and μ are constants, so Douglas has chosen the simplest type of exponential function (see § 8). On the basis of the assumption that the optimum size of enterprises is considerably smaller than the complexes he has investigated, Douglas sometimes assumes that an increase of a and K in a given proportion, for instance 1½, must lead to an increase of u in the same proportion. This restricts the function (34.1) in that it must be linearly homogeneous, which in this case means that $\lambda + \mu = 1$.

Douglas has tried to test relation (34.1) by historic and by geographic equations. From production statistics, he computed time series of a, K, and u for various countries (United States, Australia), as well as figures for a, K, and u relating to different industries in the same period.

His results are always such that he finds roughly ¾ for λ and ¼ for μ when taking the first regression equation. The conclusions he draws from the production function found in this way

$$u = ca^{\frac{3}{4}}K^{\frac{1}{4}} = c\sqrt[4]{a^3K} \tag{34.2}$$

are very important. In the first place, it can be deduced that the *distribution of the national product between labor and capital* will always be in the same proportion, namely ¾ for labor and ¼ for capital. Edelberg,* who has worked along similar lines, but who also takes the production factor of land into consideration, finds somewhat lower figures and also a small percentage for land. A second conclusion which can be drawn from (34.2) is that with a given stock of capital, the demand elasticity for labor is 4, i.e., that a wage decrease of 1 per cent

* An econometric model of production and distribution, Econometrica 4 (1936) p. 210.

will increase employment by 4 per cent. This is a long-term reaction, i.e., after complete adaptation of the production method to the new wage level. The great importance of function (34.2) therefore, is clear.

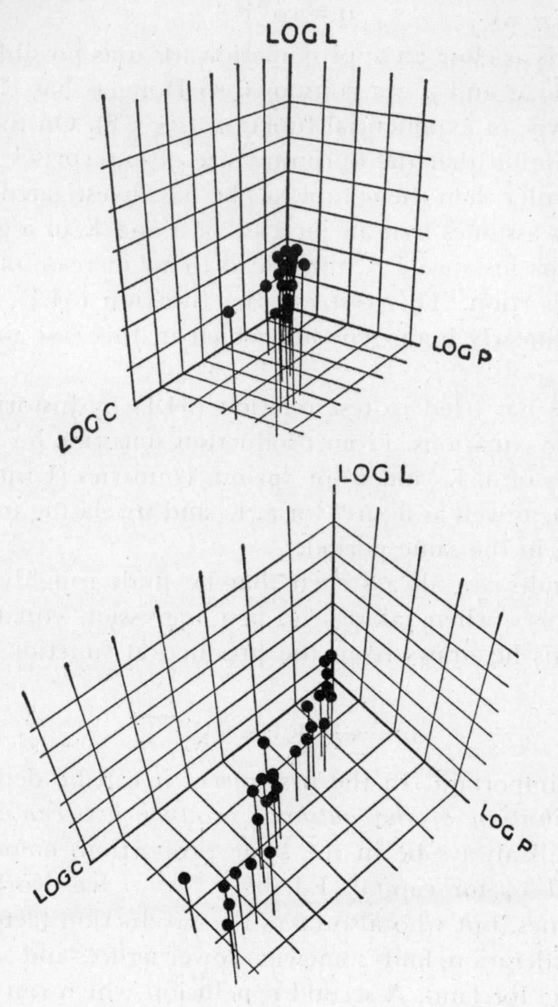

Fig. 11. Spatial representation according to Mendershausen of Douglas's statistical material for determining the production function. P: product; L: labor; C: capital. The points are nearly on one line, which makes the determination of the regression surface very difficult.

Douglas's results, however, are subject to serious criticism. As regards the historical method, Mendershausen* has pointed out that Douglas's material is to a high degree multicollinear. This also becomes clear if the other regression equations are computed. Mendershausen demonstrates this by Fig. 11, giving a spatial representation of the situation of the points. They turn out to lie practically on one line. The regression plane

$$\log u' = \lambda \log a + \mu \log K$$

(in Douglas's notation: $\log P = \lambda \log L + \mu \log C$), therefore, is to a high degree indefinite. Mendershausen concludes that, strictly speaking, Douglas's λ is nothing other than the ratio $\frac{\alpha - \gamma}{\beta - \gamma}$, where α is the yearly percentage increase of production, β of the quantity of labor, and γ of the quantity of capital.

Douglas's result, however, would again be perfectly acceptable, if it may be assumed on *a priori* economic grounds that $\lambda = 1 - \mu$. The problem is then reduced to one of simple correlation. There are, however, a number of other criticisms one may make.†

With respect to the geographic investigations, one should also be skeptical, as I have indicated elsewhere.‡ These investigations, which are of the greatest importance for macroeconomic problems, show clearly that there are serious dangers in applying the method of multiple correlation uncritically.

§ 35. Technical Development

If we want to describe the phenomenon of technical development we can make use of exponential and logistic trend lines (see § 16). The development of certain forms of technique, for instance—the length of the railway system, of the telephone

---

* On the significance of Professor Douglas' production function, Econometrica 6 (1938) p. 143.

† See D. H. van Dongen Torman: "The Cobb-Douglas Production Function," Rotterdam 1950 (in Dutch).

‡ Professor Douglas's production function, Revue de l'Institut International de Statistique, 1942: ½.

system, the number of automobiles, of radio sets, etc.—nearly takes place along a logistic curve. The growth of production in general and of labor productivity can very well be approximated by exponential curves, or by straight lines, if a logarithmic scale is used.

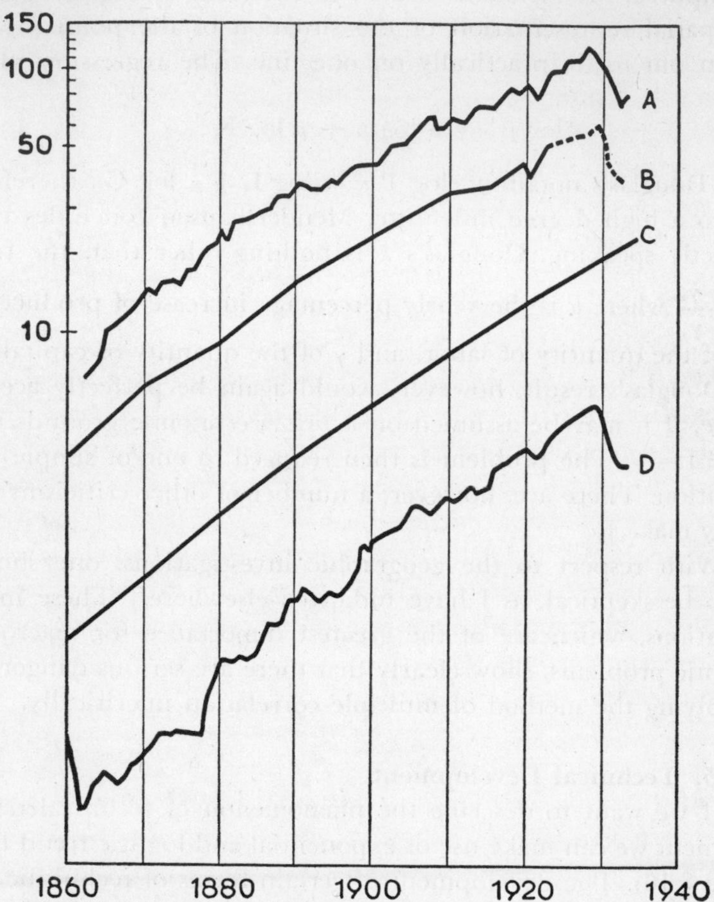

Fig. 12. Examples of nearly exponential growth curves (straight lines with logarithmic scale) for production, taken from Snyder.

A: Index of the total volume of production.
B: Index of industrial production.
C: Index of commercial transactions (real).
D: Index of payments (real; namely "clearing debits" divided by price index).

Fig. 12, taken from C. Snyder,* demonstrates this very clearly for various series representing the rate of production, whereas graphs by W. P. de Lange† show it for labor productivity. An important question is whether we can explain theoretically, exactly why an exponential curve should appear here. To answer this question, we must formulate a theory concerning the development of the economy. The first germs of such a theory can be found in Cassel's views about the uniformly developing economy in his *Theoretische Sozialökonomie*. He explains that an economy, the development of which is exclusively determined by saving sometimes actually shows an exponential development of production. If we try, however, to generalize this theory by including an increasing labor productivity, an exponential production trend is much less likely. Much remains to be done in this field of investigation.

We also mention Douglas's opinion that the increase of labor productivity in the past is exclusively a consequence of the higher capital intensity of production, and not of a change in technical knowledge. He finds no contradiction, therefore, between a development process through saving (and capital formation) on the one hand and by increased labor productivity on the other hand. We doubt whether this opinion can be maintained in the light of the increase in efficiency practically without enlargement of capital, which has come so much to the fore in the past decades.

The trend of labor productivity itself has also been a subject of econometric research. Besides the attempts concerning labor productivity in the mining industry (§ 34), which have already been referred to, we mention an investigation by Van der Schalk‡ into the influence of the number of working hours on labor productivity.

* Measures of industrial growth and their significance, in: "Beiträge zur Konjunkturlehre," Hamburg 1936.

† Labour productivity in manufacturing industry, Dutch Business-cycle Studies, December 1933, p. 10 (in Dutch).

‡ The mathematical-statistical analysis of labour productivity and its application in practice to a few branches of industry and enterprises in the Netherlands, Haarlem 1938 (in Dutch).

Fig. 12, taken from a Swedish* study, shows this trend clearly for various series representing the Swedish production. We [illegible] graphs by W. P. [illegible] labour productivity. An important question is, whether we can explain, theoretically, exactly why an exponential trend should appear. To answer this question, we must formulate a theory concerning the development of the economy. The first germs of such a theory can be found in Cassel's views about the uniformly developing economy in his *Theoretische Sozialökonomie*. He explains that an economy, the development of which is exclusively determined by saving, sometimes actually shows an exponential development of production. It is by no means [illegible], however, [illegible] this theory includes an increasing labour productivity; an exponential production trend is much less likely. Much remains to be done in this field of investigation.

We also mention Douglas's opinion that the increase of labour productivity in the past is exclusively a consequence of the higher capital intensity of production, and not of a change in technical knowledge. He finds no contradiction, therefore, between a development process through saving and capital formation on the one hand and its increased labour productivity on the other hand. We doubt whether this opinion can be maintained in the light of the increase in efficiency, especially without increment of capital, which has come so much to the fore in the past decades.

The trend of labour productivity itself has also been a subject of econometric research. Besides the attempts at explaining labour productivity in the mining industry (§ 14), which have already been referred to, we mention an investigation by Van der Schalk into the influence of the number of working hours on labour productivity.

* Measures of industrial growth and their significance, in: [illegible] Hamburg 1952.

[illegible] productivity in manufacturing industries [illegible] 1951 [illegible]

The econometrical statistical analysis of labour productivity and its application [illegible] 1948 [illegible]

6
Reactions of Business Life

§ 36. Supply of Products

We have seen in § 26 that in dealing with the supply of products and with the demand for labor and raw materials, much more objective decisions are concerned than with demand and supply functions, which only have a psychic basis. After having discussed a few technical relations regarding production, therefore, we now turn to the aforementioned reaction relations of enterprises. If short-term reactions are concerned, it is, strictly speaking, not necessary to distinguish between supply of products and demand for production factors, as these represent one and the same decision and come into being *uno actu*.

It has already been pointed out in § 9 that although the logical coherence of quantity supplied and price is different as production for the market and production to order is considered, in both cases the same magnitudes appear in the supply relation. These magnitudes generally will be the production, u; the price, p; and the cost factors of a representative firm, k.

Attempts have been made to determine supply relations for a number of divergent branches of industry. With *agricultural enterprises* the particular circumstance occurs that we can distinguish between the production plans—to be read off from the acreage cultivated—and the real production, which is influenced by the changing yields per acre. The farmer's reaction can be most accurately determined from the former. Various investigations show that prices play a decisive role and that rather high elasticities appear. Interesting figures, obtained by Bean,* indicate that these elasticities lie above 1 for the most part. He finds

* The farmer's response to price, Journal of Agricultural Economics (1929) p. 368.

at the same time, however, that lags of one or two years appear and that the elasticity becomes considerably less if the price changes are large. It can be added that this is correct for relative price changes of one product with respect to another; if all prices decrease at the same time, only a very small decrease of the total acreage cultivated results. Bean's observations, therefore, refer to substitution elasticities rather than to total elasticities.

Also for livestock products it has been found that the prices show a high correlation with the quantities supplied, but likewise after a certain time interval. The supply of hogs, for instance, is high 1½ years after a high price level,* as a result of the length of the "production process." The supply elasticity according to Hanau lies between ½ and 1. This investigation was started from an *a priori* combination of prices and costs, as has been described in § 20.

For *mining* products there is usually a high correlation between prices and quantities, almost without lags, because the production process is very short. As we have seen in § 20, the correlation can in principle be interpreted as a supply function. The elasticity of this supply function was not very high in the period before 1914, namely, in the neighborhood of 0.4.

A number of investigations concerning products of *manufacturing industry* have been carried out by the author.† We tried here to approximate the price of finished products, p, by a linear function of the price of raw materials, r, of the wage rate, l, and of the rate of the production, u. A satisfactory correlation was found both for the Netherlands after 1921 and for England between 1870 and 1914, where the regression coefficient for the u term was small. If we accept the theory as correct, these figures would point to a very large supply elasticity of the goods, namely, of the order of magnitude of 3 to 10. A lower figure was found for investment goods in the period prior to

* A. Hanau: Die Prognose der Schweinepreise, Sonderheft 18 der Vierteljahreshefte zur Konjunkturforschung, Berlin 1930.

† The coherence between the prices of imported raw materials and of finished products in the Netherlands, Dutch Business-cycle Studies 10 (1939) p. 150 (in Dutch).

1914, which is in accordance with the fact that in these branches of industry the capacity limits were reached more often.

It should be expected that the supply function in the vicinity of full employment of productive capacity shows a distinct kink. Most investigations are disappointing in this respect; obviously either the data are too rough or the production remains in these regions for so short a time that only little of it can be shown statistically. An interesting exception to this rule is an investigation by T. Koopmans* into the supply of tankers. In times of underemployment the supply, likewise, is very elastic and in periods of full employment—which were sufficiently frequent to permit of statistical research—very inelastic.

The long-term reactions, of course, are also influenced by changes in productive capacity, which appear as consequences of changes in profit possibilities. This brings us to our next point.

§ 37. The Demand for Investment Goods

Regarding the factors determining the demand for investment goods by entrepreneurs, various partial theories have been advanced, i.e., theories which accentuate only a few factors while neglecting others. As the fluctuations of investment activity play an important role in business-cycle fluctuations, many business-cycle theorists, particularly, have occupied themselves with these problems.

In this connection, the so-called acceleration principle has often been advanced during the last few years. According to this principle the demand for investment goods is determined by the increase per time unit of the production of consumption goods. In its simplest form the reasoning is very clear: if the production of consumption goods first increases from 100 to 110 and in the year afterwards from 110 to 115, we first need means of production to produce 10 units extra, and in the year afterwards, to produce five units. New investments, in this way, will decrease to half the original amount. J. M. Clark, who

* Tanker freight rates and tankship building, Haarlem 1939, p. 83.

first called this the *acceleration principle,* gives figures for the American railways, which are in agreement with it. A further investigation, however, shows that for the majority of branches of industry the principle is in conflict with the facts.*

Another one-sided theory explains the fluctuations of investment activity in particular by the fluctuations of the *interest rate.*

In this situation a synthetic research was needed, trying with the help of multiple-correlation calculations to determine the relative importance of the different factors. This was tried in my investigation for the League of Nations,† where the following explanatory variables were used:

1. the profits of business life as a whole (Z);
2. the price of investment goods (q);
3. the rate of interest (m);
4. the rate of increase of the production of consumption goods (Δ u);
5. the rate of increase of the price level of investment goods (Δ q);
6. the profit margin per unit of product (z).

Variable 1 was included to represent the influence of profit expectations, assuming, therefore, that the *expectations* will depend in a considerable degree on actual profits. The inclusion of variables 2 and 3 was based on the following reasoning: in the profits, Z, the prices of investment goods and the rates of interest of many preceding years play a role, because the depreciation allowances and the interest burden are usually based on previous investments and loans, respectively. For profits on new investments, however, the prices and the interest rate of this moment will be the determining magnitudes. These may differ considerably from the averages of previous years. These averages, by the way, show little movement as soon as they are calculated over a period of more than one business-cycle wave: they are only trends. Variable 3 was included to represent the

* J. Tinbergen: Statistical evidence on the acceleration principle, Econometrica 5 (1938) p. 164. This article is reprinted in Appendix B.

† "Statistical Testing of Business-Cycle Theories I," Geneva 1939.

theories which attribute a dominating role to the interest rate.

The basis for variable 4 was to interpret the purely technical factor embodied in the acceleration principle. Variable 5 may have influence if speculative motives—the consideration that the goods to be constructed will rise or decline in value—will lead to an earlier, or to a postponed, investment. Variable 6, finally, was included, because according to some writers the profit *margin* per unit of product rather than total profits determines the investment activity. Changes in the degree of utilization of capacity are also expressed in total profits: in dull times the profits are low, particularly on account of the low level of production. As there is more reason to expect a complete utilization for new investments than for other parts of the production apparatus, we may—according to these theorists—assume a given constant utilization of the new means of production.

The variable Z, total profits, at the same time represents the profit *rate,* i.e., the profit per unit of capital; the course of these two series is nearly perfectly parallel, because the quantity of capital, by which Z has to be divided to obtain the profit rate, has a gradual trend.

In the above list of variables, therefore, many theoretical viewpoints have been united.

In a few cases the lag was assumed *a priori* to be six months; in other cases it was assumed to be six months for the less important variables and was left "free" for the main variable, Z. This means that the lag was to be determined by the correlation calculation itself. On the average a lag of about six months was also found for Z.

The correlation calculations show that a rather good approximation of the course of investment activity, v, can be obtained with the help of these variables and that, assuming our list of variables to be correct, the variables 4, 5, and 6 play a very small role. Nearly as good an explanation is possible with 1, 2, and 3. From these variables, Z's influence is by far the greatest; q's and m's influences are secondary.

The result provides a check against economic theory: the coefficients of q and m must both be negative (see § 24, under

6). In almost all cases investigated, this requirement was actually satisfied. If we accept the theory that investment activity is mainly determined by Z, q, and m, the influences of q and m also turn out to be weak, as has been pointed out.

The influence of q can be expressed in the form of an elasticity coefficient. If we take the price of pig iron, the elasticity is 0.2 to 0.3; if the prices of finished products (e.g. machines) are taken, this elasticity would rise to 0.3 to 0.5, which still is distinctly below 1.

The accurate evaluation of this elasticity is always very difficult, because the gross correlation between q and v is positive; obviously the fluctuations in v are in the first place brought about by another magnitude (Z, according to our theory), which shows nearly the same fluctuations as q, and q's influence is inverse, but weaker. That influence, then, is the difference between v and Z's influence on v, and this difference cannot be determined accurately: small random deviations in Z and small errors in the lag used in the calculation may have a great influence on the elasticity determined.

The influences of Z and m may also be formulated as follows: the difference between the profit rate and the interest rate determines the level of the investment activity. This becomes clear from the order of magnitude of the coefficients and is not true as a matter of course. It is in accordance, however, with the well-known formulation that investments are determined by the *difference between "natural" interest and market interest* —at least if, as often happens, the natural interest is identified with the profit rate. Much more could be said about this than the scope of this book allows and so we shall not go into this further.

The fact that the market rate of interest, m, nevertheless, has a relatively small influence, is a consequence of the circumstance that the fluctuations of the profit rate are much greater than those of m.

It may finally be remarked that the influence both of the interest rate and of the acceleration principle has turned out to be more important for investments in *railway material* than for total investments. This is possibly connected with the longer life of those goods. In this connection the fact pointed out by Zimmerman* is important that before 1910 railway investments formed a much more important part of total investments than after that year.

§ 38. Substitution Elasticities

In commercial relations—which belong to the field of "objective" decisions described in § 36—competition still plays an important role and consequently also the *substitution elasticity* between products supplied by competing firms or countries. The trade of a small country in particular is strongly influenced by the price level, not only of its own, but also of competing products. To quote an example, the demand for Dutch butter in the London market depends on the prices both of Dutch butter and of Danish and Australian butter. Knowledge of these substitution elasticities is of particular importance for several problems of commercial and monetary policy. Moreover, as trade statistics provide very comprehensive data, it is difficult to understand that an attempt has not been made earlier to determine the substitution elasticities for a number of products. For the Netherlands this has been done by Derksen and Rombouts.† Although many difficulties still have to be solved when dealing with these investigations, a satisfactory result can already be recorded in a number of cases.

The authors start from the theory that the ratio of quantities of a certain product bought from the Netherlands and from other countries is determined by the ratio of the prices charged by the Netherlands and by the other countries. If the quantities are denoted by u_N and u_F respectively, and the prices by p_N and p_F, it is assumed that:

$$\frac{u_N}{u_F} = - a \frac{p_N}{p_F} + b \tag{38.1}$$

* "Saving and Investing in Economic Literature," The Hague 1941 (in Dutch).

† The influence of the price level on exports, Special Investigations of Dutch Business-cycle Studies, No. 1, The Hague 1939 (in Dutch, with English summary).

If both ratios are measured as percentage deviations from their trend, a is the substitution elasticity. This is an example of an *a priori* combination of variables (§ 20), in which a relation between four magnitudes is determined by only one regression coefficient. The combination is given by the definition of substitution elasticity (§ 20). Nevertheless, it could be asked whether the influence of still other factors should be assumed, in particular, income in the market concerned. This is possible, although of course the most important influence of income in the ordinary demand function (on u_N, therefore) is counteracted by an influence into the same direction exerted on u_F. In other words, it is conceivable that the *ratio* of the quantities bought in the Netherlands and elsewhere depends only slightly on income. The authors have made sure that in the cases they have investigated no great change would be brought about by including income as an additional variable.

In the following table a few of the values which they have found are summarized.

Article	Market	Competing Countries	Period	Substitution Elasticity
Butter*	England	Australia & New Zealand	1922-37	−2.0
Cheese	England	Canada & New Zealand	1927-37	−1.2
Cheese	Belgium	France	1927-37	−2.3
Bacon	England	All other countries	1926-37	−3.0
Coal	Belgium	" " "	1926-37	−2.0
Cotton Goods	Neth. Indies	" " "	1927-37	−4.8†
Shoes	Neth. Indies	" " "	1928-38	−2.8

* Danish and Dutch butter together.

† Average figure for separate periods.

Important investigations concerning substitution elasticities for the whole of imports and the whole of exports of a number of countries have been carried out by Tse-Chun Chang in four studies.* He explained the fluctuations of exports, in general, from fluctuations in: (1) the size of world exports, representing the income of the receiving countries; (2) the price level of export products of the country concerned; and (3) the price level of competing countries. The fluctuations in imports were explained by fluctuations in: (1) real income or employment, (2) the ratio of the import price level and the domestic price level, and (3) the size of exports. The results shown in the following table were obtained:

Country	Import Elasticity	Export Elasticity	Total
Lithuania	−0.48	−1.84	−2.32
Canada	−1.34	−0.35	−1.69
Hungary	−0.54	−1.10	−1.64
Estonia	−0.34	−1.29	−1.63
Norway	−0.86	−0.62	−1.48
Finland	−0.25	−1.23	−1.48
United States	−0.97	−0.43	−1.40
Australia	−0.67	−0.66	−1.33
France	−0.32	−0.77	−1.09
Denmark	−0.63	−0.45	−1.08
Italy	−0.27	−0.81	−1.08
Japan	−0.47	−0.60	−1.07
Germany	−0.37	−0.58	−0.95
South Africa	−0.64	−0.31	−0.95
New Zealand	−0.34	−0.52	−0.86
Sweden	−0.37	−0.36	−0.73
Switzerland	−0.26	−0.44	−0.70
Great Britain	−0.28	−0.40	−0.68
Chile	−0.32	−0.17	−0.49

Chang's figures concerning export elasticity are lower than a number of figures obtained in an investigation by the author.†

* International comparison of demand for imports, The Review of Economic Studies 13 (1945-46) p. 53; The British demand for imports in the inter-war period, The Economic Journal 56 (1946) p. 188; The British balance of payments, 1924-1938, The Economic Journal 57 (1947) p. 475; and A statistical note on world demand for exports, The Review of Economics and Statistics 30 (1948) p. 106.

† Further measurements of the substitution elasticity, Monthly Bulletin of the Netherlands Central Bureau of Statistics, 1943, p. 151 (in Dutch).

In this latter investigation, the price index of world trade was started from as a competing price index. In this respect Chang's calculations are to be preferred. As regards his evaluations of the import elasticity, some doubts may be raised in connection with the facts that he neglects the existence of the quota system, that sometimes he takes the cost of living as a competing price index, and that sometimes the employment figures are taken as an income index. Nevertheless, his results deserve confidence, because the differences between the one group of countries and the other can be explained satisfactorily. The results are particularly interesting because the balance of payments equilibrium is under certain conditions indifferent if the sum total of the two elasticities mentioned is equal to 1 and unstable if the sum total is < 1.

Another example is given in Fig. 13: it refers to the substitution elasticity of American iron and English iron imported into the United States. In this case the ratio of imports to total consumption (including imports) has been taken instead of the ratio of the quantities.

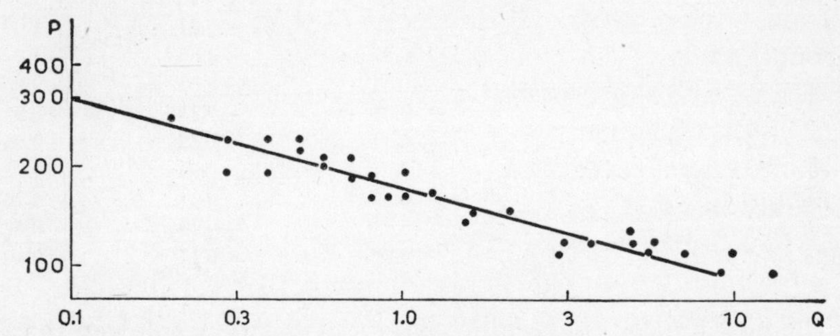

Fig. 13. Evaluation of the substitution elasticity of pig iron imported into the United States for pig iron produced there.
P: ratio of the price of imported iron to domestic price (%).
Q: imports as a % of consumption.

Although most of the figures found lie above 1, they are not as high as has often been supposed on the basis of suggestive theoretical writings concerning this subject. If the figures are correct, a price decline of Dutch products will not result in as sharp a rise of Dutch exports as has sometimes been thought. It will consequently have less importance for the promotion of exports.

There are reasons to assume that the elasticities just discussed are higher for long-run than for short-run reactions. For a more complete discussion of some evidence on this point the reader may be referred to Appendix C.

§ 39. Reaction Relations in the Financial Sphere

It took some time before reactions in the financial sector of the economy were investigated econometrically. It is not impossible that the education of many econometricians as natural scientists is a reason why they found the commodity sphere more interesting than the financial and why, consequently, they held aloof. Now, however, a few attempts to check and measure demand and supply functions are available in this field also. Keynes' theoretical work, and the discussion it has provoked, have stimulated this.

A first example is an attempt by A. J. Brown to determine a relation for the demand by the London clearing banks for various sorts of assets.* Brown subdivides these assets into four groups, namely

1. cash and short loans (C),
2. bills discounted (B),
3. investments (I),
4. advances (A),

of which 1 and 2 represent the more liquid group and 3 and 4 the less liquid group. He argues, on the ground of the liquidity theory, which we cannot entirely restate here, that the ratio both of C to B and of I to A will depend on

a. the ratio of the yields and
b. the total resources in each group which the banks have at their disposal.

If the yield of B is represented by Y_B and that of C by Y_C, he gives the relation in the following form:

* The liquidity preference schedules of the London clearing banks, Oxford Economic Papers 1 (1938) p. 49.

$$\log C/B = a_1 + b_1 \log \frac{Y_B}{Y_C} + c_1 \log (CB) \qquad (39.1a)$$

and similarly:

$$\log I/A = a_2 + b_2 \log \frac{Y_A}{Y_I} + c_2 \log (IA) \qquad (39.1b)$$

As we see, this is another application of the idea of elasticity of substitution; because the logarithmic form of the equations has been chosen, b_1 is the substitution elasticity of cash for bills, etc., and b_2 that of investments for advances. The third term denotes the influence of the resources. The author has taken the product CB instead of the total $C + B$, because, according to the theory, the total utility of C and B is involved and this will depend on CB rather than on $C + B$. The indifference curves, in other words, have the form CB as constant (rectangular hyperbolas) rather than $C + B$ as constant (straight lines). For small variations the difference will not be great, if the averages of C and B do not deviate strongly. Brown's results are:

$$b_1 = -0.26 \qquad c_1 = -0.83$$
$$b_2 = -0.66 \qquad c_2 = +1.54$$

which, on acceptance of (39.1a) and (39.1b), would point to a rather low substitution elasticity. It is remarkable that c_1 is negative and c_2 positive. This means that an increase of total resources in the more liquid group—also with unchanged yields—will lead to a relative decrease of cash, and an increase of resources in the less liquid group to a relative increase of the item investments. The author also measures the changes which the coefficients underwent during the depression period; but it would lead us too far to go into this.

A second example may be taken from my study of the business-cycle mechanism in the United States during the period 1919-1932.* It refers to the supply elasticity of money (in the sense of means of payment) by the entire banking system. The supply relation can best be regarded as a price-fixation relation (see § 9) for short money: by their interest rates the banks regu-

* "Business Cycles in the United States, 1919-1932," Geneva 1939.

late the amount of credit granted. They do this in such a way that their debt position with the Federal Reserve Banks remains within the prescribed limits. That debt position can be indicated by the amount: rediscounts minus surplus reserves, or $Bi - R^e$. The short-term interest rate m_s indeed shows a high correlation with $Bi - R^e$, as can be seen from Fig. 14. This is a good example of nonlinear correlation. If the amount of money available becomes very large, the rate of interest becomes insensitive to changes in $Bi - R^e$ (left-hand side of the figure), whereas the dependence is much stronger when the market is tight. For the period 1917-1932 the following equation was found by rough approximation:

$$m_s = 4\ (Bi - R^e) + 2 \qquad (39.2)$$

The right-hand side of this equation must be expressed in terms of the corresponding quantity of money. This correspond-

ASSETS	LIABILITIES
Gold reserve, Au	Reserves of member banks, R^r
Discounts, Bi	Surplus reserves of same, R^e
Bills of exchange and bonds bought in open market, P	Bank notes in circulation, M'

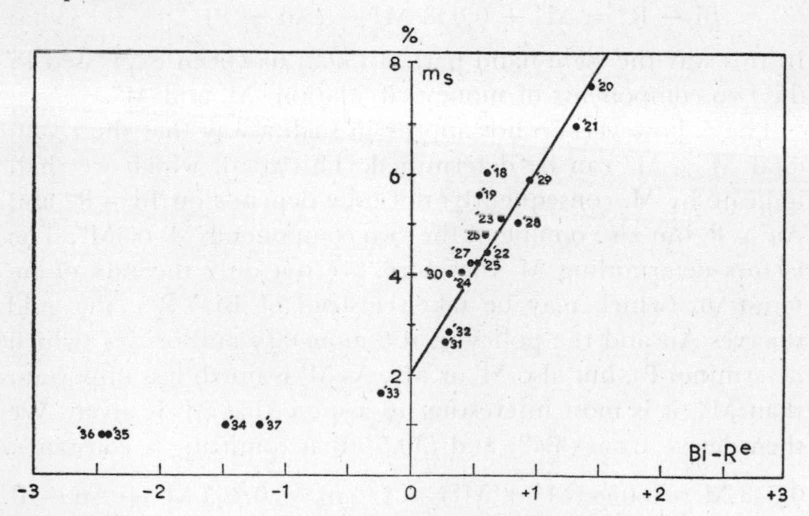

Fig. 14. The relation between $Bi - R^e$, rediscounts with the Federal Reserve Banks less surplus reserves of member banks (billions of dollars) and m_s, the discount rate in per cent.

ence is reflected in the balance sheets of the Federal Reserve Banks and in the legal reserves requirements against deposits prevailing in the United States. The aggregate balance sheet of the Federal Reserve Banks can be written as follows:

Item P has been denoted in the above way, because the credit policy of the government and the central banks manifests itself in this magnitude. The member-bank reserves keep a relation prescribed by the law with outstanding deposits M″, with which they are proportionate for each type of member bank separately (in central-reserve cities, reserve cities, and in the country). Although the relative importance of the deposits of these banks fluctuates during the business cycle, there is nevertheless a nearly linear relation between R^r and M″, which, according to simple correlation calculations, reads as follows (omitting a constant):

$$R^r = 0.038\ M'' \qquad (39.3)$$

From the balance sheet, further, it follows that

$$Bi - R^e = M' + R^r - (Au + P) \qquad (39.4)$$

which can be written in combination with (39.3), as follows:

$$Bi - R^e = M' + 0.038\ M'' - (Au + P) \qquad (39.5)$$

In this way the right-hand part of (39.2) has been expressed in the two components of money circulation, M′ and M″.

These, however, do not appear in such a way that their sum total $M' + M''$ can be determined. This total, which we shall indicate by M, consequently, not only depends on $Bi - R^e$ and $Au + P$, but also on one of the two components M′ or M″. The factors determining M, therefore, are not only the rate of interest m_s (which may be taken instead of $Bi - R^e$), the gold reserves Au and the policy of the monetary authorities (which determines P), but also M′ or M″. As M′ is much less important than M″, it is most interesting to assume that M′ is given. We then derive from (39.2) and (39.5), that (omitting a constant):

$$0.038\ M = 0.038\ (M' + M'') = 1/4\ m_s - 0.962\ M' + Au + P$$

or

$$M = 6.6\ m_s - 25\ M' + 26\ (Au + P) \qquad (39.6)$$

In this way a supply relation for money has been found, from which an elasticity can be calculated (assuming a constant M′) of approximately 0.65.

An attempt was made in the publication mentioned to determine the reactions in the whole financial sphere, as regards their main features. To this end a very rough model of this sphere has been designed, in which only broad categories have been regarded as separate assets: shares, bonds, short claims, banknotes, and gold. For other purposes, of course, microeconomic research is needed. Investment advisers, in particular, have made many investigations into the factors determining the course of separate share prices. Most of these, however, have not been published. We have already mentioned a few macroeconomic investigations in this field in § 7 and § 31.

7

The Functioning of Economic Systems

§ 40. Separate Markets (Echo Principle, Hog Cycle, Building Cycle)

Our previous discussions concerning the results of econometric research belong to what we have called earlier in this book (§ 4) the first and the second stage of investigation: formulating and testing the theory, and carrying out measurements. We have now reached the third stage, in which mathematical-economic conclusions are drawn. These conclusions refer either to the explanation of a given historic course from the data, or to the probable consequences of certain measures of economic policy. For both sorts of conclusions it is necessary to know the functioning of economic systems. Such a system may be a single market or a whole economy, possibly also a group of connected markets. The functioning is reflected in a number of equations, with the phenomena to be explained as unknowns. With one market, there are two phenomena: price and quantity sold; with a larger system there may be many more.

We shall first consider the functioning of a few types of separate markets. We choose the examples and their sequence for reasons of exposition. They facilitate somewhat the understanding of more intricate systems.

The fluctuations in a market may be caused exclusively by *exogenous* factors. Most seasonal fluctuations are examples. Butter production, for instance, fluctuates because the cows give less milk in winter. The lower milk supply and, consequently, the lower supply of butter and other products, raises the price in winter, unless a seasonal leveling has been attained by cold storage.

Another example of a market showing fluctuations which are exclusively caused exogenously is the *anchovy* market. The catch of this fish varies very greatly and one year may be a hundred times as great as in another year. The main cause is the fluctuation in temperature in the area where the young fish has to grow in the spring. The fluctuations of the catch cause fluctuations of stocks, which in their turn largely explain the enormous fluctuations both in prices and in sales. A great part of the catch, consequently, is kept for several years because old anchovy is valued higher than new.

The markets where *endogenous* causes of fluctuation are active in addition to exogenous ones are of more importance for economic science.

A very simple case is the so-called *echo principle,* which usually appears in markets of durable goods. The quantities sold at such markets are partly intended to replace old items. The quantity required for this purpose is partly determined by the quantity which has reached the maximum age, and this largely depends on quantities sold earlier. If the lifetime of the good amounts to 10 years, the production of 10 years ago determines today's demand. Other factors will usually also determine the demand for replacement. If we could abstract from these for a moment and if we could assume that the lifetime is a sharply defined number of years, it would be possible to explain a fluctuating movement, the period of which would be equal to the lifetime of the goods considered, by the repetition of earlier sales ("echo"). This mechanism shows quite a number of interesting aspects, which we cannot go further into here. We therefore refer to the literature.* An illustration of what has been discussed can be found in the study mentioned concerning the demand for automobiles (§ 28), and in Fig. 15. This figure refers to the replacement demand for ships and is taken from an article by J. Meuldijk, Jr.† The course of this replacement demand can very well be explained by a combination of earlier production and freight prices, the latter repre-

* Einarsen: "Reinvestment Cycles," Oslo 1938.

† Der englische Schiffbau während der Periode 1870-1912 und das Problem des Ersatzbaues, Weltwirtschaftliches Archiv 52 (1940) p. 524.

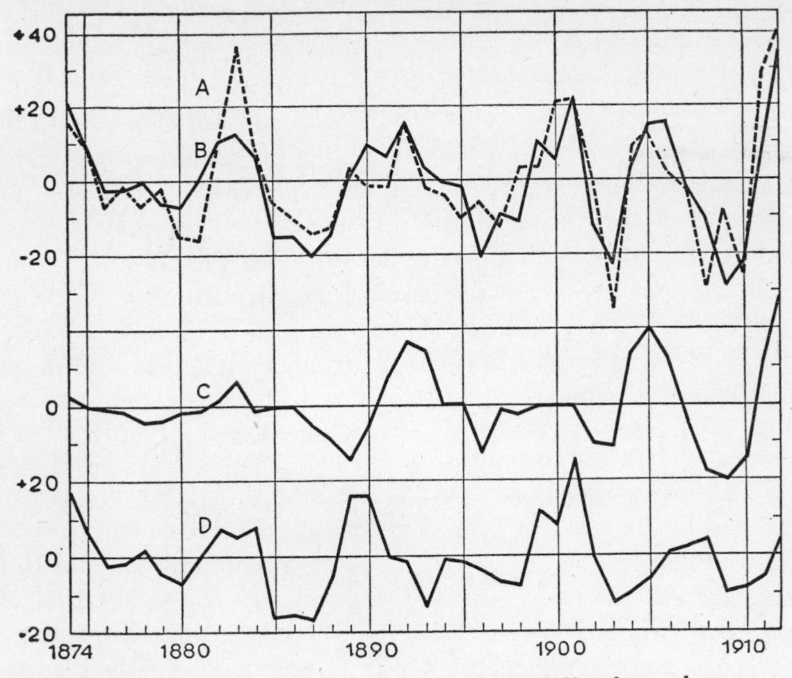

Fig. 15. Explanation of the course of shipbuilding for replacement (A) from (B), the total of the influences of: (C), the production of approximately 20 years ago, and (D) the level of freight rates, one year ago. (Taken from J. Meuldijk, Jr.: Der englische Schiffbau während der Periode 1870-1912 und das Problem des Ersatzbaues, Weltwirtschaftliches Archiv 52 (1940) p. 524.)

senting the shipping cycle at the moment itself. The fact that this factor has to be included with a lag of one year has to be ascribed to the length of the shipbuilding process.

A somewhat more complicated fluctuation mechanism is obtained, if the so-called *cobweb theorem** can be applied, which is approximately the case in the *hog market*. This mechanism presents itself in its purest shape if demand and supply depend only on the price, the former without, the latter with, a lag. If at a certain moment the price has reached a peak, this will

* The name of this theorem is due to the shape of a graph which is often used in this connection.

result in the supply also showing a peak after a one-unit lag. This, however, reduces the price at that moment to a minimum, because otherwise the demand cannot absorb the quantity supplied. This minimum price after a one-unit lag causes a minimum supply, through which at that moment the price again takes a maximum position. This situation can be compared to that of the starting point; one period has been completed. This period, however, is *double* the lag unit (see Fig. 16).

It has already been remarked that this situation appears roughly in the hog market. There are also a number of other less evident examples, where disturbances (exogenous forces) influence the picture somewhat. The well-known tendency to a two-year agrarian cycle is one of these examples.

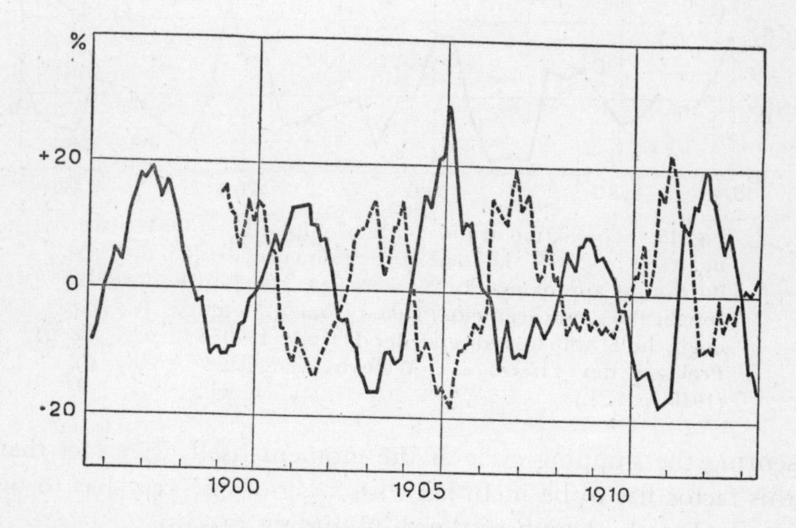

Fig. 16. Example of the operation of the "cobweb theorem": the hog market, according to Hanau.
——— Pork price, percentage deviation from trend.
– – – – Supply of slaughter-pigs, deviation from trend.

A high sugar price leads to a large cultivated area in the next year; if the yield per acre is normal, the production therefore will be high. The price, however, will be low. This low price results in a small area being cultivated and, if the crop yield is normal, a low level of production. Through this, the price rises again, and a two-year cycle has been completed. This phenomenon is often found with many agricultural products. But if the yield per acre diverges strongly from the average, irregularities appear in the movement. The latter, therefore, only maintains itself for a short time.

A type of endogenous movement which again is somewhat more complicated appears in the market of services of some durable goods, such as houses or ships. The movements usually are mixed with other elements. In its pure form the mechanism works as follows. Suppose at a certain moment there is a high price for the service in question, for instance, a high house rent. This high rent, now, stimulates, after the building period, not the total supply of houses, but the supply of *new* dwellings. This, however, does not immediately cause a low rent; the rent also depends on the total quantity of houses available, i.e., in principle, of the cumulation in time of newly built houses. As, however, the stock of houses was relatively low at the starting point—otherwise the rent would not have been relatively high—it takes a considerable time before the increased building activity leads to a relatively high stock of dwellings. Only in that case is the minimum rent to be expected and half the period has been accomplished. The movement described here, therefore, has a longer period than twice the lag unit which plays a role; normally it is even about *four times* as long.

We have already pointed out that apart from the causal relations mentioned, other disturbing factors are active here. The system, consequently, does not work itself out accurately. Such disturbing circumstances may be, for instance, that not only the level of rents, but also building costs and the interest rate influence the building activity; rent, further, is determined not only by the stock of houses, but also by the income, the growth of the number of families, etc. Only if the shortages at a certain moment are very great and if the other factors move rather narrowly in comparison to them, may this mechanism make itself felt. This seems to have been the case particularly in the United States, and the widely fluctuating waves in house building since 1830 should partly be ascribed to this mechanism.*

The considerations given above have been treated without any formula, for the benefit of the nonmathematical readers. It could be asked, therefore, whether they are examples of econometric research. They are, because their exact treatment is only possible with the help of formulas, and because the conclusions have only been found by exact treatment. These conclusions actually go considerably further into detail than has been possible within the scope of this chapter, precisely as a consequence of its nonmathematical treatment. For this, however, we again refer to the literature cited.

§ 41. The General Business-Cycle Movement

The tendencies to cyclic movements appearing in separate markets have relatively little to do with the general business-cycle movement in economic life which has been observed for years. The examples cited are more or less special cases, the importance of which is methodologic rather than real. We see from them in how many different ways cyclic movements not only may, but also actually do, come into being.

Econometrics, however, has also contributed to our knowledge concerning the causation of the general business-cycle phenomenon. By its exact way of describing a causal structure and by the possibility of measuring the different influences at least approximately, it has provided more insight in the business-cycle mechanism than verbal treatment alone can do. It has achieved this by creating a number of models of the business-cycle mechanism, which by statistical measurements have been adapted to reality as closely as possible.

The first few of these models—e.g., Frisch's†—have been set up mathematically and are consequently sharply outlined, but they are still rather distant from reality, as they are only based on measurement of a few magnitudes. Kalečki's model,‡ like-

* J. B. D. Derksen: Long cycles in residential building: an explanation, Econometrica 8 (1940) p. 97.

† In the volume: "Essays in Honour of Gustav Cassel," London 1933.

‡ "Essays in the Theory of Economic Fluctuations," London 1939.

wise, although adapted to reality to a greater extent, is still relatively simple in its assumptions, nor is it based on elementary equations which have all been tested statistically. Nevertheless, it is very instructive.

Radice's model* is entirely based on elementary equations which have been tested against reality. The same applies to Colin Clark's calculations,† who in 1937 predicted the turning point in the English business cycle, on the basis of the relations by which he described the business-cycle mechanism of that country.

In this connection we may go somewhat further into the results of two attempts by the present author to set up models for the United States‡ in the period 1919 to 1932 and for England in the period 1870 to 1914.§ In these models, in order to make them as realistic as possible, 30 to 40 variables have been included: two or three income categories, separate production (and for England import and export) indices for consumption goods and means of production, separate price indices for these two sorts of goods and their raw materials, and a number of variables from the financial sphere, etc. An equal number of elementary equations (§ 11) was set up and tested statistically. By this testing, of course, their correctness has not been proved (see § 26), but it was at least established that they were not in conflict with the data. The most interesting equations among these 30 or 40 are the demand and supply relations for the various markets included in the model. A final equation was obtained for one of the variables in the way described in § 12, from which equation the movements of the model can be derived. Nonlabor income, Z, was taken as the variable appearing in this final equation. This variable is approximately equal to the profits figure. With the help of a number of appropriate approximations a final equation in three terms was

* A dynamic scheme for the British trade cycle, 1929-1937, Econometrica **7** (1939), p. 47.

† National income at its climax, Economic Journal 47 (1937) p. 308.

‡ See Note * on page 130.

§ In a forthcoming study.

obtained, for instance, for England (where the time unit is eight months):

$$Z_t = 1.27\, Z_{t-1} - 0.60\, Z_{t-2} \tag{41.1}$$

Z here indicates the deviation from trend. The equation, consequently, only describes the movements around the trend, which is considered as given.

The reader will remember that the systematic movements are indicated in this way; as soon as a new change of data appears, a "disturbance term" should be added. We shall first consider only the systematic movements.

The coefficients 1.27 and 0.60, which, as will become clear later, determine the movements of the system, have been obtained from a great number of coefficients from elementary equations, having the significance of elasticities, marginal propensities to consume, labor quota, etc. If we consider the origin of the final equation (41.1), we might wonder how it will ever be possible to describe such a process in words alone, and without the help of symbols. We shall nevertheless try this in the following, but it can only be done approximately and very roughly. We fear, however, that no literary theory will ever be able to overcome this defect.

The way in which the numbers 1.27 and 0.60 have been obtained also entails that they are rather uncertain. This problem has been fully discussed in the publication mentioned in note * on page 138.

The character of the final equation determines the systematic movements which the system can perform, as we have already explained by a simple example in § 12. We shall clarify this further with our new case of (41.1). If only the first term would be present on the right-hand side of (41.1), the movement would show an ever-growing deviation from the trend. A cumulative process without end would appear; every deviation would be 1.27 times as great as the preceding one, either negatively or positively. A turning point would not appear, except by exogenous disturbances. It is not impossible, now, that the business-cycle movement should be regarded as caused by exogenous disturbances alone. As has become apparent from Slutzky's* studies, a system like the one under discussion may show movements of a quasi-periodic character, as a consequence of random shocks. The most important economic interpretation conceivable is that these shocks are the changing crop yields and a few very important political events (e.g., wars). The majority of business cycle theorists, however, will be of the opinion that also more systematic causes of turning points should be assumed.

If the coefficient of the term with Z_{t-1} were negative and if the one with Z_{t-2} still were absent, fluctuations would also have appeared, but only very short ones. After two time units (16 months) the picture would repeat itself: positive and negative values of Z would constantly alternate.

Only because there are two terms, is it possible that fluctuations of longer duration appear. This can only happen, however, if the values of the coefficients satisfy certain requirements. If, for instance, both coefficients are positive, no fluctuations can appear. Even if the second coefficient is smaller than the square of half the first one (in this case, smaller than 0.635^2 or approximately 0.4), no fluctuations can appear. The following example deals with the two cases:

Numerical values of Z with different t and for $Z_1 = 0$, Z_2 — 10: (A), if formula (41.1) applies, and (B), if in that formula the coefficient 0.60 is replaced by 0.30:

t	= 1	2	3	4	5	6	7	8	9
(A) Z	= 0	10	12.7	10.1	5.2	0.5	−2.5	−3.5	−2.9
(B) Z	= 0	10	12.7	13.1	12.8	12.4	12.0	11.5	11.0

This example makes it clear that a theory in words alone cannot be sufficient. It is conceivable that two theories are qualitatively the same—i.e., assume the same causes for the movements in all variables—but are only different as regards the size of the influencing coefficients. Then it is entirely possible

* The summation of random causes as the source of cyclic processes, Econometrica 5 (1937) p. 105.

that the one theory results in a movement like (A), and another theory in one like (B). In the case of (A), the theory also explains the lower turning point, with (B) it does not.

The question, now, is of great importance, which of the economic relations have mainly contributed to the presence and size of the coefficients + 1.27 and − 0.60. Only the most important outline of the complicated origin of these figures can be given here. In the coefficient 1.27, among other things, the "propensity to consume" and the investment incentive manifest themselves. If at a certain moment, profits are high, this will lead to higher expenditures for consumption and investment some time later. The lag is a consequence of the time elapsing between the reaping of the profit and its paying out, and between the receipt of the income and its spending; a consequence, also, of the duration of investment processes. The high expenditures for consumption and investment, however, will after a short time again give rise to higher profits. This manifests itself in the coefficient 1.27. It lies above 1, among other things, because prices will also have risen, as a consequence of the higher demand for goods. This price rise, moreover, often influences the profit calculation—perhaps unjustly. A sort of acceleration principle is at work here: the profit depends on the price rise and as the price level itself is also determined by earlier profits (and the demand resulting from it), the profit indirectly depends on the rise in profits at some time earlier.

This is important enough to set forth in a formula:

$$Z_t = a\,(Z_{t-1} - Z_{t-2}) + b \qquad (41.2)$$

Within brackets we have the increase of profits at some time before (namely, between $t-2$ and $t-1$); this increase exerts its influence—in addition to another factor, b—on Z_t by means of the coefficient a. Part of the coefficient 1.27 is formed by the a standing before Z_{t-1}. At the same time we see that part of the negative coefficient − 0.60 is formed by the term $-aZ_{t-2}$, which also appears in (41.2). We have just called the type of relation laid down in (41.2) a sort of acceleration principle, because, just as with Clark's principle, the level of Z_t is determined by the speed by which a certain magnitude increases. As the presence of a negative term with Z_{t-2} is of decisive importance for the appearance of a turning point, the appearance of such acceleration principles is also very important for the explanation of turning points. Although, as our investigations indicate (§ 37), it seems that no great importance should be assigned to Clark's acceleration principle for the explanation of the course of the business cycle, there are a few other relations which give rise to the mathematical form of (41.2). In addition to the aforementioned influence of price increases on the profit calculation, there is an influence—important in the United States in 1929—of share-price rises on consumption, and a tendency to keep stocks proportionate to the size of production. Production for the increase of stocks, consequently, shows a tendency to have a course parallel to the increase of production.

The negative term $-0.60\ Z_{t-2}$ should also be partly ascribed to the restrictive influence of the interest rate and of the prices of securities (see § 37). The interest rate and the prices themselves depend indirectly on Z, with a small lag; through their influence on investments and consequently indirectly on profits, the profits made some time ago work negatively on the profits of this moment. These influences, which are mentioned in several theories, however, would, according to our results, be quantitatively too weak to result in a term -0.60. They would not even reach -0.40 and therefore could not explain the two turning points of the business cycle. Together with the acceleration influences mentioned, however, they can.

If such relations appear in the mechanism, it is not necessary (contrary to general opinion) to explain the turning point by changes in the elasticity of certain markets. The changes usually thought of are rigidities in the neighborhood of full employment of productive capacity: the so-called *bottle-necks*. In mathematical language these mean a *nonlinear relation* and we have seen from the above that they are not necessary to explain turning points. They may appear in certain situations and have been noticed, for instance, in many crises before 1914. On the other hand, they need not start a declining movement. It is also conceivable that production, after having reached full capacity, stays there. Whether a reaction follows depends on the other relations in the model.

We have now given a few examples of the sort of conclusions which may be drawn from macroeconomic models regarding the generation of general business cycle waves. Besides—and this is a great difference from the old "barometers" (see § 2) based on a rough empiricism—the structure of these models can be changed in order to study in which way the movements they may show will also change. In other words, with these models it is possible to study the consequences of certain measures of economic policy.

Similarly by way of an example, we mention here the conclusions in the field of business-cycle policy (see § 13) drawn from the American model. In the first place, it has become evident that the fluctuations would be much narrower if it would be possible to curb speculation in shares. Further, a stabilization of total consumption expenditures would have particularly favorable consequences for the business-cycle movement: the movement would be considerably more damped. Stabilization of investment expenditures would help much less, on account of the fact that the absolute fluctuations in investment expenditures are smaller than those in consumption expenditures.

We only give these conclusions to arouse the reader's curiosity. It is out of the question that the whole problem of business-cycle policy could be treated satisfactorily within the scope of this book.

Model construction has been practiced intensively during the last five years in the United States; among other things, in aid of business-cycle forecasting in relation to employment policy. In particular, we mention the work of L. R. Klein, which has brought a considerable extension, especially of the income formation relation and of the relation concerning investment activity.*

* The use of econometric models as a guide to economic policy, Econometrica 15 (1947) p. 111.

Further, we refer to the investigation by M. A. Girshick and T. Haavelmo cited above (see § 27), in which a very simple dynamic model is presented which has been tested statistically with the help of the method of simultaneous equations. In this model the attention has been focused on the market for agricultural products in its relation to the economy as a whole.

§ 42. Comparative-Static Systems

In addition to models intended to analyze short-term movements (business-cycle models), comparative-static models have also been developed since the Second World War, with the purpose of estimating either the influence of certain forms of economic policy or the long-term development. Two most outstanding attempts may briefly be mentioned here; an elaborate treatment is outside the scope of this book.

In Appendix C of Sir William Beveridge's book: "Full Employment in a Free Society," N. Kaldor* has constructed a model of the English economy, with a view to estimating the influence of a few alternative methods of employment policy (additional government expenditures, financed either by loans or by direct or indirect taxes). The system, consisting of 37 equations, is relatively simple in its setup; the various income categories depend linearly on total national income and their savings, likewise, linearly on income after payment of taxes. Prices are not introduced as variables.

Colin Clark, in his "Economies of 1960,"† has made an attempt to describe the world economy in that year on the basis of an econometric model in which more than 30 countries are distinguished. The production and the population have been subdivided into primary (agriculture, fisheries, etc.), secondary (manufacturing industry and mining), and tertiary (all other) branches of industry. The system is based, among other things, on the following relations:

---

* An econometric analysis of the model is given by R. Stone and E. F. Jackson in: Economic models with special reference to Mr. Kaldor's system, The Economic Journal 56 (1946) p. 554.

† London 1942; subsequently reprinted.

1. the population is distributed over the branches of industry in such a way that the wages (equal to the marginal productivity of labor) have a fixed mutual relation;

2. the productivity in agriculture depends on the density of the agrarian population; moreover, it has a trend;

3. the productivity in the secondary and tertiary branches of industry only shows a trend;

4. the demand for agricultural products depends on the height of national income and on the price level of agricultural products.

The coefficients of these relations are determined from international statistical material. In a number of cases, certain limits of validity are assumed, outside of which other relations are valid; it is assumed, for instance, that at most 35 per cent of the agrarian population will disappear between 1935/38 and 1960.

On the basis of these relations Clark comes to an evaluation of the agrarian price level in comparison to that of products of manufacturing industry, and to an estimation of world trade in agricultural products, subdivided according to countries.

§ 43. Concluding Remarks

In this book we have tried to make the reader acquainted with the way of thinking, the methods, and the results of econometric research. We have made it our task to do this without calling into use what is sometimes called higher mathematics. It goes without saying, therefore, that only the contours of econometrics could be indicated. We have only gone very briefly into the most important investigations: insofar as possible only the principle has been discussed in every instance, together with the most important results.

Econometrics as a scientific method is so young that very much remains to be done. Moreover, we are always dependent on the statistical data which will become available.

In the field of long-term reactions, i.e., in the field of the explanation of the trend movement and of structural economic policy, very little has as yet been undertaken.* Also here, we have a vast unexplored territory for scientific work. That work is not only theoretically important. It may render good service in the search after a better economic policy or even other forms of society. It should, above all, not be inferred that this type of research only has sense in a "free" society; and that it is not necessary in a more or less "planned" economy. Also in a "planned" economy many reactions remain which are entirely or partly free, and the particulars of which should be known for an adequate influencing of the course of events. Measurement will always remain a useful activity if applied with intelligence and without bias. The comparison with what happens in a "free" economy may also be useful. Econometric methods may render many services in this field.

* Some important considerations can be found in Kalecki: "Essays in the Theory of Economic Fluctuations," London 1939.

Part IV

ECONOMIC POLICY

8

The Use of Econometric Research for the Purpose of Economic Policy (An Example)

§ 44. Object and Summary of This Chapter

The object of this chapter is:

1. to estimate, for the Netherlands, the influence of wage, tax, and price policy (including devaluation) and an increase in productivity on the balance of payments and employment;
2. to give some examples of "inefficient regulators" in economic policy; and
3. to illustrate a number of questions of methodology in economic analysis, viz.:
   a. the question when the results of economic analysis can be proved verbally;
   b. what simplifications in the analysis are possible by the introduction of new ("composed" or "derived") variables;
   c. to indicate the role of "directives" and "instruments" of economic policy in the analysis, and
   d. to illustrate the role of "boundary conditions" in modern economic analysis.

Using a new expression of Frisch's, these points will be dealt with by the introduction of a "decision model"* of a very simple nature; indeed on purpose as simple as seems possible without violating the nature of the subject (§ 45).

The coefficients used in the model are as much as possible based on statistical regression analysis for the interwar period. For this model, in order to close the balance of payments gap,

* Ragnar Frisch: "A Memorandum on Price-Wage-Tax-Subsidy Policies as Instruments in Maintaining Optimal Employment"; The University Institute of Economics, Oslo; publ. as an UN Document, April 1949.

the wage policy appears to be inefficient in that wage reductions of an acceptable size won't do the job (§ 48). The reason is that real incomes of nonworkers will rise and hence imports for their expenditures, which renders the total influence of wage reductions on the balance of payments only weak. The same appears to be true for reductions in nonlabor margins, since these raise real wages (§ 49). A combined policy, most easily obtained by a devaluation of the currency, gives somewhat better results, but still appears to be inefficient in one respect, viz. in that it increases incomes as a consequence of increased exports and hence still tends to charge imports "unduly" (§ 50). It is better, therefore, simultaneously to keep home consumption down by indirect taxation or government budget economies; by combining all these measures it appears to be possible to reach the goal by relatively small changes, viz. a 15 per cent devaluation (vis-à-vis the outside world as a whole) and an increase in indirect taxation by some 3 per cent of total national expenditure (§ 51). Some alternative tax measures are indicated (§ 52).

The same model enables us to study the effect of wage increases and changes in labor productivity on employment (§ 53). It appears necessary and possible to distinguish sharply between problems with different "side conditions," e.g. wage increases without or with automatic demands for a rise in real farm incomes or automatic financial measures to maintain balance of payments equilibrium.

It further appears that not all these results can be "proved verbally" in the usual sense of this phrase. As soon as simultaneous equations are involved this is essentially impossible (§ 54).

Finally it appears to be efficient to use, instead of the variables "wage rate" and "employment," two others, viz. "wage cost per unit of product" and "volume of production" (§ 46).

§ 45. Description of the Model and Its Alternatives

The model to be presented is a model in which all coefficients have been measured; in order to demonstrate the margins of uncertainty in the results, one central case and five alternative cases, showing different numerical values of the coefficients, have been considered. From the theoretical point of view the models represent a logical combination of two lines of thought in present-day literature with a refinement for the labor market. The two lines of thought may be indicated as the income approach, for which the Keynes-Machlup-Meade models are typical and the price approach, as given by Bickerdike,* Brown,† Joan Robinson,‡ Polak,§ Metzler,|| Faxén and Savosnick,¶ Neisser,** and others. Some of the latter authors have combined the two approaches, others have not, i.e. have assumed full employment throughout.

In our model, two products are distinguished, viz. a *national product,* sold abroad (exports) as well as at home (total expenditures) and an *import product,* used as raw material in the national product. The population is divided into *wage earners* and *entrepreneurs.* The former spend the whole of any additional income, and the latter only a certain part of it (mainly because of taxes which are supposed not automatically to be spent wholly at an increase in receipts). It appears to be possible, and attractive, to boil down the system of relations describing the model to three equations only (after elimination of a number of definition equations), which might conveniently be called

1. the demand equation for the national product by the home market;
2. the demand equation for that product by the world market; and
3. the supply or price-fixation equation for that product.

---

* C. F. Bickerdike, The instability of foreign exchange, The Economic Journal, 30 (1920), p. 118.

† A. J. Brown, Trade balances and exchange stability, Oxford Economic Papers, 6 (1942), p. 57.

‡ Joan Robinson, "Essays in The Theory of Employment," Oxford, 1947, p. 142.

§ J. J. Polak, Various unpublished reports of the International Monetary Fund.

|| L. A. Metzler, The theory of international trade, in: "A Survey of Contemporary Economics," Philadelphia, 1948, p. 210.

¶ K. O. Faxén and K. Savosnick, Växelkurs och handelsbalans, Ekon. Tidskr., 1949, p. 168.

** H. Neisser, Unpublished report of the Institute of World Affairs.

Since the purpose of the model is to discuss questions of economic policy, a number of phenomena will be considered as constants which could not be so in a model meant to explain economic history, such as world market prices, world market demand at constant supply prices, crops, etc.

Equation (1) is obtained from the demand equation proper (1, 1) and the definition of income (1, 2) by eliminating, as is usual in Keynesian analysis, total expenditure: the result is a kind of "multiplier equation."

The demand equation proper expresses that the increase in real expenditure $\bar{\bar{x}} - \bar{x}$, where $\bar{x}$ represents the mid-1949 figure of x, depends on the increases in real incomes of nonworkers $\bar{\bar{Z}}' - \bar{Z}'$, and of workers $\bar{\bar{L}}' - \bar{L}'$ in the following way:

$$\bar{\bar{x}} - \bar{x} = (1 - \sigma)(\bar{\bar{Z}}' - \bar{Z}') + (\bar{\bar{L}}' - \bar{L}') \qquad (1, 1)$$

This means that the marginal propensity to spend is $1 - \sigma$ for nonworkers and 1 for workers.

It will be clear that

$$\bar{\bar{Z}}' = \frac{\bar{\bar{Z}}}{\bar{\bar{p}}} \quad \text{and} \quad \bar{\bar{L}}' = \frac{\bar{\bar{L}}}{\bar{\bar{p}}}$$

where $\bar{\bar{Z}}$ is the nominal nonworkers' income
$\bar{\bar{L}}$ is the nominal wage bill, and
$\bar{\bar{p}}$ the price level.
Further, if Y is national income,
$\bar{\bar{Z}} = \bar{\bar{Y}} - \bar{\bar{L}}$

Indicating by $\bar{\bar{X}}$ the total expenditure and by $\bar{\bar{D}}$ the deficit on the balance of payments, we have in addition:

$$\bar{\bar{X}} = \bar{\bar{x}}\bar{\bar{p}}, \text{ and}$$
$$\bar{\bar{Y}} = \bar{\bar{X}} - \bar{\bar{D}} \qquad (1, 2)$$

which is the definition of the national income.

It follows from (1, 1) and the subsequent identities that

$$\bar{\bar{X}} = \bar{\bar{x}}\bar{\bar{p}} = (1 - \sigma)\bar{\bar{Z}} + \bar{\bar{L}} + \{\bar{x} - (1 - \sigma)\bar{Z}' - \bar{L}'\}\bar{\bar{p}} \qquad (1, 1')$$

The elimination of $\overline{\overline{X}}$ between (1, 1′) and (1, 2) and the substitution of $\overline{\overline{Z}}$ by $\overline{\overline{Y}} - \overline{\overline{L}}$ yield:

$$\overline{\overline{Y}} = (1 - \sigma)(\overline{\overline{Y}} - \overline{\overline{L}}) + \overline{\overline{L}} + c\overline{\overline{p}} - \overline{\overline{D}} \tag{1, 3}$$

where $c = \overline{x} - (1 - \sigma)\,\overline{Z}' - \overline{L}'$; (1, 3) may be written in the form

$$\overline{\overline{Y}} = \overline{\overline{L}} - \frac{\overline{\overline{D}}}{\sigma} + \frac{c\overline{\overline{p}}}{\sigma} \tag{1′}$$

which reminds us of the multiplier equation; it is somewhat more complicated because of the different behavior of workers and nonworkers.

It will appear useful to rewrite this equation after we have discussed equations (2) and (3); hence we indicate it provisionally as (1′).

Equation (2) is meant to express the balance of payments deficit *D* as a function of the relevant variables. In our "decision model" only such phenomena have to appear as variables which may vary during any change in economic policy of the Netherlands, i.e. only Dutch phenomena. According to present-day views there are two main variables influencing the balance of payments, viz. the production level *y* of the country and its price level *p*. Imports *m* will depend on both; in a linear approximation* we have then:

$$m = \mu y + \overline{m}\epsilon^{m} p \tag{2, 1}$$

where *m, y,* and *p* are measured as deviations from initial values; for *y* and *p* these initial values are taken equal to 1. Under these circumstances, μ is the marginal import quota and ϵ^{m} the elasticity of imports with respect to the Dutch price level (foreign prices being constant). Value of imports is indicated by the same figures as volume, since foreign prices are equal to 1 throughout.

* The restrictions implied in the use of linear approximations will be discussed in §§ 48, 49 and 50.

The volume of exports *e* will only depend on *p*:

$$e = -\bar{e}\epsilon^{e}p$$

if also *e* is measured as a deviation from initial value, and ϵ^{e} represents (the absolute value of) the elasticity of exports with respect to the Dutch price level. The money value of exports *E* (deviation from initial value) will be:

$$E = -\bar{e}(\epsilon^{e} - 1)\,p \qquad (2, 2)$$

From equations (2, 1) and (2, 2) we deduce

$$D = \mu y + \{\overline{m}\epsilon^{m} + \bar{e}(\epsilon^{e} - 1)\}\,p$$

or

$$D = \mu y + \delta p \qquad (2)$$

Equation (3) will be written as a "price-fixation equation"; the price level will depend on labor costs per unit of product l' (deviations from initial value which will be taken equal to 1), volume of production *y*, and possible autonomous changes π_0 of the profit margin as may be the consequences of either a government price policy or, e.g., the liberalization of international trade. Writing *p* for the price level (deviation) we have*

* This formula may be deduced in the following way. To begin with, assuming free competition, we have: price = marginal cost. The changes in marginal cost will depend on at least three factors, viz.:

1. the development in labor cost per unit of product in a fixed enterprise, viz. the marginal enterprise in 1949;
2. differences in costs due to the expansion or contraction of production, causing a shift of the marginal unit of production;
3. a number of autonomous factors such as indirect taxes, price regulations, or changes in the remuneration of nonworkers.

We shall assume that the development meant under 1 may be represented by the movements of our variable $\bar{l}'$, i.e. we assume a parallelism between average labor cost of unit of product and such costs in a fixed enterprise. The difference meant under 2 will be a function of the general level of production $\bar{\bar{y}}$; the autonomous factors will provisionally be indicated by $\bar{\bar{f}}$. Hence, marginal cost may be written as $\phi(\bar{l}', \bar{\bar{y}}, \bar{\bar{f}})$ and $\bar{\bar{p}} = \phi(\bar{l}', \bar{\bar{y}}, \bar{\bar{f}})$. This function we develop into a series, taking only the members of zero and first degree in the deviations l', y, etc.:

$$\bar{p} + p = \phi(\bar{l}', \bar{y}, \bar{f}) + l'\,\frac{\overline{\overline{\delta\phi}}}{\delta l'} + y\,\frac{\overline{\overline{\delta\phi}}}{\delta y} + f\,\frac{\overline{\overline{\delta\phi}}}{\delta f}$$

Leaving out the 1949 values which cancel, we have

$$p = l'\,\frac{\overline{\overline{\delta\phi}}}{\delta l'} + y\,\frac{\overline{\overline{\delta\phi}}}{\delta y} + f\,\frac{\overline{\overline{\delta\phi}}}{\delta f}$$

The differential coefficients are constants and the first two may be written as π_1 and π_2; the third term as a whole as π_0.

$$p = \pi_1 l' + \pi_2 y + \pi_0 \tag{3}$$

where π_1 represents the marginal wage quota, and
π_2 the "flexibility of prices," being the inverted supply elasticity.

At this moment we may return to equation (1') and rewrite it in a more convenient form. It will be possible to express both *Y* and *L* in terms of *y, p,* and *l'*. Using the symbols, as was done in (1'), in their meaning of absolute values, we have:

$$\overline{\overline{Y}} = (1 + \mu')\, \overline{\overline{y}}\,\overline{\overline{p}} - \overline{\overline{m}}$$

where μ' is the average import quota; in fact, $(1 + \mu')\, \overline{\overline{y}}\overline{\overline{p}}$ represents the gross value of the national product, from which imports have to be deducted in order to obtain the net value. Since for the Netherlands the marginal import quota happens to be equal to the average import quota, we have substituted μ for μ' in what follows.

We have also: $\overline{\overline{L}} = \Lambda \overline{\overline{l'}} y$, where Λ represents the initial value $\overline{L}$ of L; since $\overline{Y} = 1$, Λ represents the wage quota in the national product.

We shall now replace all the variables by their deviations from initial values and simplify the resulting equations by omitting initial values at both sides of each one (since they are equal) and products of deviations (since they are supposed to be small). This leads to:

$$Y = (1 + \mu)\, p + y - \mu\epsilon^m p$$

$$L = \Lambda\, (l' + y)$$

Equation (1') may, also using deviations, then be written:

$$\sigma(1 - \Lambda)\, y + D + \{1 - \bar{x} + \sigma\, (\mu + \Lambda - \mu\epsilon^m)\}\, p = \sigma\Lambda l'$$

or

$$\xi_1 y + D + \xi_2 p = \xi_3 l'$$

In this equation we shall add a political parameter ξ_0 representing an autonomous increase in national expenditure, e.g. by an increase in investment outlay or government expenditures, or by certain measures of taxation or subsidizing.* This gives to this equation the form:

$$\xi_1 y + D + \xi_2 p = \xi_3 l' + \xi_0 \qquad (1)$$

The other two equations may now be added using the same order of the variables:

$$-\mu y + D - \delta p = 0 \qquad (2)$$

$$-\pi_2 y \qquad + \ p = \pi_1 l' + \pi_0 \qquad (3)$$

All of the seven coefficients have more or less exactly been measured statistically; those appearing in equations (2) and (3) may be taken from multiple-correlation studies for the period 1923 to 1938, not only macroeconomic, but also to some extent microeconomic in character.† The coefficients of equation (1) depend, apart from μ and ϵ^m, on the structural parameters Λ and $\bar{x}$ and the coefficient σ. For the situation in 1949, Λ and $\bar{x}$ are fairly exactly known and equal to 0.55 (portion of national income going to workers) and 1.04 (national expenditures expressed in national income).‡ The coefficient σ is by far the least certain; under present conditions it seems, however, to be definitely positive. This is primarily due to the high marginal rate of taxation and the probability that an increase in tax receipts will only slightly influence the level of public expenditure. It is partly due also to the circumstance that total expenditure of the nation already surpassed its income for years as a consequence of the war and the resulting desire to do away with dissaving.

In view of the uncertainty margin in some of the coefficients and in particular σ, a number of alternative models have been

* A more detailed treatment will be given in § 52.

† For *exports* see J. B. D. Derksen and A. L. G. M. Rombouts, The influence of prices on exports, De Ned. Conjunctuur, Special Memorandum Nr. 1, The Hague 1939. For *imports* see J. Tinbergen, The fluctuations of the Netherlands imports, 1923-1938, Stat. en Econometr. Onderzoekingen 3 (1948), p. 52 (Dutch with an English summary). For *prices* see J. Tinbergen en A. L. G. M. Rombouts, De samenhang tussen de prijzen van ingevoerde grondstoffen en die van afgewerkte producten in Nederland, De Ned. Conjunctuur 10 (1939), p. 150 (Dutch).

‡ See Centraal Economisch Plan 1949, The Hague (Dutch), p. 20.

used, which are characterized by the following values of the coefficients (where the alternative values have been printed in italics):

	Model Nr.	*1*	*2*	*3*	*4*	*5*	*6*
$1-\sigma$	marginal prop. to spend	0.7	*1.0*	*0.5*	0.7	0.7	*0.9*
ϵ^m	price elasticity of imports	0.3	0.3	0.3	*0.5*	0.3	0.3
ϵ^e	price elasticity of exports	2.0	2.0	2.0	*3.0*	2.0	2.0
π_1	marginal wage quota	0.3	0.3	0.3	0.3	*0.5*	0.3

The variation in the last coefficient may be interpreted not so much as a variation in the marginal wage quota proper but more as the tendency for certain trade margins to move in sympathy with direct (mostly labor) costs.

Model Nr. 1 is considered to be the most likely representation of the year-to-year reactions of the Dutch economy.

From the above-listed values of the fundamental coefficients the following values for the dependent coefficients in the equations may be found:

Model Nr.	*1*	*2*	*3*	*4*	*5*	*6*
$\xi_1 = 0.45\,\sigma$	0.135	0	0.225	0.135	0.135	0.045
$\xi_2 = -0.04 + \sigma(0.99 - 0.44\epsilon^m)$	0.217	-0.04	0.389	0.191	0.217	0.046
$\xi_3 = 0.55\,\sigma$	0.165	0	0.275	0.165	0.165	0.055
$\delta = m\epsilon^m + \bar{e}(\epsilon^e - 1)$	0.53	0.53	0.53	1.02	0.53	0.53

The coefficients μ and π_2 have been taken equal to 0.44 and 0.125 throughout; the first since it seems to be pretty exact and the second since its influence on the results appeared to be only small, within the probable limits of variation.

For the reader's convenience the initial (1949) values of the various variables may be summarized here:

$$\underline{y} = \underline{p} = \overline{l'} = \overline{Y} = \overline{1}; \overline{x} = 1.04; \overline{m} = 0.44; \overline{e} = 0.40; \overline{D} = 0.04;$$
$$\overline{L} = \overline{L'} = 0.55; \overline{Z} = \overline{Z'} = 0.45.$$

§ 46. Choice of Variables; Boundary Conditions

Before discussing the use that has been made of the models, a few preliminary remarks may be made about what seems to the author to be a feature of efficiency in the choice of the variables and equations. The complaint is rather general that the older models used in econometrics are often too complicated to be understood. On purpose therefore a very simple setup has been chosen here, where only the most strategic variables are left. As the characteristic parameter for the labor market, whose inclusion was essential for the subjects to be dealt with, the *index of labor cost l' per unit of product* has definite advantages in comparison to the *wage rate l*. Essential for the whole argument is the influence of wages on prices at the one hand and labor income on the other hand. Now for prices l' is decisive indeed rather than l; whereas total labor income may either be written as the product of l' and y or as the product of l and employment a. Introduction of l into the "central system" of the three equations, therefore, would have meant the introduction of a. The choice of l' enables us to avoid this. Of course a may and will be considered later on; but it need not be included into the central simultaneous kernel of relations. This seems to be a good example of an efficient choice of a "composed" or a "derived" variable able to simplify the system. The choice of D instead of imports and exports separately, although more familiar, seems to be another example. Both are examples of what may be called the "art" of scientific analysis and are of some interest for the understanding by general economists of econometrics.

Another remark may be made before using our equations. They have only a restricted "range of validity"; as soon as some of the variables surpass certain limits or boundaries they are no longer valid. Such *boundary conditions* may be of a different nature and there may be several of them, partly overlapping, for the same variable or set of variables. A few examples will be given. One is the condition that y cannot surpass the value y^F corresponding with full employment. If in any problem a solution for y would be found greater than y^F, equation (1) no longer applies and instead we have to replace it by:

$$\mathbf{y} = \mathbf{y}^{\mathbf{F}}$$

At the same time (3) should be changed so as to express that p may rise more than indicated by (3).

Other boundary conditions are of course that neither y nor p or l' be less than -1 (or, in absolute amount, negative). Long before such a limit would be reached, however, certain psychologic or political boundaries would have been attained, the exact place of which is not known and must be left to the judgment of the reader.

The role of these boundary conditions may be very important; in fact they may sometimes far more influence the situation than our equations. They may even be such as to exclude any solution at all if their number, together with the number of valid equations, surpasses the number of unknowns.*

§ 47. Directives and Instruments; the Strategy of Economic Policy

With the traditional setting of the problem, the political parameters (in our example l', ξ_0, and π_0) are considered as given and the economic phenomena proper (in our example y, D, and p) as unknown. We then ask: what are the consequences of a given increase in wage rates l', or of a given increase in government expenditure ξ_0, etc.† and our equations enable us to answer such questions easily. Since, however, an economic policy has a certain purpose, it seems more appropriate to invert the roles of these two classes of variables. In order to clarify the matter entirely, we introduce the concepts of "*directives*" and "*instruments*" of economic policy. If the wage rate is used to obtain a closed balance of payments, we call the wage rate the instrument

---

* There is an interesting development of economic analysis toward the discussion of such situations, as is, e.g. clear from the recent work on linear programming.

† It is not essential, in this respect, that, as a simplification, we have considered wage rates as autonomous and not as consisting of an autonomous and a dependent component, viz. a component determined by the automatic reactions of workers on prices, etc. Under present social and political conditions this seems to be a feasible approximation to reality.

of this policy and the directive is that particular value of the variable D which corresponds with equilibrium (in our case $D = -0.04$). The directives are, with this new setting of the problem, the data, and the instruments are the unknowns. This is characteristic of the decision models. Also, now our equations may be used to determine the unknowns, provided that their number is not too large or too small. This latter remark reminds us of the necessity, in this case in particular, of a correct statement of our problems and the choice of a correct number of unknowns. Among these, some of the old unknowns may remain, if the number of unknown political parameters is smaller than the number of equations. It may be observed finally that further political parameters may be introduced; in fact one could say, e.g. that the Marshall help represented such a parameter in equation (2). The parameter l', in addition, may be split up into two components, the wage rate l and the index of productivity h (we shall again take $\bar{h} = 1$), in the following way:

$$l' = l - h \tag{4}$$

where under the present conditions each of these components is, to some extent, an autonomous parameter.

Each of the political parameters can be determined by a restricted number of "pressure groups": l' by trade unions (or more precisely by trade unions, employers, and government together), π_0 by employers (more precisely by employers and government), ξ_0 by government (and parliament). Economic policy, therefore, is a strategic game in the sense of Morgenstern and Von Neumann. Recent experience in this field shows a number of interesting examples of this play of chess: devaluation as a pure act of government, followed by a demand for 5 per cent wage increase by the workers. The government may be compelled to decrease subsidies as a further response, etc.

Actual economic policy will therefore differ from some well-advised welfare planning based on an attempt to indicate an "optimum solution" (see § 51).

§ 48. Isolated Wage Policy; Consequences of the Double Function of Wages

As a first example of the various problems one may alternatively formulate let us consider isolated wage policy. The well-known question how wage-rate changes influence employment may at once be answered by our system of equations. We shall assume proportionality between employment and volume of production *y;* we could have supposed a general linear relationship as well. Solving our equations for *y* we have:

$$y = \frac{\begin{vmatrix} \xi_3 l' + \xi_0 & 1 & \xi_2 \\ 0 & 1 & -\delta \\ \pi l' + \pi_0 & 0 & 1 \end{vmatrix}}{\begin{vmatrix} \xi_1 & 1 & \xi_2 \\ -\mu & 1 & -\delta \\ +\pi_2 & 0 & 1 \end{vmatrix}} = \frac{\{\xi_3 - \pi_1 (\delta + \xi_2)\} l' + \xi_0 - (\delta + \xi_2)\pi_0}{\xi_1 + \mu + \pi_2 (\delta + \xi_2)} = \eta l' + \eta' \xi_0 + \eta'' \pi_0 \qquad (5)$$

The numerical values for η, η', and η'' are:

Model Nr.	*1*	*2*	*3*	*4*	*5*	*6*
η	−0.09	−0.29	0.00	−0.27	−0.31	−0.21
η'	1.50	2.00	1.28	1.38	1.50	1.80
η''	−1.12	−0.98	−1.18	−1.67	−1.12	−1.03

It should be kept in mind that this formula is only a correct approximation for small values of the political parameters l', ξ_0, and π_0. Even then η, η', and η'' could have been unreliable, if the determinant in the denominator were close to zero; this, however, does not appear to be the case.

From the results it is clear that the elasticity of the demand for labor (coinciding with η) is very modest according to this model. A closer study of the numerical values obtained for the other variables shows that this is due to the well-known double function of wages, viz. that they are on the one hand an element of consumer demand with a high propensity to spend and, on the other hand, a cost and price element.

A second problem on wage policy arises if, as is advocated in certain quarters, this policy is proposed in order to restore balance of payments equilibrium. This means assuming $\xi_0 = \pi_0 = 0$ and asking for what value of l' the condition $D = -0.04$ is fulfilled. This is an example of the (partially) inverted problem referred to in § 46; D now being given and l' unknown. The other political parameters ξ_0 and π_0 are, however, given and hence the other variables y and p must be considered as unknowns: they cannot be chosen freely.

We might solve the present problem by solving, similarly to (5), our system (1) to (3) for D and putting $\xi_0 = \pi_0 = 0$ and $D = -0.04$. A somewhat shorter way consists, however, of rewriting our equations:

$$\left.\begin{array}{l} \xi_1 y - \xi_3 l' + \xi_2 p = -D = 0.04 \\ -\mu y \qquad\qquad - \delta\, p = -D = 0.04 \\ -\pi_2 y - \pi_1 l' + \quad p = 0 \end{array}\right\} \qquad (6)$$

and solving for l'; leading to:

$$l' = \frac{0.04\,(\xi_1 + \mu + \delta\pi_2 + \pi_2\xi_2)}{-\xi_1\delta\pi_1 - \xi_3\mu - \xi_3\delta\pi_2 + \xi_2\mu\pi_1} \qquad (7)$$

the numerical values of which are:

Model Nr.	*1*	*2*	*3*	*4*	*5*	*6*
$l' =$	-0.35	-3.75	-0.25	-0.26	-0.37	-0.77

One general remark should be made here before interpreting these results. Most of them are outside the range of what could be considered small changes; hence the values are only exact solutions to the linearized system of equations. They will be somewhat different from the solutions of the nonlinear equations from which we started; they may even be quite different. We shall not, however, make use of the numerical results as such.

The interpretation of the result for model 2 is that it is meaningless in that it surpasses the possible boundary condition that l' in absolute value shall be positive. It is not meaningless, however, in that it shows that no equilibrium in the balance of payments can, in this model, be obtained by small wage reductions.

For the other models too the results show that small wage reductions cannot do the job. Even the real wage reductions would be quite different from small, as the figures for p, obtainable from (6), show:

Model Nr.	*1*	*2*	*3*	*4*	*5*	*6*
$p =$	-0.10	-1.00	-0.08	-0.07	-0.17	-0.21

Wage rates may therefore be said to be bad regulators of the balance of payments under present conditions in the Netherlands (and probably in many other countries). A closer study of the other variables shows that the reason is that wage reductions tend to increase real incomes of nonworkers and thus to burden the balance of payments which partly compensates the favorable direct effects; hence such a strong reduction is necessary.

It is interesting to note that this failure of wage rates as "single regulators" of the balance of payments is not due to the phenomenon of "critical elasticities" of external trade, frequently discussed.* This we see from the denominator of (7) which does not vanish for positive values of δ; in fact, when we vary δ it only vanishes for:†

$$\delta = \delta_0 = \mu \frac{\xi_2 \pi_1 - \xi_3}{\xi_1 \pi_1 + \xi_3 \pi_2} \tag{8}$$

the numerical value of which is negative for all models. This difference between wage rates and the general price level or the rate of exchange is also due to the dual role of wages just mentioned and expresses itself *inter alia* in the appearance of l' in equation (1). If it did not appear there it would only influence D through p and the case of critical elasticities would apply.

---

* See L. A. Metzler, The theory of international trade, in: Ellis, "A Survey of Contemporary Economics," Philadelphia, 1948, p. 210.

† This argument is not quite exact, since ϵ^m also influences ζ_2; it is only exact if we consider ϵ^e as subject to variations. Since ϵ^e is the more important of the two, there is no serious objection against doing so.

§ 49. Isolated Price Policy

As a counterpart to an isolated wage policy we may now consider an isolated price policy, i.e. a policy of deliberate lowering of price margins, say by price control or by a liberalization of international trade tending to increase competition. In our formulas this comes to handling π_0 as a political parameter and asking for the consequences. We shall consider only the question, what decrease in π_0 would be necessary in order to fill the gap in the balance of payments? Since the method of answering this question is similar to the one used in the preceding section we need only give the numerical results which are:

Model Nr.	*1*	*2*	*3*	*4*	*5*	*6*
π_0 (necessary for $D = -0.04$)	$+1.11$	-1.14	$+0.60$	-0.54	$+1.11$	$+5.7$

The meaning of these apparently meaningless figures is that in none of the models a price fall within the limits set by reality, or by the range of validity of our equations, will be able to close the gap. Even in model 4, where the decrease is less than 1, it surpasses nevertheless the margin left after deduction of wages (30 per cent) and imports (31 per cent). In model 2 it is more than unity and in the other models only a price rise would lead to a (possibly unstable) equilibrium in the balance of payments. If we restrict ourselves—as we should—to the regions of validity of the equations, the answer must be that the influence of prices on the balance of payments is small and of doubtful algebraic sign. A closer examination leads to the explanation of this result by two major factors: first, there is the counterpart to the influence of wages. A fall in prices lowers nonlabor incomes but raises real wages, leading to extra imports. Secondly, there is the question of critical elasticities, referred to at the end of the preceding section. The analytical expression for π_0 in this problem being

$$\pi_0 = \frac{0.04\,(\xi_1 + \mu + \pi_2\delta + \pi_2\xi_2)}{\mu\xi_2 - \delta\xi_1} \tag{9}$$

we find that its denominator becomes equal to 0 for $\delta = \delta_0 = \frac{\mu\xi_2}{\xi_1}$, being a positive figure not far from the actual value of δ. The introduction of wages into our model has therefore brought the critical elasticity of the balance of payments with respect to prices to a higher level and in fact to the neighborhood of δ.

For practical policy our conclusion is therefore that neither wage policy nor price policy should, as an isolated policy, be applied in order to close the gap in the balance of payments. Each of them would disturb the equilibrium between the two big classes of society too seriously and as a consequence be ineffective.

§ 50. Devaluation

It seems natural therefore to think of a combined policy of lowering prices and wages at the same time, in order to preserve this "social equilibrium" and consequently get an efficient tool to close the balance of payments. The combination may be tried with different "weights"; but by far the most practical form of this type of policy would seem that of a devaluation of the national currency. This in fact comes to lowering, in the same proportion, wage rates and all other national cost items expressed in foreign currency. For our formulas this would mean that the percentage fall in prices would be less than that of wages since 31 per cent of prices in the initial situation is imports; hence we would have the condition

$$\lambda l' = 0.69\, l' = p \tag{10}$$

Substituting this condition into our equations and taking $\xi_0 = 0$, we obtain:

$$\left.\begin{aligned} \xi_1 y + D + \xi_2 \lambda l' &= \xi_3\, l' \\ -\mu\, y + D - \delta\lambda\, l' &= 0 \\ -\pi_2 y \qquad + \lambda l' &= \pi_1\, l' + \pi_0 \end{aligned}\right\} \tag{11}$$

Again we may study, in the traditional way, the influence of devaluation on y and D, e.g. by solving these equations, now considering l' as given. The third equation would be superfluous for finding y and D, but would give us π_0. Again it is easier, however, to impose a given value of D and instead consider l' as an unknown. The structure of the equations then becomes a simpler one from the mathematical point of view; the third equation, being the only one which contains π_0, may be disregarded as long as we are not interested in π_0 and the two others yield us y and l'. It is particularly interesting to solve for l', indicating at once the percentage of devaluation which would be necessary if devaluation were the only policy pursued. Its analytical expression is:

$$1' = \frac{0.04\ (\xi_1 + \mu)}{-\xi_1 \delta \lambda - \mu \xi_2 \lambda - \mu \xi_3} \tag{12}$$

and its numerical values are:

Model Nr.	*1*	*2*	*3*	*4*	*5*	*6*
l' (devaluation)	−0.41	−1.46	−0.31	−0.21	−0.41	−0.72

Apart from the figure for model 2 these figures are already less unrealistic than those obtained in the case of wage policy or price policy separately. Nevertheless they are still pretty high, even in the central model. A closer study of the values found for the other variables in this case shows that devaluation as the only policy to obtain balance of payments equilibrium is still not very efficient. This may be illustrated by the figures of the following table.

VALUES FOR THE OTHER VARIABLES IN THE CASE OF DEVALUATION

(Degree of devaluation* necessary to equilibrate the balance of payments.)

	Model Nr.	*1*	*2*	*3*	*4*	*5*	*6*
p	price level	−0.28	−1.00	−0.22	−0.15	−0.28	−0.50
y	volume of production	0.25	1.12	0.17	0.24	0.25	0.51
x	real expenditures	0.13	0.81	0.07	0.18	0.13	0.34
Y	national income	−0.12	−0.19	−0.11	+0.07	−0.12	−0.14
L	wage bill	−0.09	−0.18	−0.08	0.02	−0.09	−0.12
Z	other income	−0.03	0.00	−0.03	0.05	−0.03	−0.03
L'	real wage bill	0.07	0.37	0.04	0.10	0.07	0.16
Z'	real other income	0.09	0.44	0.06	0.11	0.10	0.19
M	imports	0.07	0.36	0.05	0.08	0.07	0.16
E	value of exports	0.11	0.40	0.09	0.12	0.11	0.20

* As indicated above.

Again, these figures should not be taken too literally; the reservations made in § 48 are again valid. They only show two things; first, that a small degree of devaluation will not be sufficient, and second, what the ratios between small changes in the wage-and-price level on one side and the corresponding changes in the other variables will be.

From the table it is clear that devaluation will automatically lead to a considerably higher volume of consumption and production; the most obvious reasons being that larger exports lead to larger incomes and hence larger consumption. Of course, these findings are subject to the qualification that they are not outside the region of validity of our equations. Under the actual conditions of the Netherlands, e.g. with almost full employment, a further rise of production by 25 per cent would hardly be possible at short notice. Apart from this it would seem more efficient to maintain consumption as far as possible until the balance of payments would be in equilibrium and only then to increase it. Evidently this will not happen automatically by devaluation. It should be aimed at on purpose, i.e. by an additional political parameter.

§ 51. Combined Wage, Price, and Tax Policy: the "Optimum" Solution

It is here that we may introduce our third parameter, ξ_0, one interpretation being that by a decrease in subsidies or an increase in indirect taxes, home prices may be raised in comparison to export prices, tending to keep consumption on the predevaluation level. The same might be done by a direct decrease in other government expenditures.

Almost the same problem, and even a somewhat simpler mathematical version of it, arises if by mere technical necessity we have to keep down the volume of production on the predevaluation level and if we wish to make room for the increased exports by pressing consumption somewhat down. In this latter case the problem is: given D and y, given also that $p = \lambda l'$, how shall we choose ξ_0, l', and π_0? The role of data and unknowns in our system of equations has now been completely inverted. And the three equations enable us to find the degree of devaluation l', the reduction ξ_0 in national expenditures, and π_0 and from them all other variables. The interesting thing from the mathematical point of view is that even equation (2) immediately yields l', the only unknown appearing in that equation; equation (1) then enables us to find ξ_0 and equation (3) to find π_0. It is easily found that for models 1, 2, 3, 5, and 6 the degree of devaluation is now:

$$l' = \frac{-0.04}{\lambda\delta} = \frac{-0.04}{0.69 \times 0.53} = -0.11 \qquad (13)$$

and for model 4:

$$l' = \frac{-0.04}{0.69 \times 1.02} = -0.06$$

The reduction of national expenditure appears to be very near to -0.04 everywhere, being equivalent to an increase in home prices by about 4 per cent.

The problem we started this section with is a little bit more complicated. Here we may express all the unknowns, i.e. the three political parameters, ξ_0, l', and π_0 and all the variables except D, p, and y in terms of y which now acts as a mathematical parameter.

We find:

$$\left.\begin{aligned} l' &= -\frac{\mu y + 0.04}{\delta\lambda} \\ \pi_0 &= -\pi_2 y - \frac{(\lambda - \pi_1)(\mu y + 0.04)}{\delta\lambda} \\ \xi_0 &= \xi_1 y - \frac{(\xi_2\lambda - \xi_3)(\mu y + 0.04)}{\delta\lambda} - 0.04 \end{aligned}\right\} \qquad (14)$$

Using equation (1, 2) and expressing l' and p $(=\lambda l')$ in y with the aid of (14) we find:

$$x = y + (0.04 - \mu + \mu\epsilon^{m})\left(\frac{\mu y + 0.04}{\delta}\right) - 0.04 = 0$$

Putting this expression equal to 0, we find y and hence, by (14), the political parameters. The results are:

Model Nr.	*1*	*2*	*3*	*4*	*5*	*6*
y volume of production	0.08	0.08	0.08	0.05	0.08	0.08
l' degree of devaluation	−0.20	−0.20	−0.20	−0.09	−0.20	−0.20
ξ_0 incr. in national expenditure	−0.027	−0.034	−0.021	−0.030	−0.027	−0.032

It is interesting to note that

1. the necessary reduction of national expenditure lies within the range of real possibilities, whereas
2. the resulting increase in production seems possible at short notice;
3. the degree of devaluation now necessary is of the order of magnitude of the actual relative devaluation that took place in Sepetmber 1949.*

In fact, this is the only case of those so far considered where small values for the unknowns are found and, hence, some reliance can be placed upon the numerical values. It is the only case where, on the other hand, this is necessary; in the other cases only a negative use needed to be made of the results.

There is some reason to speak of an optimum solution now since (a) some sort of equilibrium between workers' and non-workers' incomes is preserved, (b) the increase in production is devoted to the balancing of foreign accounts before admitting an increase in consumption, which (c) makes it possible to devalue only slightly. One could, however, formulate other opti-

* The guilder devalued 30 per cent with respect to the dollar, but only 13 per cent with respect to the average of foreign currencies when weighted according to Dutch exports, and 20 per cent when weighted according to imports.

mum solutions and of course this depends upon the practical choice one makes as to the relative weights of the various interests concerned. Some alternative choices were made and the corresponding solutions calculated. One was to postulate that real incomes of workers and nonworkers should be affected proportionately; it results in almost the same solution as the one presented. Others might be tried, according to whether one judges the labor share in national consumption too small or too large (it is, in the Netherlands, considerably larger than before World War II).

Also in another, and perhaps even more important, respect our solution represents an "optimal" solution; it is an attempt to handle the three political parameters at the same time with one single directive. In this respect it is fundamentally different from the situation which would develop as a result of the strategic game between the various "pressure groups" mentioned before (including the government as the representative of the general interest). Each of these groups acts on different directives. It would be interesting, and in fact constitutes an item on the author's agenda, to find out what type of results emerges.

Dealing with the "inverted" problems typical for "decision models" we may observe at this moment that there is, in our special case, one of the possible problems which is not soluble, viz. the problem to find the values of the three political parameters if the variables y, D, and p are given. This is due to the special circumstance that in equation (2) no political parameter enters and that hence (2) cannot be fulfilled if all three variables are given. This is again an illustration of the many anomalies from general theory that may occur if the equations have special forms: a possibility too often forgotten by the mathematical economists of the Lausanne school and only detectible by a specific choice of the equations. Even if these are only approximations to reality there will be only a very narrow range of possible combinations of y, D, p.

§ 52. A Closer Examination of Tax and Subsidy Policy

We may introduce somewhat more explicitly some elements of tax and subsidy policy by writing:*

τ' for the excise tax rate, to be applied to the value of home sales $\bar{\bar{X}}$;

θ'_1 for the profit tax rate, to be applied to gross profits $\bar{\bar{Y}} - \bar{\bar{L}}(1-\theta_2)$;

θ'_2 for social charges, to be applied to total wages $\bar{\bar{L}}$, as an additional payment to be made by entrepreneurs (these charges may be also such taxes on wages as are paid by entrepreneurs, even if formally assessed to workers); and

θ' for all benefits received by workers, expressed equally as a multiplier to $\bar{\bar{L}}$.

We have accordingly to define more exactly some of our variables which are affected by the tax system. Let $\bar{\bar{L}}$ and $\bar{\bar{Z}}$ represent wages and other income *after tax*, let $\bar{\bar{Y}}$ be national income *"at factor cost,"* $\bar{\bar{X}}$ be home sales, and $\bar{\bar{p}}$ be prices *excluding excise tax.*

The following changes have to be made in our equations:

$$(1, 1): \bar{\bar{x}} - \bar{x} = (1 - \sigma)(\bar{\bar{Z}}' - \bar{Z}') + (\bar{\bar{L}}' - \bar{L}') + \bar{\theta}'\bar{\bar{L}}' - \bar{\theta}'\bar{L}'$$

$$\text{where } \bar{\bar{Z}}' = \frac{\bar{\bar{Z}}}{\bar{\bar{p}}(1 + \tau')} \text{ and } \bar{\bar{L}}' = \frac{\bar{\bar{L}}}{\bar{\bar{p}}(1 + \tau')}$$

$$\bar{\bar{Z}} = \{\bar{\bar{Y}} - \bar{\bar{L}}(1 + \theta'_2)\}(1 - \theta'_1)$$

(1, 2): remains unchanged.

$$(1, 1'): \bar{\bar{X}} = \bar{\bar{x}}\bar{\bar{p}} = (1 - \sigma)\frac{\bar{\bar{Z}}}{1 + \tau} + \frac{\bar{\bar{L}}}{1 + \tau} + \frac{\theta'\bar{\bar{L}}}{1 + \tau} + c'\bar{\bar{p}}$$

$$(1, 3): \bar{\bar{Y}} = (1 - \sigma)\frac{\{\bar{\bar{Y}} - \bar{\bar{L}}(1 + \theta'_2)\}(1 - \theta'_1)}{1 + \tau} + \frac{\bar{\bar{L}}(1 + \theta')}{1 + \tau'} - \bar{\bar{D}} + c'\bar{\bar{p}}$$

* I have added primes to these symbols in order to avoid confusion with the symbols used by Frisch (Mathematical Appendix to Memorandum on Price-Wage-Tax-Subsidy Policies as Instruments in Maintaining Optimal Employment). These are all conceived of as multipliers to national income at market prices. Our symbols are rates in the practical sense.

where $c' = \bar{x} + (1 - \sigma)\,\bar{z}' - (1 - \theta'_0)\,\overline{L}'$ and θ'_0 is the value of θ' prevailing in 1949.

So we get for equation (1):

$$(1 + \tau')\xi_1 = \tau' + \sigma + \theta'_1 - \sigma\theta'_1 + \Lambda\,\{-\}$$
$$(1 + \tau')\xi_2 = (1 + \mu - \mu\epsilon^{m})(\tau' + \sigma + \theta'_1 - \sigma\theta'_1 - c(1 + \tau')$$
$$(1 + \tau')\xi_3 = -\Lambda\,\{-\}$$
$$(1 + \tau')\xi_0 = -\tau' - \sigma - \theta'_1 + \sigma\theta'_1 + (c - 0.04)(1 + \tau') - \Lambda\,\{-\}$$
$$\text{where } \{-\} = \{-\sigma\,(1 + \theta'_2)(1 - \theta'_1) + \theta'_2 - \theta'_1 - \theta'_1\theta'_2 - \theta'_2\}$$

For small tax rates we may neglect their products and we find:

$$(1 + \tau')\xi_0 = -\tau'(1.04 - c) - \theta'_1\,(\sigma - 1 - \Lambda - \Lambda\sigma) - \theta'_2\,(\Lambda - \sigma\Lambda) + \theta'\Lambda - \sigma + c + \Lambda\sigma - 0.04$$

Assuming $\sigma = 0$, we have, for the case in which no private hoarding takes place,

$$\xi_0 = \frac{1}{1 + \tau'}\,\{-\tau'(1.04 - c) - \theta'_1(1 - \Lambda) - \Lambda\theta'_2 + \theta'\Lambda\}$$

In that case, $c = 0.04$ and the "weights" with which the various tax rates now appear in this political parameter may be easily understood: an increase in τ' decreases, in the same proportion, national expenditure since it "presses" upon the total of them; increases in θ'_1 and θ'_2, do so for the part of national income going to nonworkers and workers, respectively, whereas an increase in θ', on the other hand, stimulates national expenditure in the same intensity as θ'_2 would press it down. With the degree of approximation used here, all these changes can be substituted in the proportions indicated. As soon as the tendency to hoard is introduced by making σ greater than 0, their substitutability is changed as indicated in the last formula but one. If supply of labor had been relevant (with the situation of supply pressure, we consider, it is not), still other differences would have been found. See Frisch's memorandum just quoted.

§ 53. The Influence of Wages upon Employment under Various Side Conditions

In § 48 we discussed the consequences and possibilities of wage policy as regards the balance of payments. An important further aspect of wage policy is its influence on employment. Our equations enable us to compute the influence of an autonomous change in wage rates on employment, if a relation between the volume of production and employment is added. As long as labor productivity remains unchanged, they are simply proportional and may be represented by the same index y. As soon as changes in labor productivity h (also considered as an index number with $\bar{h} = 1$ and measured as deviations from this value) are introduced we have to distinguish between y and employment a (with $\bar{a} = 1$, say). Their relation is

$$a = y - h \qquad (15)$$

At the same time, then, we have to distinguish between the true wage rate l ($\bar{l} = 1$) and the index of labor cost per unit of product l', their relation being

$$l' = l - h \qquad (4)$$

as was stated in § 47.

Under the prevailing conditions we may and will, in fact, assume that changes in h are autonomous, depending as they do on (1) the psychologic-political attitude of certain groups of workers, and (2) such entrepreneurial initiatives as the intro duction of work classification, better industrial relations, or the organization of many plants.

To begin with, we will assume that labor productivity is constant. The influence of the wage rate on employment, other political parameters remaining constant, may then be found as indicated in § 48, equation (5). Under present conditions there are good reasons, however, to drop the assumption of other constant parameters, and take into account, when considering the consequences of wage policy, the probable reactions of the government and possibly of others. This comes to considering the consequences for employment of wage changes with "side conditions." Of course these consequences are different from those expressed in equation (5). An important special case is the one in which we assume that the government, by tax measures, tries to preserve the balance of payments equilibrium. In this case we have as data: l', $D = -0.04$, and $\pi_0 = 0$. Our unknowns are y, in which we are particularly interested, p, and ξ_0. The equations, written in the relevant order, are:

$$\left.\begin{aligned} \xi_1 y + \xi_2 p - \xi_0 &= \xi_3 l' + 0.04 \\ -\mu y - \delta p \quad &= +0.04 \\ -\pi^2 y + p \quad &= \pi_1 l' \end{aligned}\right\} \qquad (16)$$

Since ξ_0 does not interest us in particular, we have only to eliminate p from the last two equations, leading to

$$y = -\frac{0.04 + \delta' \pi_1 l}{\mu + \delta \pi_2} \qquad (17)$$

The corresponding conjectural elasticity of the demand for labor appears to be considerably larger than was found in § 48, viz. -0.31 in all models, except in model 4, where it amounts to -0.54.

We may also express y as a function of the real wage rate $l - p$ instead of l. This leads to an elasticity of about -0.4 (-0.7 in model 4; -0.6 in model 5).

As another problem consider the case where the government and perhaps the entrepreneurs together respond to the wage policy by changing both ξ_0 and π_0 so as to maintain (1) balance of payments equilibrium, and (2) "social equilibrium" as we understood it in the case of devaluation. This comes to taking as given $D = -0.04$, and $p = \lambda l'$ and l' and as unknown ξ_0, π_0 (which do not primarily interest us now), and y. We may now use equation (2) and find:

$$-\mu y - \delta\lambda l = 0.04$$

$$y = -\frac{0.04 + \delta\lambda l}{\mu} \qquad (18)$$

yielding an elasticity of -0.83 (in model 5: -1.60).

Let us now suppose that labor productivity is no longer constant, but constitutes another policy parameter in the hands of workers and employers. Instead of l' we have now to introduce two other data, viz. l and h, whereas y has to be replaced by $a + h$, according to (15). In the two problems just considered this yields us:

Bal. of paym. equil. by tax measures $a + h =$

$$\frac{0.04 + \delta\pi_1 (l + h)}{\mu + \delta\pi_2} \qquad (17')$$

Bal. of paym. equil. and "social equilbrium" by tax and price

$$\text{policy } a + h = -\frac{0.04 + \delta\lambda (l + h)}{\mu} \qquad (18')$$

This leads to the following numerical results:

	Models 1 to 3, 5, 6	*Model 4*
(17′)	$a = -0.31l - 0.69h - 0.08$	$a = -0.54l - 0.46h - 0.08$
(18′)	$a = -0.83l - 0.17h - 0.09$	$a = -1.60l + 0.60h - 0.09$

We may also calculate p as a function of the data and hence use the real wage rate $l_R = l - p$, instead of l, yielding:

	Models 1 to 3, 6	
(17″)	$a = -0.42l_R - 0.59h - 0.08$	$a = -0.73l_R - 0.28h - 0.07$
(18″)	$a = -2.7l_R + 1.7h - 0.09$	$a = -5.2l_R + 4.2h - 0.09$

Model 5

$$a = -0.58l_R - 0.43h - 0.07$$
$$a = -2.7l_R + 1.7h - 0.09$$

These results deserve careful consideration. It is interesting to note, first, that generally the autonomous influence of labor productivity on employment is, in the short run, negative, with the exception of the second case in model 4. It is obvious that this is correlated with the elasticity of demand. This negative influence of labor productivity on employment is no difficulty only if the value of *a* would otherwise (i.e. without the considered change in *h*) have surpassed full employment and would therefore have been impossible. Another interesting feature of our results is that the elasticity of employment with respect to real wages is always higher than the elasticity with respect to nominal wages, a well-known fact that explains a large part of the discrepancy between Douglas' findings and those of various other authors. It is also noteworthy that the elasticity of employment with respect to real wages is, in absolute value, well above one in all models in the second case, that of balance of payments equilibrium and "social equilibrium."

§ 54. Summary; Is It Possible to Translate Our Analysis into Verbal Deductions?

We may briefly summarize our findings. We constructed a simple model intended to approach short-run reactions (i.e. reactions within the next few years) of the economy of a small country upon autonomous changes in wage, price, and budget policy as well as in labor productivity. We used numerical values (in six alternatives) believed to be valid for the Netherlands. The essence of the model is a combination of the basic ideas of Keynes-Machlup on the influence of real income on the balance of payments, the influence of prices in this respect, and the role of wages for prices and workers' income. An appropriate choice of the main variables led to a very simple system with production volume, price level, and balance of payments deficit as representing the economic phenomena, unit wage cost, autonomous profit margin, and autonomous part of national expenditure as "political parameters." Various problems of economic policy were dealt with. With given "directives" the values of the parameters were the unknowns. It appeared that closing the balance of payments cannot very efficiently be done by wage reductions alone or profit reductions alone. Their combination, in the special form of devaluation, appeared more efficient, although still not very attractive. Double the devaluation applied in September 1949 might have been necessary to close the gap. Budget policy (in either of three forms: decrease of subsidies, increase in indirect taxes, or reduction of expenditure generally) should be added. An "optimum solution" is presented, which seems to be within the range of practical possibilities. That solution may be made even more acceptable by increases in labor productivity.

Finally, the influence of wage rates and labor productivity, considered as autonomous variables, on employment is studied. A distinction should be made between a number of cases according to whether the other political parameters do or do not react. Other parameters being equal, the elasticity of the demand for labor is found to be very weak. It is higher, however, if the other parameters are supposed to change in response to wage increases, e.g. in order to maintain balance of payments equilibrium and "social equilibrium." The elasticity may then approach or even surpass unity. If the real wage rate instead of the nominal rate is considered to be the action parameter, the elasticities are higher. The influence of changes in labor productivity on employment is negative as long as the demand elasticity is below one, otherwise it is positive.

Having summed up our main findings, we now ask whether this analysis, in view of the interest for practical politics it may arouse, and a certain aversion of mathematics, can be given in nonmathematical form. The answer clearly depends on what exactly is meant by nonmathematical analysis. It is of course possible to replace every equation by a series of verbal statements but by doing so we would certainly not get an easy-reading exposition of our analysis. I am inclined to consider as "verbal treatment" a sequence of statements (including calculations) each of which is based on one or more of the preceding statements. An example may be: "A wage rate fall of 1 per cent, production remaining constant, leads to a 0.3 per cent fall in prices. This price fall, production remaining constant, improves the balance of payments by an amount $\delta \times 0.3$. Since we assume production constant and imports increase, a decrease of so and so much in consumption must have occurred. This may have been obtained by a decrease in subsidies of so and so much." Characteristic of this piece of logic is that it is one-dimensional. It does not and cannot involve a simultaneous relation between two or more variables. Hence verbal treatment is only possible for such problems where the system of relations involved is of the "consecutive" type, i.e. where one equation only contains one of the unknowns, a second equation contains one more unknown, a third equation again one more, etc. This is the type of system considered by Bentzel and Wold* for other purposes. Of the problems dealt with in our present paper some are of this type, viz. the first one in § 51 (given D, y, and $p = \lambda l'$, and unknowns ξ_0, l', and π_0) and the second in § 53 (given D, l', and $p = \lambda l'$, and unknowns y, ξ_0, π_0). These may therefore be treated verbally and in fact the above example of verbal treatment refers to the former of these two. The other problems treated are not, however, of this type. Some simultaneous relation comes in.

I see a confirmation of my viewpoint in the fact that literary economists, when dealing with simultaneous problems, have to recur to graphical treatment, which is a substitute for proof: the usual demand-and-supply scheme is the best-known case in point.

There is of course one other escape: dynamization with sequence analysis. It is needless to say that matters are often unduly complicated by this method. As a practical method, the one followed in § 50 may be recommended, where the numerical results are given in a table enabling every reader at least to test that the figures satisfy the equations and further enabling him to understand why (in that particular case) the influence of devaluation on the balance of payments is only restricted.

---

* R. Bentzel and H. Wold, On Statistical Demand Analysis from the View-Point of Simultaneous Equations, Skandinavisk Aktuarietidskrift, 1946, p. 95.

APPENDIX

A.

The Use of Correlation Analysis in Economic Research*

§ 55. Introductory

This article tries to give a summary of the methods of correlation analysis, developed during the last decennia, and the use that may be made of them in the field of economic research. It does not contain anything new, but may be of some value to economists, when they have to judge results of statistical investigations or to plan such investigations.

The need for quantitative insight in economic relations is now generally felt. There are some simple possibilities of gaining this insight, consisting in the direct measurement of the variables whose relation must be studied. An example is that of family budget statistics for the relation between incomes and expenditures.

In other cases a simple comparison between two series of figures may be sufficient. An example is the relation between the price of certain crop products and the available supply of such products. Here it may be assumed that price fluctuations can be explained by supply fluctuations only and hence a simple scatter diagram will be a useful tool.

As a rule, however, the fluctuations in any variable x will be caused by fluctuations in more than one other variable: y, z, etc. and one of the most important problems therefore arising in statistical analysis of economic phenomena is how then to find the relation between the "variable to be explained" x and the "explanatory variables" y, z, etc.

---

* Ekonomisk Tidskrift, 49 (1947), 173-192. Reprinted by the courtesy of the publisher.

§ 56. Multiple Correlation Analysis

In principle a solution is possible by the use of multiple correlation analysis. Under certain conditions this type of analysis

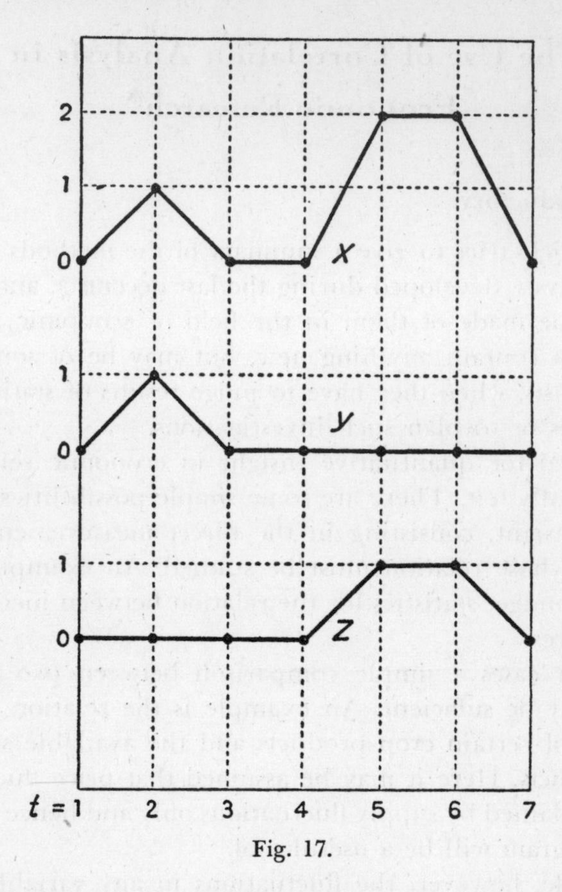

Fig. 17.

is able to tell us what are the most likely values of the coefficients *a* and *b* to be used in the expression:

$$x' = ay + bz + \cdots \tag{56.1}$$

which may be called the "explanation" of *x*.

This equation, which provisionally has been given a linear form, is called a regression equation and *a* and *b* are called regression coefficients. It is the intention of this "explanation" that the consecutive values of x' for all the time units in the period considered are as near to the corresponding values of x as possible.

The ideal situation presents itself if the values of x, y, and z are such that it is possible to obtain complete equality of the corresponding values of x' and x. This may be the case without the existence of a parallelism in the movements of y and z (restricting ourselves to the case of two explanatory variables, y and z). If so, there will only be one pair of values a and b which yield us the equality of x' and x (see Fig. 17, where a very simple case has been represented; it will be immediately evident that only for $a = 1$ and $b = 2$ equality of x and x' can be reached).

The choice of the variables y, z, etc. which have to explain the fluctuations in x, must be made by the economist. Once this choice has been made—which means that a theory of the fluctuations of x has been presented—the task of the statistician, when applying multiple correlation analysis, is twofold: He may *test the theory* and if this theory can be accepted he may *measure the coefficients* a and b, which may be called the strength with which the variables y and z act on x.

As to the testing of the theory, two extreme cases may present themselves:

(1) if x and x' are badly correlated, the theory is erroneous or at least incomplete;
(2) if the correlation between x and x' is complete, the theory does not contradict the facts.

If the theory be accepted by the economist, the statistician is now able, under certain conditions, to measure a and b. Generally speaking there will be only one pair of values a and b by which the highest correlation between x and x' is obtained. These values of a and b may be calculated by the method of "least squares," making $\Sigma\,(x' - x)^2$ a minimum. The regression equation so obtained is called the first (elementary) regression equation. The obtained values are considered as the most likely ones. If other values of a and b would be assumed to prevail, x and x' would be less well correlated and this is a less probable situation, once that the economist makes us believe that the theory put forward is correct.

From the foregoing it will be clear that the statistician never can give a *proof* of any economic theory.

Measurement of a and b will sometimes be impossible, even if a very good fit between x and x' is found.

The simplest case presents itself if y and z themselves are exactly correlated. In that case there will not be only one pair of values a and b for which a good fit is obtained, but an infinity of them. Any part of the influence of y may be replaced by part of the influence of z. Sometimes this situation is the consequence of the properties of the economic system under consideration: it may be, e.g., that there is a second relation between y and z which is the cause of their correlation.

Example: x represents consumption outlay, y total income, z the price level. The two relations may be:

$$x = ay + bz \text{ (demand equation)} \qquad (56.2)$$

and

$$z = cy \text{ (relation determining price level)} \qquad (56.3)$$

More complicated situations in which the coefficients a, b, c, etc. are not measurable may arise in more complicated systems. Generally these cases are described as cases of "multicollinearity" (Frisch). In cases where there is not complete correlation between the explanatory variables a, b, etc. are not completely uncertain, but to some extent uncertain (see § 57).

T. Koopmans has summarized the logic of multiple correlation analysis in the following elegant way.* Unconditional conclusions can only be negative: the rejection of some theory. For

* T. Koopmans, The Logic of Econometric Business Cycle Analysis, Journal of Political Economy, April 1941, p. 157.

positive conclusions additional information is needed. This information is subject to the principles of:

(a) statistical censorship: the additional information must not be contradictory to observation;
(b) scientific efficiency: it must not be a consequence of assumptions already made or of data already used;
(c) the solid base: it must be as plausible as possible;
(d) the sufficient base: it must be sufficient to draw the conclusions.

As a rule the following hypotheses will be made when constructing the relation to be tested. The influences *that are not included* in the relation are:

(i) accidental and small or
(ii) included in the trend term or
(iii) present only in individual years which are excluded from the analysis.

As to the *included* variables it will usually be assumed that:

(iv) these act in a given mathematical way, usually represented by a linear formula;
(v) the lags included are given or must at least be positive and
(vi) some of the regression coefficients have a given algebraic sign or a value within a given interval.

§ 57. Determination of Uncertainty in Results

In the above only the extreme cases are mentioned in which the correlation between x and x' is either absent or perfect and in which the correlation between y and z is moderate or perfect.

In reality various types of intermediary cases may be found. This means that it will only very seldom be possible to find exact values for a and b or to conclude that a and b are perfectly uncertain.

In most cases a and b will be only uncertain to some extent. Various methods have been developed for the judgement of the degree of uncertainty:

(A) R. A. Fisher assumed that the lack of complete correlation must be attributed to errors of measurement in x. Each set of observations may be considered as a sample drawn at random from a large population of possibilities: sometimes large errors in x will be made, sometimes smaller. The results will be uncertain because of the errors in the samples. If all the possible samples would be drawn, a frequency distribution of a and b would be found, characterized by a certain standard deviation which is a measure of the uncertainty in a and b. These standard deviations may be calculated provided that the following conditions are fulfilled:

(1) the values of the independent variables y and z are given and do not change from one sample to the other;
(2) the consecutive errors in x are mutually independent;
(3) their frequency distribution is normal.

At present we do not think so much of errors of measurement in x; far more important is the influence on x of the explanatory variables not included in the regression equation. This influence will usually be assumed to behave as an error of measurement.

(B) R. Frisch approached the problem from another angle. He developed his theory since Fisher's formula becomes inexact, if condition (3) is not rigorously fulfilled and if at the same time there is a high correlation within the set of "explanatory" variables: y, z, etc.

Frisch assumes that:

(1) every variable is composed of a systematic part and an error;

(2) there is perfect correlation between the systematic part of x at one side and of y, z, etc. at the other side;
(3) there is no correlation between any error component and the systematic ones;
(4) there is no correlation between the error components mutually.

He shows that under certain conditions the "true regression coefficients" (being the regression coefficients between the systematic parts) are between the regression coefficients one obtains when taking the first, second, third, etc. elementary regression equation and solving for x in the case of the second, third, etc.

By the second regression equation we mean the equation obtained if we try to approximate y by a linear combination of x, z, etc. and use the method of least squares.

One gets the impression of the limit of uncertainty by drawing the so-called "bunch maps" in which the values found for one and the same regression coefficient from the first, second, third, etc. elementary regression equation are plotted. If the limits do not differ very much, the results are considered highly trustworthy. If on the other hand they are rather different, it is difficult to make a decision as long as one does not know what relative weight should be given to the errors in the various variables.

(C) T. Koopmans, developing both theories and using some results obtained by Van Uven, distinguishes between errors of sampling and errors of weighting. He shows that sometimes the limits of Frisch's method give too unfavourable an impression of the degree of uncertainty.

Taking, e.g. the third regression means that the whole discrepancy between the observed and the calculated value of x is ascribed to errors in the variable z. If now the influence of z on x is only weak, this would come to assuming that the errors in z are very large as compared with the fluctuations in z itself. In many cases where z is rather accurately known, this hypothesis may be rejected beforehand. This rejection is made automatically by Koopmans since he introduces a priori a hypothesis on the extreme values of errors to be accepted.

As we already observed, in most economic problems (though not in all) the errors of measurement are far less important than the errors introduced into the relation by the simple fact that the influence of a number of unknown explanatory variables is neglected. This means that as a rule the largest errors must be assumed in x and that they have the significance of the non-specified influences on x. If so, the use of the first elementary regression equation is most appropriate.

§ 58. Simultaneous Relations

All the foregoing methods are based on the hypothesis that there is only one relation between the variables studied.

T. Haavelmo directed attention to the fact that in almost every economic problem more than one relation must be assumed to exist between the variables under consideration. Price and quantity in one market, e.g. have to obey both the demand and the supply equation. In this case Fisher's assumption (1) is no longer fulfilled. This may be exemplified by the following simple case.

Let q be the quantity sold and bought in a certain market and p the price. Then the demand equation may be written as

$$q = \alpha p + u \tag{58.1}$$

and the supply equation as

$$q = \beta p + v \tag{58.2}$$

where u and v are the unexplained parts of q, comparable with Fisher's "errors."

The most appropriate statistical hypothesis to be made now is that u and v are two independent random variables with a common two-dimensional frequency distribution. Each set of real observations represents one combined sample of u and v.

Solving for p and q we find

$$p = \frac{-u + v}{\alpha - \beta} \tag{58.3}$$

and

$$q = \frac{-\beta u + \alpha v}{\alpha - \beta} \tag{58.4}$$

From these equations we see that p is not independent of u which means that in repeated samples p cannot be assumed to be constant.

It is easily found that the most likely values of the regression coefficients a and b approximating α and β are now no longer found by applying the least squares method to each of the equations separately. On this basis important further methods and theorems have been developed by Haavelmo and others at the University of Chicago.*

In more complicated cases it is very useful to make a distinction between the simultaneous variables which have to be explained by the set of equations and the so-called "predetermined" variables which may also be found in the equations. Predetermined variables may be either data or lagged values of the simultaneous variables. Their common property is that they remain actually the same in repeated samples, since they do not depend on the random variables u and v, etc. In the systems of equations describing dynamic economic systems such lagged values of the variables will often appear among the explanatory variables in the equations.

---

* For a very clear and simple summary of the essence of the method see T. Koopmans, Statistical Estimation of Simultaneous Economic Relations, Cowles Commission Papers, New Series, No. 11, Chicago 1945 (reprint from J. A. S. A.).

From the foregoing it will be clear that the new method will give the same results as the least squares method if:

(a) the right hand side of the relations contains only predetermined variables. This is always the case if the relations are given the so-called "reduced form," meaning that they have been solved for the simultaneous variables. In contradistinction, the original relations, representing the most direct economic connections between the variables, will be called the structural relations or equations.

In the case of a single market being described by a demand and a supply relation

$$q = \alpha p + \gamma d + u \tag{58.5}$$
$$q = \beta p + \delta s + v \tag{58.6}$$

where d represents the demand factors and s the supply factors, the reduced forms will be

$$p = \pi_1 s + \pi_2 d + \cdots \tag{58.7}$$
$$q = \varkappa_1 s + \varkappa_2 d + \cdots \tag{58.8}$$

These equations are sometimes described as the "price equation" and the "turn-over equation" or the "sales equation." The price equation expresses the price and the sales equation the quantity sold as a function of demand factors and supply factors only. In the price equation q does not appear; in the sales equation p does not appear. Statistical approximations of these latter equations therefore may be obtained by the old least squares method.

Sometimes it will be possible to determine, e.g. the demand relation from the price and the sales equation. Since the demand equation is a relation in which no term with s appears, we may obtain it if we eliminate s from (58.7) and (58.8). This is possible exactly only if there is one term with s. If there are several variables of s it will generally not be possible or only approximately be possible.

On the other hand, if the number of relations in the system is larger than the number of *s*'s to be eliminated + 1, an infinity of results would be obtained, meaning that the demand equation cannot be determined.

The results obtained by the new simultaneous equation methods are not different either from the results of the least squares method if (b), the case studied by Bentzel and Wold,* presents itself.

(b) In this case the structure of the system of equations is such that the simultaneous variables x, y, z, etc. may be found in succession without the necessity of solving any simultaneous pair of relations. This will be the case if one equation contains only one of the variables, a second equation only one other aside from the one already mentioned, etc. Lagged variables may appear everywhere.

It is interesting to note that this particular type of system of equations just coincides with the most complicated system of equations accessible to literary economists; verbal solution of economic problems only being possible if this successive solution is possible.

(c) The last case to be mentioned where the new method yields the same results as the least squares methods is the case in which all correlations are complete. This means that the results obtained by the new method and those obtained by the old one will not diverge very much if good fits are obtained.

§ 59. Some Further Remarks on the Reduced Form Method

From the foregoing it is seen that the chief advantage of the reduced form method is that the least squares calculation may be applied which is much simpler than the simultaneous equations method.

* R. Bentzel and H. Wold, On Statistical Demand Analysis from the Viewpoint of Simultaneous Equations, Skandinavisk Aktuarietidskrift 1946, p. 95.

The chief disadvantage of the reduced form method is that the relations as a rule contain more terms than the structural relations and that not so much is known beforehand of the values of the coefficients.

It is therefore more difficult to test economically the results obtained. In the case of the demand equation it is certain beforehand that no supply factors have to occur in that relation; in the supply function no demand factor should occur; in the price or the sales equation, however, both types of factors are coming in.

Sometimes (but not always) the sign of some of the terms in the reduced form relations will not be known beforehand.

The reduced form equations are not the same as the "final equations" of a dynamic system. The final equation for y, e.g. expresses y as a function only of lagged values of y, whereas the reduced form equation for y includes lagged variables of any kind. In the final equation longer lags will be included. If the disturbances of each structural equation are nonautocorrelated, the reduced form will also not have autocorrelated disturbances but the disturbances in the final equation may be autocorrelated (J. Marschak).

§ 60. General Remarks on Application of Correlation Method

(1) Immeasurability.

A general objection often made against statistical analysis of economic relations which in fact applies to all quantitative formulations of economic relations, is the immeasurability of a number of economic phenomena. It must be admitted that there do exist immeasurable economic phenomena.

Of course statistical analysis can only be applied to measurable ones. It should not be forgotten, however, once we are to analyse the explanation of the fluctuations of some measurable phenomenon, that all influences exerted on such a phenomenon are, in principle, measurable. The influence, e.g. of "psychological factors" or of expectations on the fluctuations of a price or of consumption are in principle measurable.

This does not mean that it is always easy to measure these influences. In practice they may sometimes be approximated by functions of lagged variables: the influence, e.g. of expectations may be represented by a function of past price increases.

(2) Variability of coefficients.

It is often maintained that the method of multiple correlation is too rigid since it assumes the regression coefficients to be constant. It is very easy, however, to replace those coefficients by functions of other variables which means that they will be variable.

Of course the variability of the coefficients should be systematic. Otherwise one may prove anything. Assuming variability of coefficients to be unsystematic would mean to renounce scientific analysis.

On the other hand it may be observed that experience supplies us with cases of a remarkable constancy of regression coefficients.

(3) Curvilinearity.

A further generalisation of our method consists of replacing the linear formulae by more general mathematical types. This means that instead of the linear relations curvilinear ones are introduced.

Mathematically this is not at all impossible. Experience shows, however, that in a majority of cases it is very hard to find systematic deviations from linearity.

(4) "Results too uncertain to be used."

Often results of statistical analysis are considered to be of little value since their uncertainty is rather large according to what standard deviations or bunch maps show us.

It should be kept in mind, however, that even then the most likely values of the regression coefficients are those found by the calculations. An explanation based upon such calculations still has the advantage of not being contradictory to observations, which is more than can be said of quite a number of theories.

(5) Multicollinearity with cyclical analysis.

As to the application of multiple correlation analysis to the explanation of cyclic movements the general objection is made that in this case the chance for multicollinearity is very high.

This would be true if the time shape of the cycles in various economic phenomena would be the same. During the period 1919–1932 in the U. S., however (to quote an example), the time shape of cycles in

(i) commodity prices,
(ii) stock prices,
(iii) production, and in
(iv) interest rates

were quite different and hence it was not so difficult to distinguish between the influences exerted by each of these variables on some other phenomenon.

(6) Problems solvable even in the case of multicollinearity.

Even if multicollinearity exists in the relation we are interested in, we may sometimes solve the problems put before us.

As a simple example the following may be quoted. The demand for butter may depend on income, price of butter, and price of margarine. The two latter variables are intercorrelated, meaning that we are not able to separate their influences. As long as the relation between butter prices and margarine prices is not changed, it will be possible, however, to find what the influence of a government price policy on the demand for butter will be.

Another example: by extrapolating the theoretical values x' for some variable x into a period where a new additional cause for fluctuations in x has been added, it is sometimes possible to find what the influence of this additional cause has been.

This procedure too may be applied in cases of multicollinearity between the other factors determining x'. An example will be given later (see § 61).

(7) Importance of a correct economic analysis.

It cannot be emphasized enough that the first thing to be done in any particular application is to give a correct economic analysis of the relation to be investigated. The emphasis is the more necessary since many young investigators seem to overlook this.

Two things should be carefully kept in mind: first, the necessity to know exactly what relation one really is interested in and second to know what factors enter into this relation.

Sometimes investigators are themselves not very clear about the type of relation they investigate: whether a demand or a supply relation or perhaps a price or sales equation.

In many cases it pays better to have exact figures on one of the factors hitherto neglected than to use very elaborate statistical methods.

The number of papers in *Econometrica* devoted to the description of practical results is still too small in comparison to the number of papers dealing with theoretical subjects!

(8) Difference between short-run and long-run influences.

One of the important practical topics of the day is the question of the difference between reactions during the business cycle and reactions likely to take a longer period.

During the business cycle the demand for durable goods, e.g. will show an income elasticity which is probably larger than the income elasticity in the long run which presumably may be the income elasticity to be found from family budget statistics. The demand for labour may depend on wage rates in at least two different ways. There will be a more or less immediate reaction in which the influence of wage rate on the degree of capitalisation does not play a very large role; there will also be a long-run influence of wage rates on the degree of capitalisation.

Important parts of our practical programs must be devoted to the analysis and distinction of these two types of dependency.

(9) Independency of consecutive observations.

Once it was believed that more exact results for the regression coefficients could be obtained by taking monthly figures instead of annual ones because of the larger number of observations.

What matters, however, is the number of independent observations. If the series considered are "inert," monthly data will not be new independent data.

For each statistical series there seems to be one minimum "natural" time unit, for which the independency of consecutive residuals is a fact. For crop figures, e.g. this time unit might be one year. Since random series show apparent cycles of three time units, one may even wonder whether or not the short American cycle or Kitchin may be explained by crop variations simply.

(10) Importance of having data for all relevant variables.

Multiple correlation analysis is impossible if the data are not available for all relevant variables to be included in the relations investigated. It is an illusion that one could obtain results without this condition being fulfilled. Attempts of earlier investigators to do without this necessary information have not as a rule succeeded.

A typical example may in my opinion be found in the statistical investigations quoted in Prof. Iversen's well-known book on international capital movements. The fluctuations in prices, incomes, the items of the balance of payments, etc. of the countries investigated will be the consequences not only of the capital movements that took place but also of other factors. One cannot hope to find the influence of capital movements on these phenomena without studying simultaneously the effects of these other factors.

This seems to explain why most of the authors quoted hardly succeeded in reaching conclusions, as is rightly pointed out by Prof. Iversen. It would be highly interesting if investigations along the lines of multiple correlation analysis could be substituted for the earlier attempts.

§ 61. Some Successful Examples

In recent decades a number of successful multiple correlation analyses have been published.

It is sufficient to quote the important analyses made of the demand relations for agricultural products in the United States and recently in other countries (in Sweden by Prof. Wold). Other important attempts deal with the demand for services and industrial products as well as the demand for groups of commodities such as food as a whole, consumption as a whole, and investments as a whole. The various recent investigations on the propensity to consume are examples in point. These results deserve particular attention if they form groups of consistent results.

A simple but interesting example seems to be the following. Various authors investigated the demand for tramway transport; for Dutch and Danish towns price elasticities of about 3/4 were found, whereas for Stockholm and Marseille an elasticity of about 1/4 resulted. The difference seems plausible because of the severe competition of bicycles in the Dutch and Danish towns, where they are much more numerous than in the two other towns mentioned.

The results are not always in the values found for some regression coefficient. They may also be in the extrapolations made for a period in which one new factor acts. The difference between observed and extrapolated theoretical values may then be considered to be a measure for the influence of the new factors. In Figs. 18 to 21 this procedure is exemplified. An attempt is made to explain the fluctuations in imports into the Netherlands. Imports are subdivided into raw materials and finished products. Consumers' goods and investment goods are considered separately. Imports of raw materials as well as those of finished products are assumed to depend on:

(i) the volume of production,
(ii) the price level of finished goods in the Netherlands and
(iii) the price level of imported finished goods.

A fairly good fit is obtained for the period 1923–1933.

To start with 1934 a quota system was introduced. The extrapolated values show very important deviations from the observed ones. The deviations are different for raw materials and for finished goods: the imports of finished products fell short of expectations according to the formula, whereas the imports of raw materials surpassed the extrapolated values. This is quite natural: a quota system has the intention to stimulate home production at the expense of imports of finished products. The four figures therefore show consistent deviations and these deviations may be taken as a measure for the influence of the quota system.

§ 62. Conclusions of Political and Scientific Importance

In rare cases only will it be possible for scientific analysis—and hence also for multiple correlation analysis—to contribute directly to political decisions. In most cases the formulation of

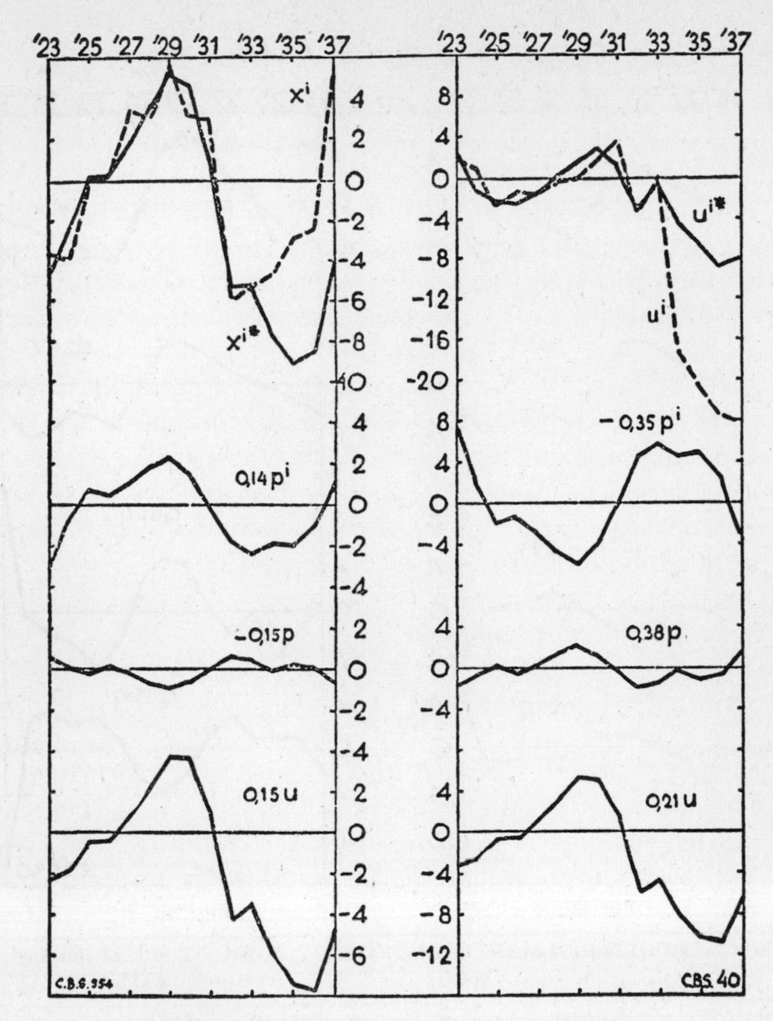

Fig. 18.

x^i	actual imports of raw materials for consumer goods
x^{i*}	calculated imports of raw materials for consumer goods $= 0.15u + 0.14p^i - 0.15p$
$0.15u$	influence of the volume of Dutch production of finished consumer goods
$0.14p^i$	influence of the price level of imported finished consumer goods.
$-0.15p$	influence of the price level of Dutch finished consumer goods

Fig. 19.

u^i	actual imports of finished consumer goods
u^{i*}	calculated imports of finished consumer goods $= 0.21u - 0.35p^i + 0.38p$
$0.21u$	influence of the volume of Dutch production of finished consumer goods
$-0.35p^i$	influence of the price level of imported finished consumer goods
$0.38p$	influence of the price level of Dutch finished consumer goods

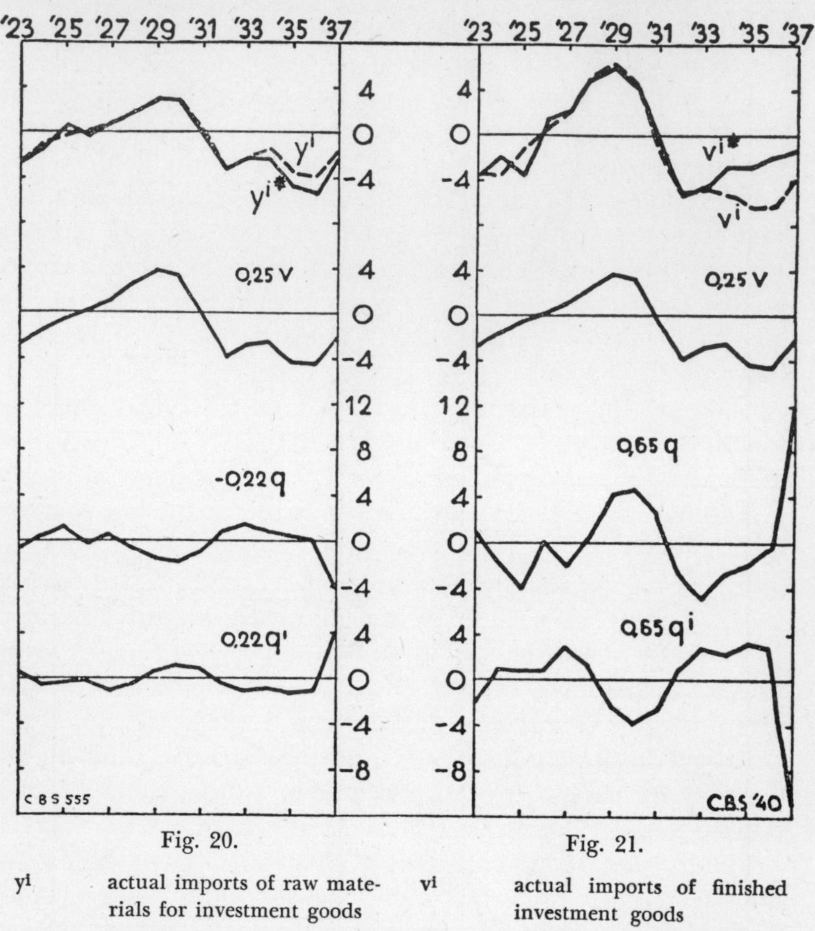

Fig. 20. Fig. 21.

y^i	actual imports of raw materials for investment goods
y^{i*}	calculated imports of raw materials for investment goods $= 0.25\,v - 0.22\,q + 0.22\,q^i$
$0.25\,v$	influence of the volume of Dutch production of investment goods
$-0.22\,q$	influence of the price level of Dutch investment goods
$+0.22\,q^i$	influence of the prices of imported finished investment goods

v^i	actual imports of finished investment goods
v^{i*}	calculated imports of finished investment goods $= 0.25\,v + 0.65\,q - 0.65\,q^i$
$0.25\,v$	influence of the volume of Dutch production of investment goods
$0.65\,q$	influence of the price level of Dutch investment goods
$-0.65\,q^i$	influence of the prices of imported finished investment goods

qualifications and the further consideration of practical complications will be necessary.

The indirect importance seems, however, to be clear. Examples of an almost direct bearing of the results of correlation analysis on practical policy are to be found in the field of agricultural policy. Price forecasts, the calculation of subsidies, etc. have often been based on correlation calculations. An important attempt outside the sphere of agricultural policy was the one to predict the employment level in the United States for the last quarter of 1945 which attempt has been so well analysed by Lawrence R. Klein.*

Cases of a more indirect practical importance may easily be found. The example represented in figures 19 to 21 was part of an attempt to give an appraisal of Dutch commercial policy.

Another example was an analysis made of the tin market† showing that the restriction of production had a considerable influence on the price of that product.

Many investigations upon the effect of devaluations after 1930 and the revalorisation of the Danish and Norwegian crowns in 1925 contributed very much to our knowledge and will be useful to the work of the International Monetary Fund.

Recent investigations of the influence of wage rates on the demand for labour will contribute to future business cycle policy.

Finally some recent results of correlation analysis may be quoted which for the time being are of scientific interest only but which may be of practical importance as well at some later stage. The rather low figure found for elasticities of substitution in international trade may lead to a better knowledge of the nature of the equilibrium in the balance of payments.

A study by Dr. Verdoorn‡ seems to show that the shift from variable to fixed costs was not very important during the last

---

* L. R. Klein, A Post-Mortem on Transition Predictions of National Product, Journal of Political Economy LIV (1946), p. 289.

† M. J. Schut, Tinrestrictie en Tinprijs, Haarlem 1940.

‡ P. J. Verdoorn, De Verstarring der Productiekosten, Haarlem 1943.

half century contrary to what was generally believed but in agreement with Prof. L. von Mises' point of view.

A closer consideration by Dr. Witteveen* of the price equations obtained so far seems to show that prices are not fixed by producers on the basis of marginal costs: possibly a support of the findings of the Oxford Institute of Statistics.†

---

* H. J. Witteveen, Loonshoogte en Werkgelegenheid, Haarlem 1947.

† R. L. Hall and C. J. Hitch, Price Policy and Business Behaviour, Oxford Economic Papers No. 2, May 1939, p. 12.

B.

Statistical Evidence on the Acceleration Principle*

§ 63. Theoretical Introduction

1. Much attention has recently been given to the so-called "acceleration principle" or "the Relation" as Mr. Harrod† calls it. Developed by Professors Aftalion, Bickerdike, Bouniatian, Carver, Fanno, Kuznets, and Pigou, it has been given special attention by Professor J. M. Clark in his splendid survey *Strategic Factors in Business Cycles;*‡ and has obtained a place in many theories of the business cycle. Professor Haberler,§ from whom part of the above references are taken, also uses it in his own synthesis of theories; Mr. Harrod regards the acceleration principle and the multiplier principle acting in combination as the chief forces in trade cycles. Quite recently Dr. Chait¶ has developed a theory implying as special cases both the acceleration principle and the multiplier principle.

2. The principle in its simplest form can be best seen in a simplified example.** Let the value of the yearly output of (say) shoes be 100. The cost of the fixed capital equipment required for this output may be 500, 10 per cent of which must be re-

* Economica, V (May 1938), 164-176. Reprinted by the courtesy of the publisher.

† R. F. Harrod, The Trade Cycle. An Essay. Oxford, 1936.

‡ Cf. also J. M. Clark, "Business Acceleration and the Law of Demand," Journal of Political Economy, XXV, pp. 217-235. (1917.)

§ G. Haberler, "Prosperity and Depression," A Theoretical Analysis of Cyclical Movements. Geneva, 1937, League of Nations.

¶ B. Chait, Les fluctuations économiques et l'interdépendance des marchés. Brussels, 1938.

** Taken from Haberler, loc. cit., p. 84.

placed each year. Then, new machines at the cost of 50 must be constructed each year for replacement. Now, suppose the demand for shoes rises, so that production must be increased by 10 per cent to 110 a year. If there is no excess capacity and if methods of production are not changed, this increase necessitates an increase of 10 per cent in the stock of fixed capital; that is, an additional production of machinery of 50, being an increase of 100 per cent. In this simplest form the principle states that percentage changes in the *production* of consumers' goods are equal to percentage changes in the *stock* of capital goods. As the latter is usually considerably larger than the annual *production* of capital goods, the corresponding percentage changes in the latter are much larger than the percentage changes in the production of consumers' goods. The principle has two aspects between which it is useful to distinguish:

(a) the correlation aspect: there must be correlation between new investment in durable capital goods and the *rate of increase* in consumers' goods production;

(b) the regression aspect: the percentage fluctuations in consumers' goods production are *equal* to the percentage fluctuations in the stock of capital goods. The first aspect states something about the correlation coefficient between two variables; the second aspect about the numerical value of the regression coefficient.

3. There is some doubt about the causal direction of the relation mentioned. Sometimes causality is not considered at all; the principle is only meant to explain the difference in intensity between consumers' goods production and producers' goods production. In other cases, however, the principle is meant to explain investment fluctuations. Changes in consumption are then taken as given; fluctuations in investment activity are deduced. In any case this seems to me the more interesting aspect of the matter and, at the same time, the kind of relationship we need for business cycle theory.

4. In its more rigorous form, the acceleration principle can only be true if the following conditions are fulfilled.

(a) Very strong decreases in consumers' goods production must not occur. If the principle were right, they would lead to a corresponding disinvestment and this can only take place to the extent of replacement. If annual replacement amounts to 10 per cent of the stock of capital goods, then a larger decrease in this stock than 10 per cent per annum is impossible. A decrease in consumers' goods production of 15 per cent could not lead to a 15 per cent decrease in physical capital as the acceleration principle would require. It is interesting that this limit is the sharper the greater the duration of life of the capital goods considered.

(b) There should be no abrupt changes in technique leading to a sudden increase in the amount of capital goods necessary to the production of one unit of consumers' goods.

In its more rigorous form, the principle is equivalent to saying that a constant part of productive capacity is idle and that entrepreneurs never increase production of consumers' goods before having increased correspondingly their capacity. In the case of this constant part being zero—i.e. full occupation of capacity at any moment—this is, at least for increases, a necessity; in all other cases this policy would have to be followed deliberately, and there are hardly enough reasons to suppose this occurs in reality.

In particular there are reasons to expect the principle to break down in times of heavy decreases in production [see what was said under (a)] as well as in the periods immediately following such decreases, until production has reached capacity again. It is only at that moment that the *necessity* of the principle's action recurs.

5. The acceleration principle may, however, be given a less rigorous form. Instead of equality of percentage changes in consumers' goods production and capital goods' stock there may

be assumed to be only proportionality or even only a linear relationship. This means that there would still be correlation but that the regression coefficient would be less than one. Two reasons exist for giving the principle its less rigorous form:

(a) During a period of increasing production, not all firms and not all branches attain at the same moment the point of full capacity. Suppose that for the individual firms the principle acts only—and then of course in its rigorous form—when full capacity is reached; then to a given increase in total production for all firms a smaller percentage increase in total stock of capital goods may correspond. Something similar may happen with heavy decreases in production: some firms may show decreases going beyond the critical one mentioned in 4 (a), others may remain within the critical boundary. Supposing that in such times all firms simply do not replace worn-out capacity, there will again be a percentage decrease in physical capital stock which is smaller than the percentage decrease in consumers' goods production. (This statement holds, of course, equally well for any individual firm going beyond the critical decrease.)

Of course, it is not at all certain in these circumstances that the regression coefficient will have to be the same for every moment. Much depends on the distribution of decreases over firms and on the distribution of idle capacity over firms. But there will be a tendency to a regression coefficient below one. It may be added already here that in fact the material used by Professor Clark in his first exposition of the principle showed this very clearly; the regression coefficient being about one-half instead of one. It may also be added that the magnifying effect may, nevertheless, still exist. If the rigorous acceleration principle would lead to percentage fluctuations in capital goods production ten times as large as those in consumers' goods production, then in the less rigorous form these percentage fluctuations would still be five times as great.

(b) A second reason for the less rigorous form of the acceleration principle might be that even with idle capacity a firm would expand its plant proportionally to the rate of increase in consumers' goods production, but not by an equal percentage. This would mean that there would not be an immediate necessity for investment but that the willingness to invest would depend chiefly on the rate of increase in consumers' goods production.

It seems important to remind the reader that we have been considering three situations in which a firm may find itself:

(i) full capacity used and increasing production;
(ii) heavily decreasing production, as defined under 4 (a);
(iii) all other situations.

If the less rigorous acceleration principle were caused only in the way indicated under 5 (a), at least part of the firms should be in the situations (i) and (ii) during most of the period studied. There is reason to doubt whether this is so for the post-war period or even for many pre-war years. If this doubt is justified. the only way in which the principle could still be fulfilled would be the one indicated under 5 (b). The behaviour of entrepreneurs assumed there seems, however, less natural than the behaviour assumed under 5 (a). Therefore I think there must be already for theoretical reasons some doubt as to the validity of the acceleration principle. In my opinion an explanation of investment fluctuations by profit fluctuations* is more natural, and for this reason a comparison between these two competing explanations has been made in some of the cases considered. It would, however, lead us too far to go into a detailed consideration of the relationship between profits and investment.

6. One further amendment of the acceleration principle may be mentioned for reasons of completeness. Dr. Staehle, in a private discussion, suggested that the correlation would exist between new investment activity and the *shift in the demand curve* for consumers' goods instead of the increase in the actual quantity demanded or produced. This seems indeed more natural especially in the following situation: suppose that, with

* To be called shortly "the profit principle."

full capacity used, demand increases, but as productive capacity cannot be expanded immediately, the quantities produced cannot rise correspondingly. Prices will rise instead. Nevertheless it is natural to assume that there will be new investment. Dr. Staehle's hypothesis can be given an especially convenient form if the elasticity of demand is unity (which, approximately, will be the case for "all consumption"): then the shift in demand curve is simply equal to the change in the money value of consumption or consumption outlay. Therefore his device would simply be equivalent to saying that new investment is correlated with the rate of increase in consumption outlay.

§ 64. Statistical Verification

7. Depending on the statistical material available, in some cases both aspects—the correlation and the regression aspect—have been tested, whereas in other cases only the correlation aspect could be considered. The regression aspect can only be investigated if figures on the stock of physical capital goods are available and this is only the case for individual branches. The following industries have been taken:

(a) Railways: United Kingdom, pre-war, Fig. 22. France and Germany, pre-war, Fig. 23.
(b) Cotton spinning: United Kingdom, pre-war, Fig. 24.
(c) Shipping: United Kingdom, pre-war, Fig. 25.

As, however, for business cycle theories the behaviour of industry as a whole is of considerable interest, general indices have also been considered. Here the only possibility seems to be comparing the *production* index of investment goods or durable goods with the rate of increase in the index of consumers' goods production. In many respects this is a less reliable comparison, as production of investment goods does not necessarily—although probably—fluctuate parallel to new investment. Replacement, which is included also, may show different fluctuations. It will, however, usually show less pronounced changes.

8. The railway charts have been drawn according to the following principle. The dotted line always represents the deviations from trend (nine-year moving averages) of the percentage rate of increase in rolling stock. For each of the countries it has been drawn twice; it has been compared with a full curve which has everywhere been drawn at such a scale as to give the best fit. The upper full curve represents the fluctuations in the rate of increase of traffic, the lower full curve the profit rate (both as deviations from their nine-year moving averages). The upper graph therefore gives "the explanation of new investment by the acceleration principle," the lower one "the explanation of new investment by the profit principle." The lag of new investment has been taken 1½ year, except for the profit principle for Germany, where it is 1 year. These lags seem to correspond fairly well to the lags in the curves, and, what is more important, they are about equal to the lag between orders and deliveries found for American figures.

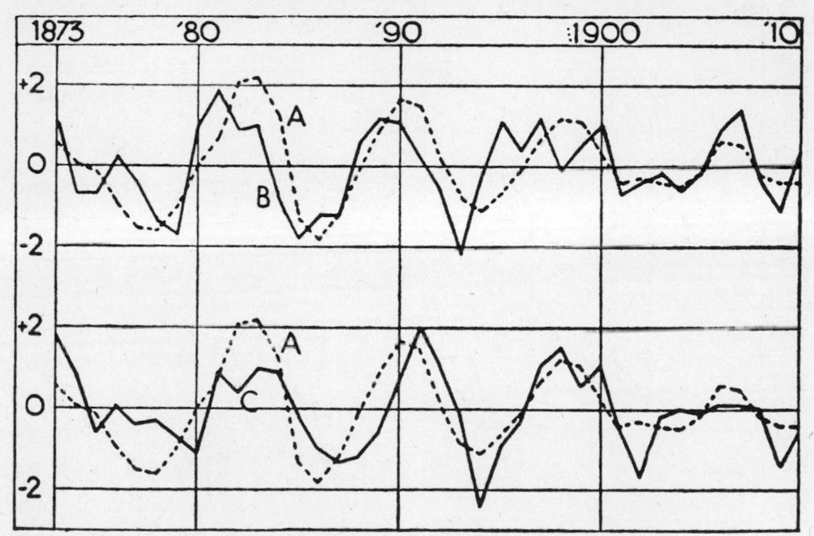

Fig. 22. Railways, United Kingdom. A, Percentage rate of increase in rolling stock (average of locomotives and cars weighted roughly according to their average prices in a base period). B, Percentage rate of increase in traffic, 1½ year before, drawn on such a scale as to yield the best fit with A. **C, Profit rate, 1½ year before, drawn as B.**

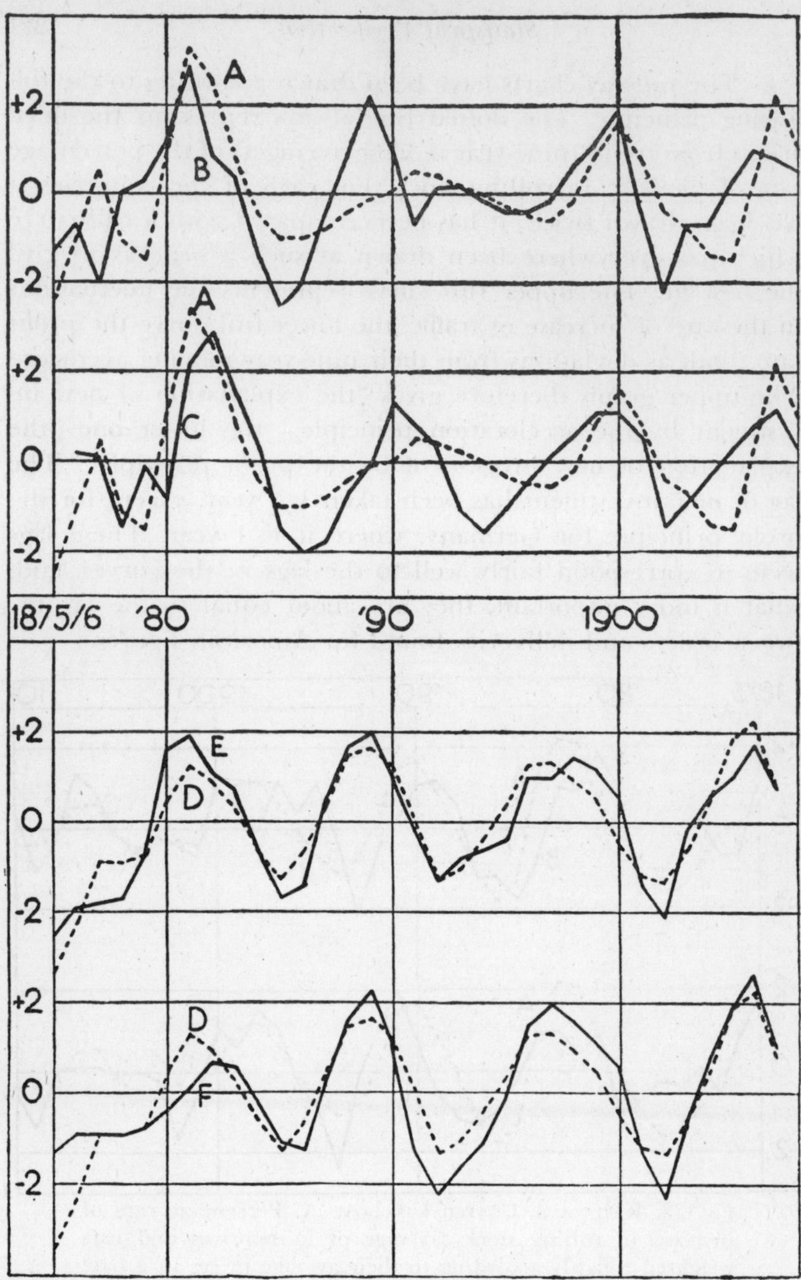

Fig. 23. RAILWAYS, FRANCE (A, B, C) AND GERMANY (D, E, F). A, D, Percentage rate of increase in rolling stock. B, E, Percentage rate of increase in traffic (B, 1½ year before; E, 2½ year before), drawn as B in chart 1. C, F, Profit rate (C, 1½ year before; F, 1 year before), drawn as B.

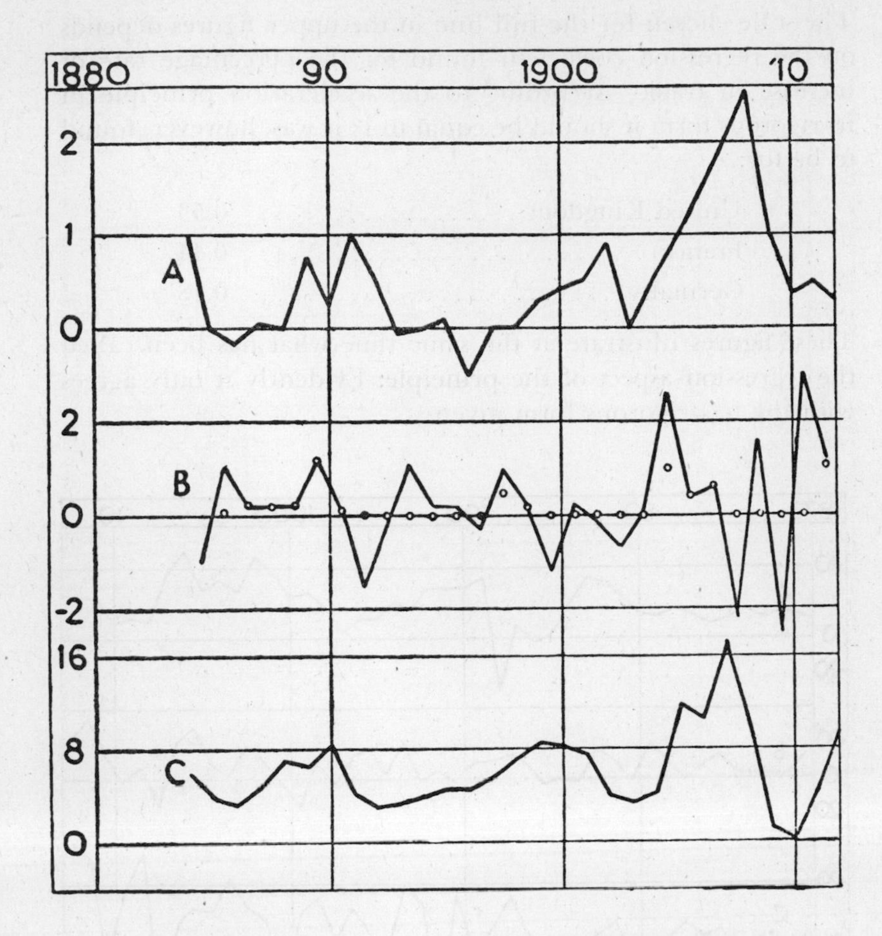

Fig. 24. Spinning, United Kingdom. A, Net increase in number of spindles (millions). B, Rate of increase in cotton consumption (million cwt). O, "Corrected curve," i.e. (i) every negative figure replaced by zero, (ii) the subsequent positive figures replaced by zero as long as former maximum in consumption not yet reached again, (iii) the first figure after the former maximum has been surpassed replaced by difference between new maximum and former maximum. C, Average spinning profits (£1,000.–). Figures taken from D. H. Robertson, A Study of Industrial Fluctuations.

The scale chosen for the full line in the upper figures depends on the regression coefficient found for the percentage rate of increase in traffic. According to the acceleration principle in its rigorous form it should be equal to 1; it was, however, found to be for:

United Kingdom	0.53
France	0.44
Germany	0.48

These figures illustrate at the same time what has been called the regression aspect of the principle. Evidently it only agrees with the less rigorous form given.

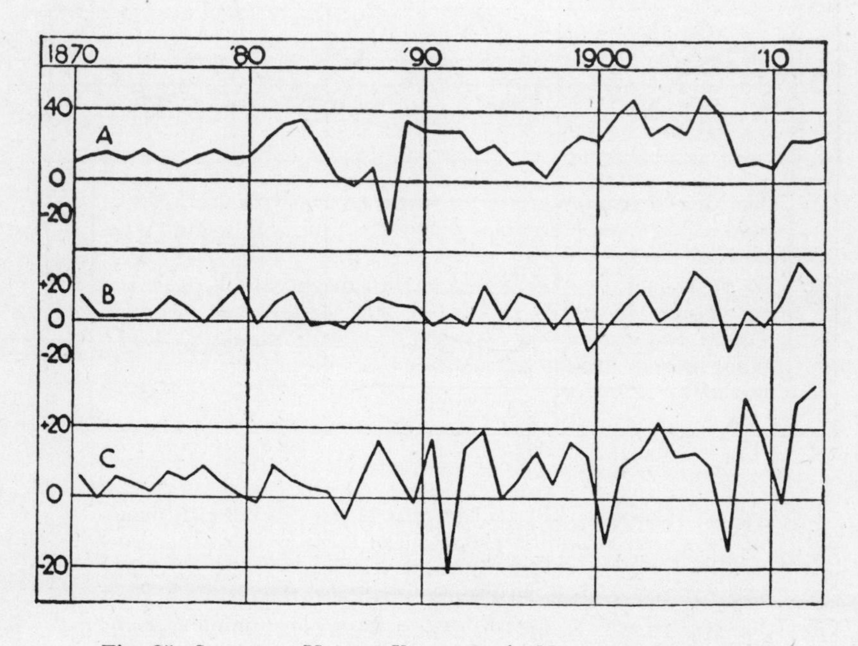

Fig. 25. SHIPPING, UNITED KINGDOM. A, Net rate of increase in total tonnage, 10,000 tons (sailing tons counted for one-third). B, Net rate of increase in total British tonnage entered, million tons. C, Rate of increase in "transport index," indicating ton-miles of transport for chief sea transport commodities (cereals, coal, wood, oil, nitrate). Taken from De Nederlandsche Conjunctuur, March, 1934.

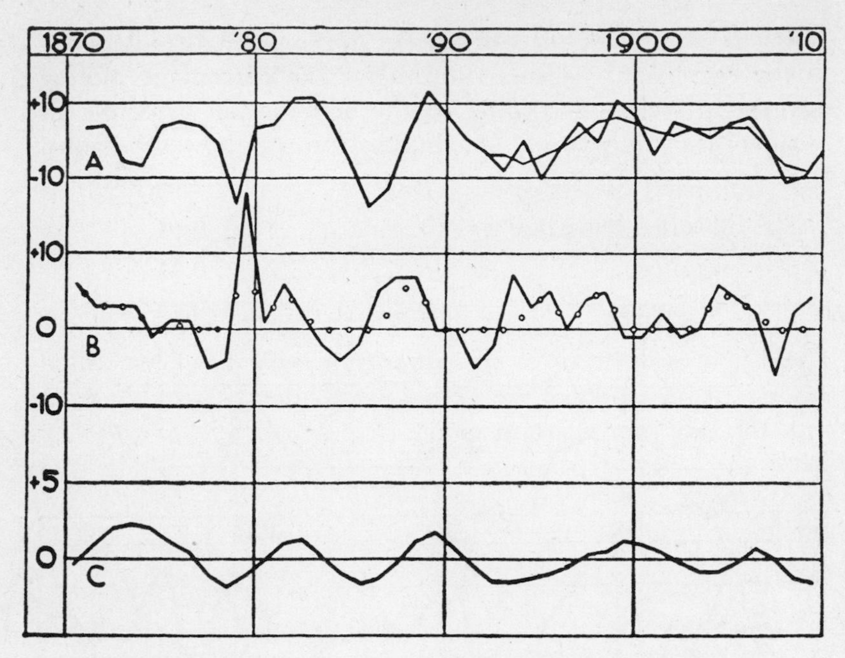

Fig. 26. GENERAL ACTIVITY, UNITED KINGDOM. A, Consumption of pig iron, percentage deviations from trend (nine-year moving average); taken account of pig iron in steel, of changes in stocks and after deduction of iron in exports. B, Rate of increase in industrial production (O, corrected figures, see Fig. 24, two-year moving averages); Hoffmann's index. C, Non-labor income, deviations from trend (Stamp's figures for taxed income).

As to the correlation aspect, it is immediately seen from the charts that the correlation is only high for the case of Germany (as it was for the U.S.A. during the period studied by Professor Clark*); for the U.K. and France, however, it is rather low. But the correlations obtained for the profit principle are by no means higher.

* It was not in the period studied by S. Kuznets: "Relation between Capital Goods and Finished Products in the Business Cycle," Economic Essays in Honor of W. C. Mitchell, New York 1935, p. 209.

It has been tried to improve the correlation by a correction, consisting in two sorts of changes in the figures for the rate of increase in traffic:

(i) putting equal to zero any negative number and the positive numbers following it, as long as the last maximum in traffic has not yet been reached;

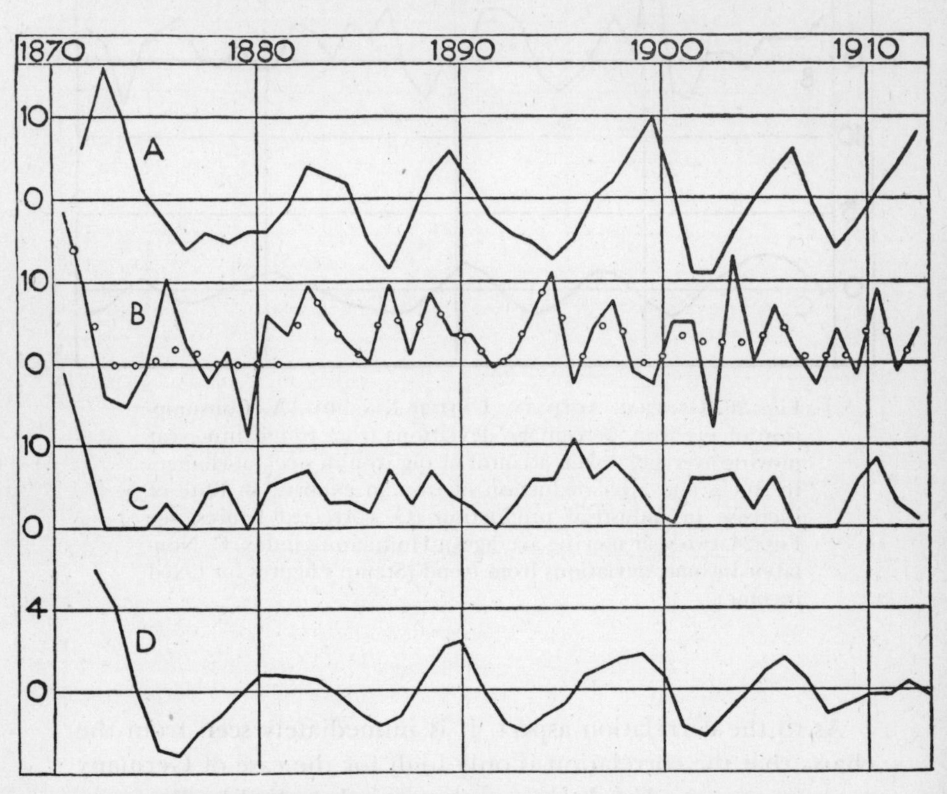

Fig. 27. General Activity, Germany. A, Consumption of pig iron, percentage deviations from nine-year moving average, two-year moving average; taken account of iron in steel and after deduction of iron in exports. B, Percentage rate of increase in industrial consumers' goods production (O, corrected figures, see Fig. 24, two-year moving averages). C, Percentage rate of increase in total industrial production, corrected figures, see Fig. 24. D, Dividends of all societies, percentage of capital, deviations from nine-year moving averages.

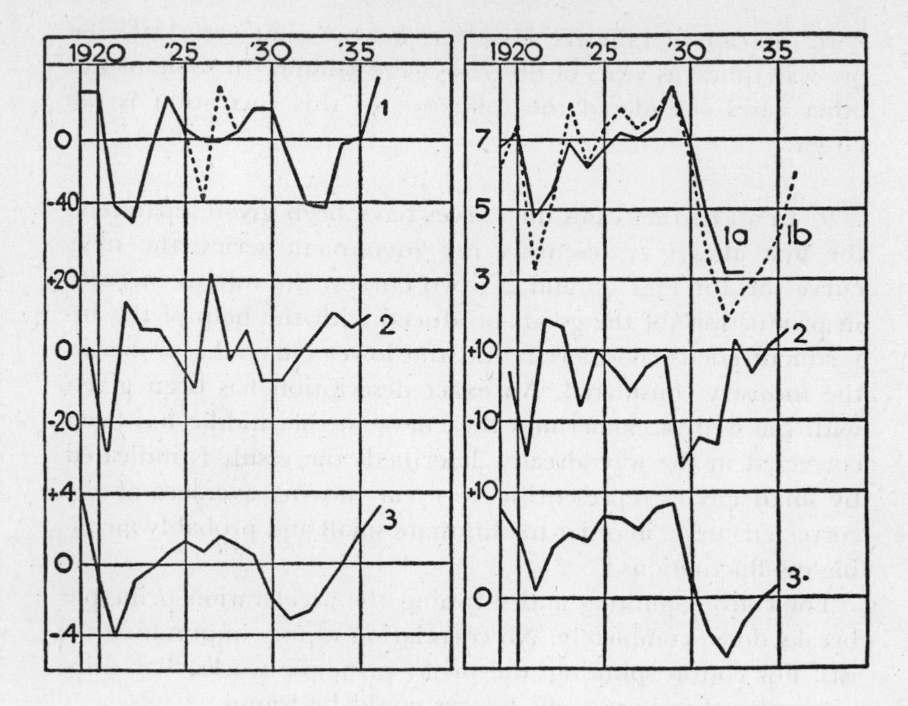

Fig. 28. General Activity, U.K. and U.S.A. U.K.: 1. Consumption of iron, percentage deviation from rectilinear trend; taken account of iron in steel, iron in exports deducted. . . . . actual figures 1926 and 1927; – – – "corrected" figures (corrected for coal miners' strike). 2. Rate of increase in industrial production, 1929 = 100; before 1928 taken from Hoffmann, since from B.o.T. 3. Profits, percentage of capital, deviations from rectilinear trend; Economist. U.S.A.: 1a. Deliveries of producers' durable commodities, Kuznets, 10^9\$ of 1929. 1b. Pig iron production in five million long tons. 2. Rate of increase in industrial production, F.R.B, 1923–5 = 100. 3. Profits of all corporations, 10^9\$, Stat. of Income.

(ii) in those years where a previous maximum in traffic is passed again the rate of increase in traffic is reduced to the extent the new maximum surpasses the previous one.

This correction evidently corresponds to the difficulties mentioned under 4 (a).

In the case of railways, however, it works out very little for pre-war times, as years of decrease were seldom. In some of the other cases considered the influence of this correction is far larger.

9. In all further cases the curves have been given separately, the first always representing the investment series, the next curve (or, for Figs. 25 and 27, two curves) the rate of increase in production (of the goods produced with the help of the investment goods considered) and the lower curve the profits in the industry considered. An exact description has been given with the figures. Sometimes the curve in the middle has been corrected in the way already described; the result is indicated by small circles representing two-year moving averages of the corrected curve, in order to eliminate small and probably meaningless fluctuations.

For cotton spinning and shipping the acceleration principle breaks down completely. No correlation of any importance exists. For cotton spinning, the profit principle works. For shipping no satisfactory profit figures could be found.

Considering the four general cases, where, however, the figures for net investment are not available in any form, I think they are all rather bad for the acceleration principle. One could doubt in the case of the United Kingdom (pre-war), Fig. 26, but even there the explanation by the profit principle certainly gives better results; and in all cases the fit obtained with the acceleration principle would certainly be poor. One has, of course, to be careful with the interpretation of the correlation between profits and investment, which could as well be such that investment determines profits, instead of the other way round. Then the mere fact that their mutual correlation is better than the one required by the acceleration principle would not prove much. There are, however, reasons for believing in the interpretation given* and then it seems that a better ex-

* These will be given in the report on the League of Nations investigations into the subject.

planation of investment is possible than the poor one yielded by the acceleration principle.

10. Summarising, it may be said that the acceleration principle cannot help very much in the explanation of the details in real investment fluctuations, with the possible exception of railway rolling stock.* As a rather rough principle with the chief object of explaining the tendency to more intense fluctuations in durable goods production it remains of value; but that tendency seems to be half as large as would be expected.

---

* Mr. D. H. Robertson draws my attention to the fact that railways have to carry any freight offered and for that reason might react more exactly in the sense of the acceleration principle.

C.

Long-Term Foreign Trade Elasticities*

§ 65. Importance of Long-Term Elasticities of Imports and Exports

The elasticity of the volume of imports or exports of any one country with respect to its price level may be either conceived of as a short-run elasticity or as a long-run elasticity. In the first case we think of the reaction of that volume which materialises within some short period, say one year; in the second case we think of the total reaction during a long period. From this it follows, however, that these concepts can only be exact if we indicate the periods. And this aspect of the phenomenon is only fully dealt with if we conceive of the volume x_t in question (imports or exports) during time unit t as a function of price levels during a whole range of preceding time units t, $t-1$, $t-2$, $t-3$, etc. In principle this range should be infinitely long:

$$x_t = \epsilon_o p_t + \epsilon_1 p_{t-1} + \epsilon_2 p_{t-2} + \cdots\cdots = \sum_{o}^{\infty}{}_i \epsilon_i p_{t-i} \qquad (65.1)$$

In this case, the short-run elasticity could be defined as:

$$\epsilon_s = \epsilon_o \frac{\bar{p}}{\bar{x}}$$

if $\bar{x}$ and $\bar{p}$ are the particular values of x and p for which we want to know the elasticity; and the long-run elasticity as:

$$\epsilon_L = \frac{\bar{p}}{\bar{x}} \sum_{o}^{\infty}{}_i \epsilon_i$$

* Metroeconomica, I (December 1949), 174-185. Reprinted by the courtesy of the publisher.

The reasons for the lagged reactions included in our equation (65.1) may be, e.g. that a certain change in price level induces a change in some production process, but only after certain machines now in operation are worn out. Or it may take some time before a switch in imports or exports is effectuated since every switch involves certain costs, which one is only prepared to incur, if the change in price level is considered to be a lasting one, not only a temporary one.

It will be remembered that our equation (65.1) represents a case of what Irving Fisher introduced as a distributed lag.

It seems useful to distinguish between short-term (however defined) and long-term elasticities of foreign trade. It may be useful in many other instances also; our special interest for foreign trade elasticities may be made clear by reminding the reader of some present-day problems for which they are of especial importance. The main problem for Western European countries nowadays is how to balance their foreign accounts. One of the methods used recently has been devaluation; other ones may be wage reductions or increases in productivity. In any of these cases the degree of success will depend on the reaction of imports and exports of the country concerned on the price change provoked. It is a well-known fact that success may even be completely absent if the sum of the elasticities of imports and exports is about one only. Recent statistical investigations* have made it plausible that these elasticities are in fact in many cases as low as that. The consequence would be that not very much could be expected from these methods to

---

* Hinshaw, R., American Prosperity and the British Balance of Payments Problem, The Review of Economic Statistics, XXVII, 1945; J. Tinbergen: Some measurements of elasticities of substitution, The Review of Economic Statistics, XXVIII, 1946; Tse Chun Chang, International Comparison of Demand for Imports, The Review of Economic Studies, XIII, 1945-46; The British Demand for Imports in the Inter-War Period, The Economic Journal, LVI, 1946; The British Balance of Payments 1924-1938, The Economic Journal, LVII, 1947; A Statistical Note on World Demand for Exports, The Review of Economics and Statistics, XXX, 1948.

equilibrate the balance of payments. The implications of this consequence are far-reaching. They might mean that only by permanent quantitative import restrictions equilibrium may be maintained. Before drawing this conclusion we must, however, ask whether the elasticities as found by the statisticians just quoted are not only short-run elasticities and whether long-run elasticities are not higher. To this question this paper is devoted.

§ 66. Long-Term vs. Short-Term Elasticities

The measurement of elasticities as performed by the authors just mentioned is based on multiple correlation analysis of the year-to-year fluctuations in imports or exports as dependent variables. The independent variables used in the explanation of these fluctuations are, in most cases, some index of home prices (or export prices), some index of foreign prices, and some index of national income of the importing country. Sometimes more variables are included, one of them being an indicator of quantitative restrictions applied. No attempt has so far been made, however, to include lagged values of the price series and hence the measurements must essentially be seen as attempts to measure the short-run value of elasticities. In some cases, where the correlation is very strong—as for a number of separate, well-defined commodities such as wheat, cotton or pig-iron—it may be seen from the figures, however, that the short-term influence explains the fluctuations to a great extent and that influences with small lags, say up to three years, cannot be very large. If they had been so, the correlation would have been a lagged one, easy to detect from the graphs. Much longer lags should evidently be introduced here, in order to get total elasticities much in excess of the figures reported by the authors.

Nevertheless it is probable that the long-run elasticities are higher, and perhaps much higher, than the short-run elasticities. There are various reasons for believing this. A number of the factors making for a relatively low elasticity work only tempo-

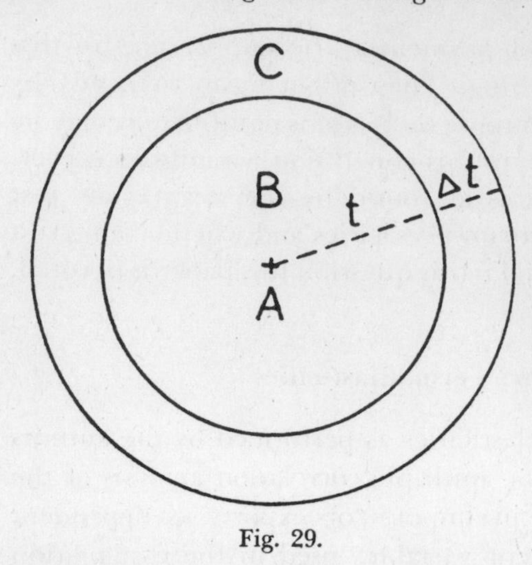

Fig. 29.

rarily. Existing contracts may prevent an immediate shift of demand to the cheapest supplier; after the contracts have expired this factor no longer works. Ties of a psychological or political character may hinder the shift. But after some psychological inertia has been overcome, this may change also. The shift may require the introduction of new machinery—as we already stated—this will therefore last until the old machinery has sufficiently been written off. A switch always causes costs of information, etc. It will not be undertaken therefore, as has been already observed, if the price change is considered a temporary one. But as time proceeds and the price change happens to be a lasting one, there will come a moment where also this cost of switching will no longer work as an obstacle.

Hence there are many reasons for expecting a lagged reaction, surpassing the immediate reaction. There remain, however, factors which are working also in the long run to prevent a complete shift to the cheapest supplier. And it may sometimes be possible to make a priori estimates of the long-term elasticity based on the nature of these factors. The simplest example is that of *distances,* causing differences in *transport costs.*

The existence of distances puts a maximum to the increase in demand caused by a given decrease in prices. Only the customers for whom under the new circumstances extra transport costs will be lower than the price reduction effected will be attracted. This may be illustrated by Fig. 29. Assume that the customers of a small country A are evenly spread over the circle

B. Potential new customers are supposed to be spread with the same density outside that circle. If now a price reduction Δp is applied, the customers in a ring C, of width Δt, will be attracted if transport costs over that distance are equal to Δp. What is the resulting elasticity of demand? Evidently it is equal to $\epsilon = \frac{\Delta x}{\Delta p} \frac{p}{x}$, where

$$\frac{\Delta x}{x} = \frac{\text{surface of ring}}{\text{surface of circle}} = \frac{2\pi t \Delta t}{\pi t^2} = \frac{2\Delta t}{t} = \frac{2\Delta p}{t}$$

Hence $\epsilon = 2\frac{p}{t}$

Now if we know something about $\frac{t}{p}$, i.e. the ratio of transport costs to total price, we are able to estimate the elasticity under the simplified conditions assumed. For such bulk goods as wheat and pig iron, transport costs between, e.g. South America and the European coast are of the order of magnitude of 10 per cent of the price. In such a case we would have $\epsilon = 20$. For piece goods the ratio of transport costs to price will probably be lower, leading to even higher elasticities.

There are, however, other factors making for inelasticity even in the long run. One may be *differences in qualities* due to inherent differences in soil, climate or technical skill of the population. These differences are not only important for separate commodities but even much more so for the whole of a country's "export basket." Its composition can only be changed gradually and within certain limits and this is probably the most powerful reason for long-term elasticities to be lower than the figure just quoted as an example. The differences in quality may take the special form of technical risks, i.e. the risk of quality divergencies or the risk of interruption of supply.

Another major class of factors is that of *political factors*. Regardless of distances or other purely technical and economic reasons for cheapness a country's exports may be in demand or not in demand if that country is or is not a part of a political group. The most outstanding examples one meets when studying the structure of international trade are those of the ties between a country and its overseas territories; the most important case being that of the British Empire. Whereas Germany's and America's customers are mainly the countries in their immediate neighbourhood, Britain's customers are often the Empire members.

§ 67. Measurement from Long-Time Series

From these a priori considerations it appears to be of much interest to measure long-term elasticities of imports or exports. What ways are open to us? There seem to be several, although each of them is beset with special difficulties. The first possibility would seem to use time series over a long period. A formula of the type of (65.1), when the necessary other explanatory variables are added, could be tested by the usual methods of multiple correlation only if we have long series of figures at our disposal. Even then it may prove to be a very risky procedure. There may exist, on closer theoretical examination, a number of factors influencing the observed movements which are hardly accessible to measurement. In the long run factors may be variable which are not so in the short run, especially such factors as quality, technical uses made of the commodity in question, etc. Not all of them will be relevant to our problem, i.e. to the relative competitive position of the countries considered. This can only be judged by insiders. As an example with, at first sight, a good chance of success we will take the demand for British pig iron by the United States during the period 1879–1914. As variables we take:

Q_t quantity of pig iron imported into the United States as a percentage of total American consumption;

P_t import price (including duties) as a percentage of home price in the United States;

v_t an index representing the cyclic situation, viz. production of pig iron as a percentage of its trend value.

It was attempted to explain the fluctuations in log Q_t in two ways, viz. once by the fluctuations in log P_t and log v_t and once by those in log P_t with a distributed lag and in log v_t. In order to account for the distributed lag the following variables were added to log P_t and log v_t: log P_{t-1}, log P_{t-2}, log $\overline{P}_{t-3/6}$ and log $\overline{P}_{t-7/10}$, where $\overline{P}_{t-3/6}$ indicates the average price for the years t-3 to t-6 inclusive and $P_{t-7/10}$ the average price for the years t-7 to t-10 inclusive.

The results of the calculations are shown in Figs. 30 and 31 and in table 1, where R represents the multiple correlation coefficient.

TABLE 1. REGRESSION COEFFICIENTS AND $1 - R^2$ IN THE EXPLANATIONS OF LOG Q_t

Explanatory Variables	$\log P_t$	$\log P_{t-1}$	$\log P_{t-2}$	$\log \overline{P}_{t-3/6}$	$\log \overline{P}_{t-7/10}$	$\log v_t$	$I\text{-}R^2$
	Regression Coefficients						
Case I	– 3.6	*	*	*	*	– 1.6	0.106
Case II	– 3.1	– 0.2	– 0.1	– 0.4	– 0.7	– 1.1	0.044

* *Not included.*

It appears that the correlation, although already high in case I, is considerably increased by the introduction of the lagged terms, all of which appear with the correct sign. The long-term elasticity as estimated by case II would amount to $-(3.1 + 0.2 + 0.1 + 0.4 + 0.7) = -4.5$ as against 3.1 when measured by the first member in the same equation or 3.6 when measured by case I. The difference between short-term and long-term elasticity (assuming that no longer lags than a ten-year one would exist) would be only moderate.

The same procedure was used in an analysis of the imports of raw cotton into the United Kingdom comparing imports of American and Indian cotton. Here it appeared impossible to obtain a satisfactory explanation of the fluctuations in the ratio between these two imports.

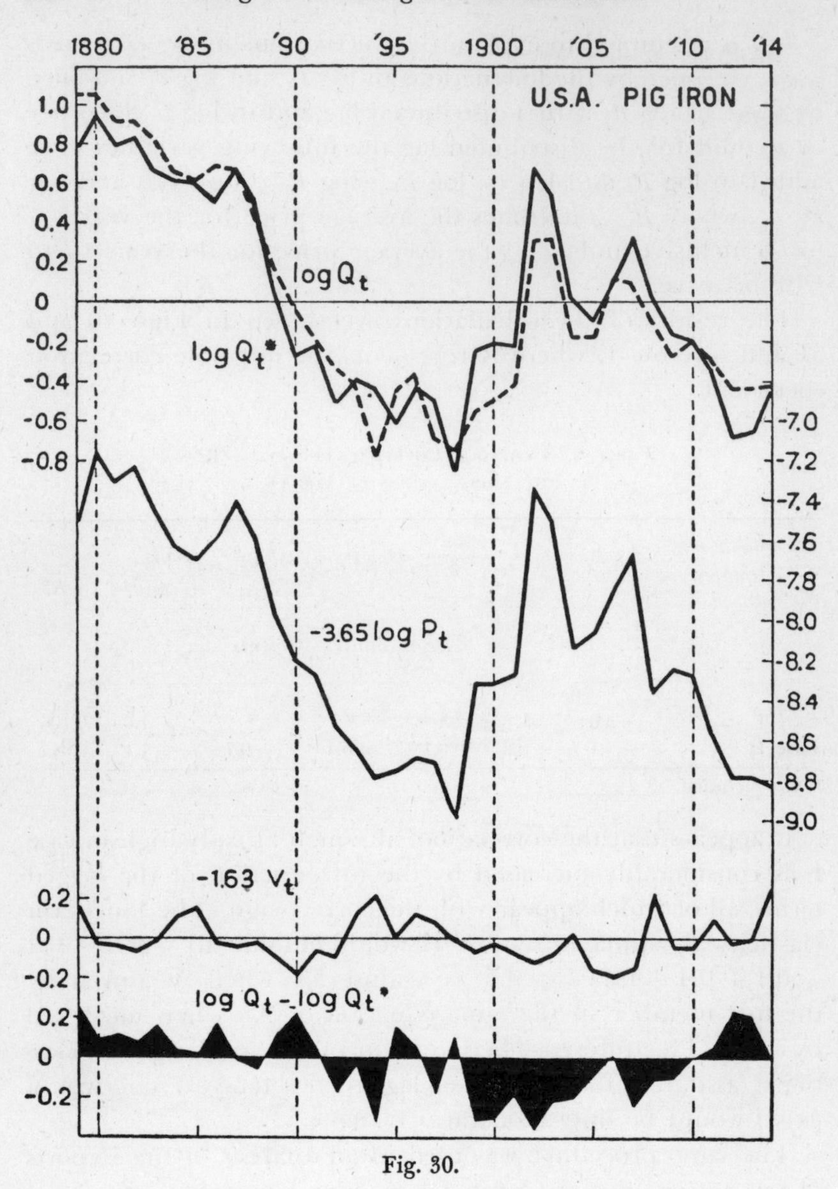

Fig. 30.

An even cruder procedure would consist of a simple comparison of two rather distant time units. This was done for total exports of manufactured articles by a number of coun-

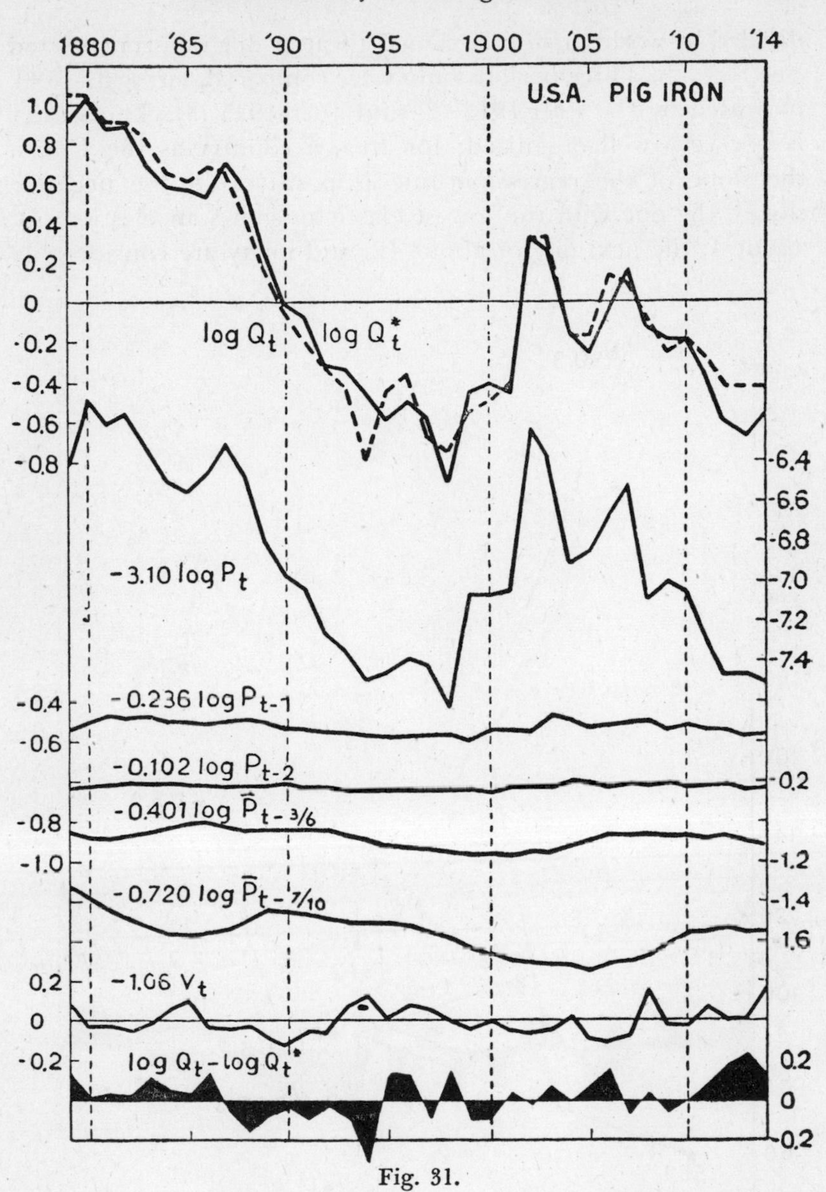

Fig. 31.

tries. These exports, expressed as a ratio to world exports of manufactures (volume figures) were compared with relative prices of these products (price index for country considered divided by world price index) and a scatter diagram constructed (see Fig. 32). Three periods only were compared, viz. 1881-1890, indicated by (1), 1901-1913 (2) and 1926-1935 (3). The scatter is not very well organized; for such a country as the U.S.A. the slope of the regression line is positive. Of the negative slopes, the one with the lowest elasticity shows an elasticity of about 4; the next one of about 12, and many are considerably

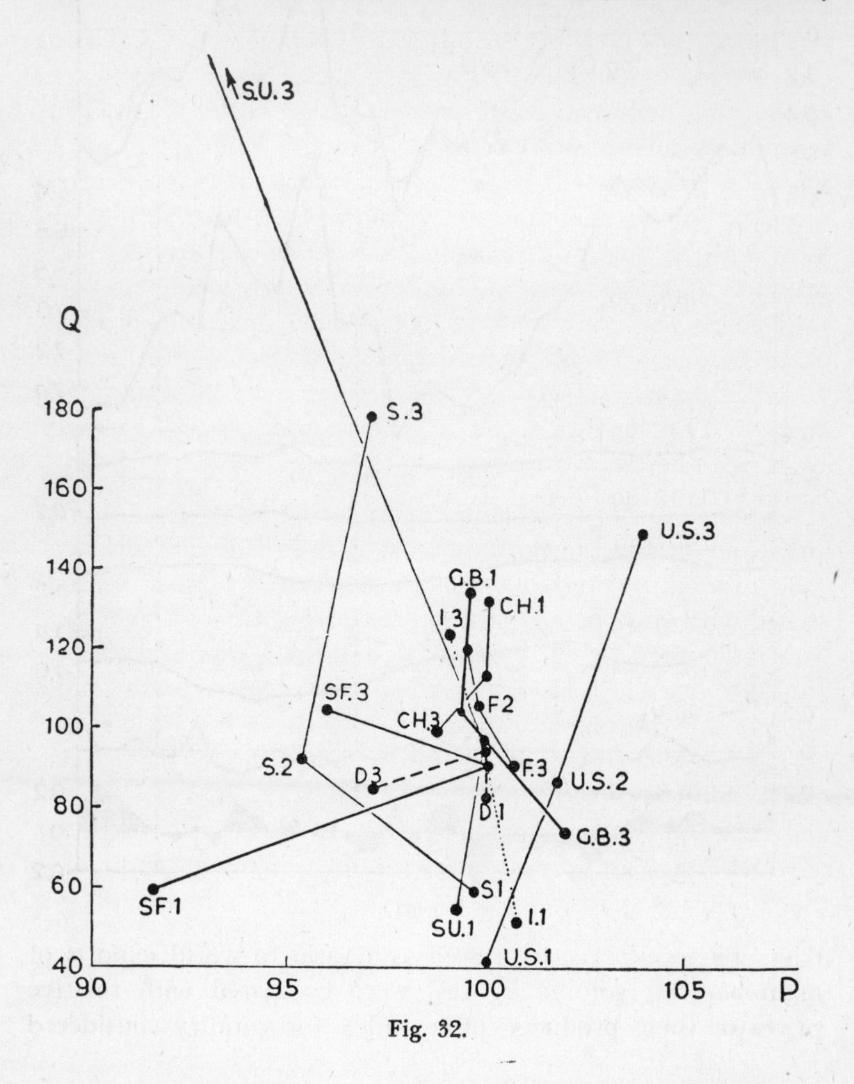

Fig. 32.

higher. These measurements are of little value, however, as long as it is impossible to explain the deviations in the scatter. It seems probable that the price index-numbers are none too good and can hardly take into account the changes in quality that the products under review must have shown.*

§ 68. Measurements from Cross-Section Studies

The other way to measure long-term elasticities is by using cross-section figures, i.e. by comparing different cases observed at the same moment, just as we do, e.g. when deriving long-term income elasticities of consumer demand from family budget statistics. In our case it comes to comparing different countries whose products for some reason or another are different in price. This we may still do in various ways. First we may compare products which for the supplying countries have a different price ratio. This was done by MacDougall who compared products of the United Kingdom and the United States, the relative costs of which diverge widely because of differences in relative efficiency.† The figures suggest a fairly high elasticity, although exact price figures are lacking.

Another possibility consists in comparing relative prices and quantities of the same commodity sold in different markets, price differences varying from one market to another because of distances and perhaps for other reasons as well. This has been attempted by the present writer for a number of commodities, one of which is pig iron. The relative shares in the imports into various countries were calculated (i.e. ratio of imports from the United Kingdom to total imports from U.K., U.S.A., and Germany) and the resulting percentages classified and represented by the intensity of the shade in three maps of which Fig. 33 is an example. From these maps it can be seen that the market shares vary from almost O to almost 100 per

* Most of the figures have been taken from Industrialization and Foreign Trade, League of Nations, 1945.

† Private communication by Mr. MacDougall.

cent and are greatly dependent on the relative distances from the three supplying countries considered.* For our purpose it is of particular interest to note that starting from a market supplied mainly by one of the big three, we have to go only a relatively small distance in order to arrive at a market supplied mainly by one of the others. Small distance meaning that the freight difference corresponding with this distance is only about 5 to 10 per cent of the price. This means that the market share may move by about 80 per cent because of a price change by say about 8 per cent, corresponding with an elasticity of the order of magnitude of 10.

A more direct and more accurate attempt was finally made by collecting figures on imports and import prices of pig iron into a number of importing countries and comparing, for the pairs Germany/U.K. and U.S.A./U.K. the relative quantities imported to and relative import prices charged to the buying countries. The results are shown in Figs. 34 and 35 and in table 2.† In order to eliminate the possible political ties existing between the supplying and the buying countries, two calculations of elasticities were made in each case, the second excluding British territories among the customers.

TABLE 2. CROSS-SECTION ELASTICITIES FOR RELATIVE IMPORTS OF PIG IRON IN A NUMBER OF COUNTRIES
(FIRST ELEMENTARY REGRESSION; DIAGONAL REGRESSION COEFFICIENTS IN BRACKETS)

		Supplying Countries Compared	
		Germany/U.K.	*U.S.A./U.K.*
Including British territories	1913	−3.9 (−8.3)	−2.0 (−14.6)
	1929	−9.5 (−15.3)	−6.2 (−11.2)
	1932	−1.6 (−5.0)	−3.4 (−5.3)
Excluding British territories a	1913	−1.9 (−7.5)	−1.3 (−15.9)
	1929	−6.5 (−14.4)	−0.1 (−16.0)
	1932	−1.6 (−5.0)	−3.1 (−5.2)

a Australia, Canada, and Union of South Africa.

* With the political exceptions already mentioned, in particular for Britain.

† The full statistical material will be supplied by the author on request.

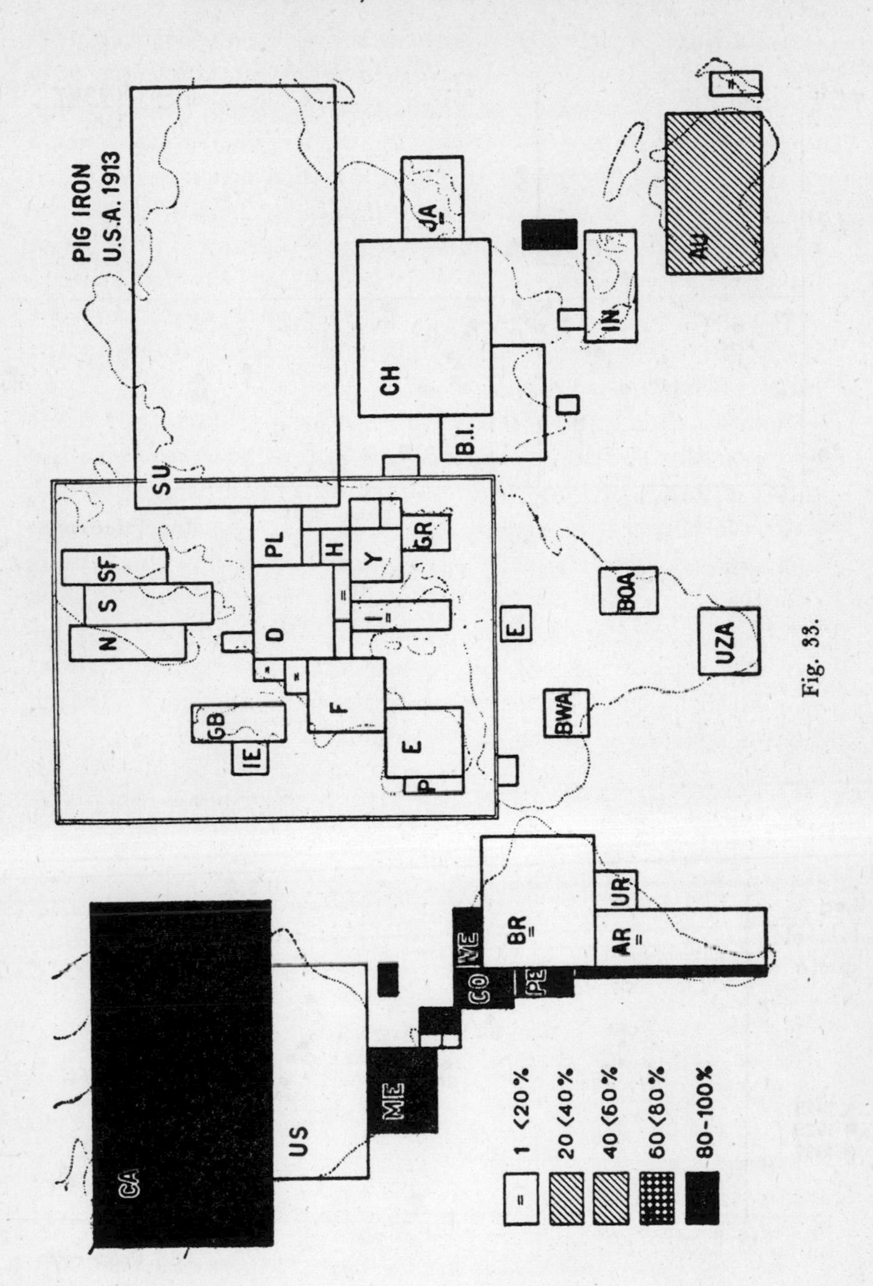
PIG IRON
U.S.A. 1913
SU
JA
CH
B.I.
IN
AU
PL
H
Y
GR
SF
S
N
D
F
GB
IE
E
P
E
BOA
UZA
BWA
BR
UR
AR
VE
CO
PE
ME
US
CA
1 <20%
20 <40%
40 <60%
60 <80%
80-100%

Fig. 33.

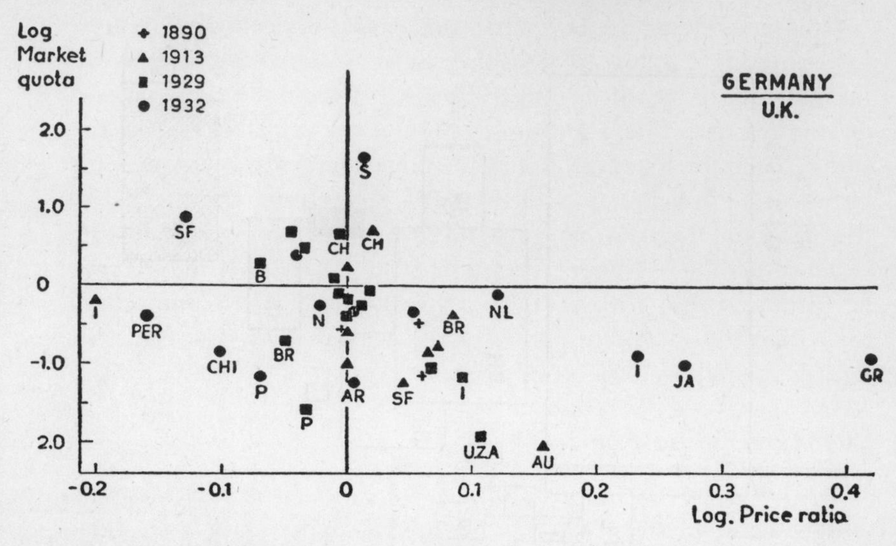
Log
Market
quota
+ 1890
▲ 1913
■ 1929
● 1932
GERMANY
U.K.
2.0
1.0
0
-1.0
2.0
-0.2
-0.1
0
0.1
0.2
0.3
0.4
Log. Price ratio
S
SF
CH
CH
B
I
N
NL
PER
BR
CHI
BR
P
AR
SF
I
I
JA
GR
P
UZA
AU

Fig. 34.

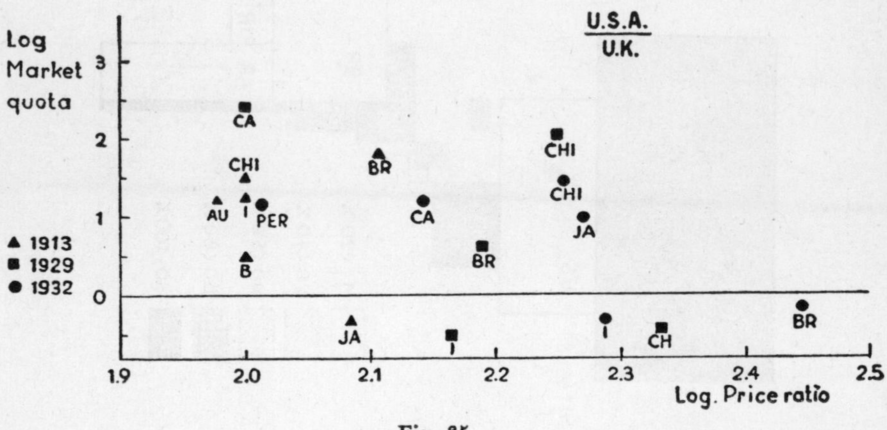
Log
Market
quota
U.S.A.
U.K.
3
2
1
0
▲ 1913
■ 1929
● 1932
1.9
2.0
2.1
2.2
2.3
2.4
2.5
Log. Price ratio
CA
CHI
BR
CHI
CHI
AU
I
PER
CA
JA
B
BR
JA
I
I
CH
BR

Fig. 35.

It is interesting to note that the exclusion of British territories among the buyers does not, as one might have expected, increase elasticity. More interesting still it is, however, that the elasticities found here are not as high as our a priori considerations (based on distances alone) would suggest; the average value being − 3.4 for the first elementary regressions and − 10 for the diagonal regressions; and their median values − 2.6 and − 9.8 respectively. When considering these figures it should not be forgotten that they refer to a very well-defined commodity, for which the short-run elasticity also surpasses, necessarily, the figures for export baskets as a whole.

§ 69. Concluding Remarks

In this paper in honour of Constantino Bresciani-Turroni whose work on the measurement of elasticities has been generally admired, an attempt has been made to measure long-term substitution elasticities of imports as distinguished from short-term elasticities. Two methods are tried, viz. one using long time series and "distributed lags," and one using "cross-sections." Their application to the case of pig iron leads to figures of − 4.5 and of − 3.6 to − 10, respectively. From the first method as well as from previous measurements of short-term elasticities it seems probable that these higher elasticities refer to reactions that require at least a couple of years.

BIBLIOGRAPHY*

Mathematics: R. G. D. Allen: "Mathematical Analysis for Economists," London 1935;

Mathematical Economics: E. G. Evans: "Mathematical Introduction to Economics," New York 1930; P. A. Samuelson: "Foundations of Economic Analysis," Cambridge, Mass. 1947;

Mathematical Statistics: T. C. Koopmans: "Statistical Inference in Dynamic Economic Models," New York 1950;

Econometrics: H. T. Davis: "The Theory of Econometrics," Bloomington 1941; C. F. Roos: "Dynamic Economics," Bloomington 1934.

* Additional references will be found in each of the books mentioned here.

INDEX

Page numbers followed by a lower case n refer to footnotes in text.
Page numbers in italics refer to illustrations.